LIQUID SOCIETY AND ITS LAW

Liquid Society and Its Law

Edited by
JIŘÍ PŘIBÁŇ
Cardiff Law School, Cardiff University, UK

Routledge
Taylor & Francis Group
LONDON AND NEW YORK

First published 2007 by Ashgate Publishing

2 Park Square, Milton Park, Abingdon, Oxfordshire OX14 4RN
52 Vanderbilt Avenue, New York, NY 10017

Routledge is an imprint of the Taylor & Francis Group, an informa business

First issued in paperback 2020

British Library Cataloguing in Publication Data
Liquid society and its law. - (Applied legal philosophy)
1. Bauman, Zygmunt, 1925- 2. Sociological jurisprudence
3. Sociology - Philosophy 4. Civilization, Modern - 21st
century
I. Přibáň, Jiří, 1967-
340.1'15

Library of Congress Cataloging-in-Publication Data
Přibáň, Jiří, 1967-
Liquid society and its law / by Jiří Přibáň.
p. cm. -- (Applied legal philosophy)
Includes index.
ISBN 978-0-7546-7072-8
1. Bauman, Zygmunt, 1925- 2. Sociological jurisprudence. 3. Law--Philosophy. 4. Sociology. 5. Postmodernism--Social aspects. I. Title.

K370.P75 2007
340'.115--dc22

2007007395

ISBN 978-0-7546-7072-8 (hbk)
ISBN 978-0-367-60363-2 (pbk)

Contents

Series Editor's Preface

The objective of the Applied Legal Philosophy series is to publish work which adopts a theoretical approach to the study of particular areas or aspects of law or deals with general theories of law in a way which focused on issues of practical moral and political concern in specific legal contexts.

In recent years there has been an encouraging tendency for legal philosophers to utilize detailed knowledge of the substance and practicalities of law and a noteworthy development in the theoretical sophistication of much legal research. The series seeks to encourage these trends and to make available studies in law which are both genuinely philosophical in approach and at the same time based on appropriate legal knowledge and directed towards issues in the criticism and reform of actual laws and legal systems.

The series will include studies of all the main areas of law, presented in a manner which relates to the concerns of specialist legal academics and practitioners. Each book makes an original contribution to an area of legal study while being comprehensible to those engaged in a wide variety of disciplines. Their legal content is principally Anglo-American, but a wide-ranging comparative approach is encouraged and authors are drawn from a variety of jurisdictions.

Tom D. Campbell
Centre for Applied Philosophy and Public Ethics,
Charles Sturt University, Australia

List of Contributors

Zygmunt Bauman is Professor Emeritus at the University of Leeds and Warsaw University. He is author of numerous books in the sociology of modernity and postmodernity, such as *Modernity and the Holocaust* (1989), *Postmodern Ethics* (1993), *Liquid Modernity* (2000) and *Society under Siege* (2002).

Vito Breda is Lecturer in Law at Cardiff University. His areas of research include constitutional theory, European law theory and jurisprudence. He has contributed to journals such as *European Law Journal* and *Res Publica.*

Emilios Christodoulidis is Professor of Legal Theory at the Law School of the University of Glasgow. His research interests lie in the philosophy and sociology of law and in political and constitutional theory.

Pablo S. Ghetti is Lecturer in Law, University of Exeter, UK. He has contributed to journals such as *Law & Critique*, *Law, Culture and the Humanities*, and *Journal of Law and Society*. His major work is *Direito e Democracia sob os Espectros de Schmitt – Uma Contribuição à Crítica da Filosofia do Direito de Jürgen Habermas* [Law and Democracy under the Spectres of Schmitt – A Contribution to the Critique of the Philosophy of Law of Jürgen Habermas] (2006).

Pierre Guibentif is Associated Professor at ISCTE (Instituto Superior de Ciências do Trabalho e da Empresa) and at the Universidade Nova, both in Lisbon; main research interests and domains of publication: sociology of law, social policies in the EU, social theory and the law.

David Nelken is Distinguished Professor of Legal Institutions and Social Change at the University of Macerata, Italy, Distinguished Research Professor of Law at Cardiff University and Visiting Professor of Law at the London School of Economics. Publications include *Adapting Legal Cultures* (ed. with J. Feest, 2001) and (ed. with V. Gessner) *European Ways of Law* (ed. with V. Gessner, 2007).

Andreas Philippopoulos-Mihalopoulos is a Reader in Law, University of Westminster. His research includes critical theory, autopoiesis, environmental law, European law, law and literature, gender, and art. He edited *Law and the City* and is author of *Absent Environments* (both published by Routledge in 2007).

Jiří Přibáň is Professor of Law at Cardiff University and Visiting Professor of Legal Philosophy and Sociology at Charles University, Prague. He is author of *Dissidents* *of Law* (2002) and *Legal Symbolism* (2007). His areas of research include social theory and law, jurisprudence, theory of constitutionalism and human rights.

Anton Schütz teaches Law and legal philosophy at Birkbeck School of Law, University of London. Most of his current publications are related to the modalities of law's presence and presentation in contemporary accounts of the Christian/post-Christian West and its cultural and religious history.

Grażyna Skąpska is Professor of Sociology at Jagiellonian University in Krakow, Poland. She co-edited *A Fourth Way? Privatization, Property, and the Emergence of New Market Economy* (with G.S. Alexander, 1994) and is a member of the editorial boards of *Droit et Societe* and *Ius et Lex*. Her research areas include postcommunist constitutionalism, law and social change and contemporary social theory.

Acknowledgements

The editor wishes to thank Zygmunt Bauman and all contributors for their participation, cooperation and enthusiasm without which this volume would never be completed. Cardiff Law School generously funded the initial conference *Liquid Society and Its Law*, organised in Cardiff in September 2005, and the subsequent work on this book. Richard Moorhead kindly supported the whole project and Julia Craske's organizational help was essential for its success. Finally, the editor is very grateful to Sian Edwards for her language editing of the manuscript.

Introduction

Theorizing Liquid Modernity and Its Legal Context

Jiří Přibáň

This book has been inspired by social theory of Zygmunt Bauman, especially his recent explorations of the 'liquidity' of our postmodern society and human lives. The metaphors of 'liquidity' and 'fluidity' were elaborated by Bauman in his highly influential book *Liquid Modernity* (2000) and followed up, especially in *The Individualized Society* (2001), *Liquid Love* (2003) and *Liquid Life* (2005), in an attempt to grasp the current state of modern society, its changes and position in the history of modernity.

The notion of liquidity is an addition to the comments on 'postmodernity', 'second modernity', 'reflexive modernity' or 'late modernity' in philosophy and social theory in the last three decades. It reflects the diminishing role of the spatial dimensions of social life and highlights the central importance of the flow of time and social change. In the time-space duality, it is time associated with change, flexibility, mobility and overall 'lightness' that matters in liquid society. Information moves with the speed of the electronic signal and has eroded territorial state power. Power has become extraterritorial and the powerful are now those able to disengage themselves from local obligations. International law and nation state legal systems significantly contribute to this strategy of disengagement and growing social liquidity. Increasingly mobile and evasive forms of power coincide with new forms of legal regulation and domination.

In this volume of essays, European social theorists of law and socio-legal scholars, joined by Zygmunt Bauman himself, aim at addressing both the metaphorical and conceptual meaning of 'liquidity', 'fluidity' and 'lightness' and their possible usage within the context of legal science. Law has been commonly associated with predictability, security, safety, trust, reliability, and manageability and considered a solid ground strengthening the bonds and institutions of modern society. Nevertheless, legality has clearly been part of the process of the ever-growing domination of instrumental rationality and rational cost-effect calculation that 'melts' all social obstacles and obligations standing in its way. Law, therefore, can hardly establish foundations for public or political life that could integrate and stabilize society as a whole. Law has adapted to social liquidity and accommodated the techniques and operation of deregulation, devolution and disengagement.

Bauman's critical sociology

Bauman's theoretical approach is highly unorthodox and critical of the existing canon of sociology. Drawing on the sociological legacy of Georg Simmel and the hermeneutical turn in social sciences, Bauman has rehabilitated the essay as a form of sociological writing and his style successfully combines rigorously sociological views with playful and seductive ideas and remarks. Instead of theoretical unity and the persistence of the same critical judgements, his books relentlessly emphasise the intellectual need to cope with emerging social problems, crises, contradictions and paradoxes and highlight sociology's role in facilitating responses to them. In modern 'human-made' society, social theory assumes the critical (and therefore ethical) role of an invitation to incessantly re-make human ingenuity and good will and thus contribute to the public debates and political dialogues and the compromises achieved in the meeting place of the *agora* (Bauman 2002, 25).

Bauman rejects the fruitless methodology of current social sciences and claims that there is no predefined distinction between common sense and scientific knowledge. The social scientists' first job is to bear moral responsibility for their work and words. Although Adorno and Horkheimer's theoretical notions and ideas do not play a major role in Bauman's social theory until the publication of his *Modernity and the Holocaust* (1989), the ethos of critical theory has always been present in Bauman's work. According to him, critical sociology is a pleonasm and social research should always be an ethically responsible research reflecting mundane reality, everyday life experiences, and common knowledge.

Talking of the sociologist's job, Bauman quotes the Czech poet Jan Skácel on the poet's plight: 'To write, means for the poet to crush the wall behind which something that "was always there" hides' (Bauman 2000, 202). He invokes this task of the poet and says of the sociologist's job that:

> we ought to come as close as the true poets do to the yet hidden human possibilities; and for that reason we need to pierce the walls of the obvious and self-evident, of that prevailing ideological fashion of the day whose commonality is taken for the proof of its sense. Demolishing such walls is as much the sociologist's as the poet's calling, and for the same reason: the walling-up of possibilities belies human potential while obstructing the disclosure of its bluff (Bauman 2000, 203).

This strong statement should not be misleadingly interpreted as the modernist image of the 'true' reality hiding behind the walls of the 'false' reality. Bauman is always on the side of the ontology of the actual and takes sociology as a cultural activity that is an element of 'the self-reflective, self-monitoring quality of human action' (Bauman 1992, 216). The scientific sociological need for the ontology of truth thus necessarily coincides with the need for the ontology of the actual. These two ontological endeavours both inform critical sociological thinking and Bauman only points to the need to tear down all cognitive and social 'necessities' when he comments on the picture of the sociologist/poet demolishing the walls of ignorance of 'the obvious and self-evident'.

Bauman is critical of the concept of social theory and sociology as a theoretical enterprise paving solid rational pathways and orientation points in postmodern society.

His sociological hermeneutics does not offer the illusion of theoretical knowledge that has right answers for social problems. Instead, Bauman's hermeneutical method uses common sense and experience as forms of socially constructed reality and supplements them with their sociological reflection. Social sciences are based on 'secondary hermeneutics' – they are never-ending interpretations of human lives and social experiences already interpreted by people and established in common knowledge. Social sciences and humanities can only be constituted because there already is knowledge available and ready to be interpreted in social reality.

In the past, social sciences supported the illusion that they are solid signs and the only genuine guidance to modern social life and its changes. In the postmodern liquid condition, the arrogance and falsity of this rationalistic illusion have been unmasked. The role of critical theory and sociology thus needs to be reconsidered. When discussing Derrida's deconstruction, Bauman, for instance, uses the metaphor of putting anti-freeze in the car's radiator before the winter (Bauman 2006, 108–9). According to Bauman, it is critical theory's job to avoid the situation in which all scientific and social knowledge would be considered 'frozen' and final, universally valid and based on transcendental grounds, to be unreservedly accepted by all participants in theoretical or any other social discourses.

Critical sociology and hermeneutics protect us against solid interpretations and understanding. Bauman praises the title of Gadamer's book, *Truth and Method* (2003), as deeply ironic because there is no method leading us towards the objective notion of truth, and suggests that people look for heuristic principles to establish compromise-driven understanding rather than the monopoly of truth (Bauman 2006, 108). According to Bauman, Gadamer's hermeneutics is an attempt at redefining philosophy's task:

> as one of interpretation, a search for meaning, making 'the other' comprehensible, making oneself understandable – and thus facilitating an exchange between forms of life – and opening up for communication worlds of meaning which otherwise would remain closed to each other (Bauman 1987, 144).

Bauman's sociology may subsequently be taken as an attempt to supply empirical proofs of Gadamer's philosophical hypothesis that human understanding is prompted by the mutual fusion of cognitive horizons established and constantly redrawn in the process of the historical accumulation of communally shared life experience. Sharing experience is essential for the constitution and development of mutual understanding, and sociology contributes to this process by reflecting on those experiences and their horizons. The concept of sociological truth is inseparable from common truths and, together with them, helps to clarify and redefine our horizon as the departure point of our dialogue, understanding and civilised coexistence with others.

Liquid modernity as a social and political crisis

Bauman's concepts of postmodernity and liquid modernity provide original insights and reflexive explanations of the process of functional differentiation and the ever-growing domination of instrumental reason. Liquid modernity means the progressive unravelling of the systems of economy, politics, ethics, law and education which makes any prospect of shifting, reforming and ultimately stabilizing current postmodern society impossible. The Hobbesian problem of the existence of a social order, which gave form to modern social theory and sociology, lacks centrality and urgency in liquid modernity. There is no system externally (social structure) and internally (culture) binding individuals to their social settings (Bauman 2002, 26). Dreams of social engineering and revolutions (working-class, managerial, etc.) collapsed in the final decades of the twentieth century dubbed by Bauman (referring to Polanyi's seminal book *The Great Transformation* published in 1944) the 'Great Transformation Mark Two', characterised by the disembodiment of labour, exterritorial capital, elusive power and 'no more salvations by society' (Bauman 2000, 120–3; Bauman 2002, 33).

For Bauman, postmodernity is modernity that has lost its ideals and illusions of one historical direction of social development pre-determined by 'objective' laws of human history. The sociology of postmodernity explains ways of life in this world without historical orientation and social laws. Life in postmodernity is best described by the image of a desert – it is life without paved paths and clearly signed motorways giving us a strong sense of safety and orientation to our movements (Bauman 1993). In the desert, all ways, signs and orientation points are constantly shifting. Our footprints disappear in the first desert wind, yet they bear witness to our existence and thus serve as orientation signs on our social journeys in the increasingly fragmented, contingent and unstable postmodern reality.

Bauman's essays occasionally read like critical comments on Ernest Gellner's 'modular man' (Gellner 1996) stripped of his circular belief in the superiority of the Western form of life, reason and culture (Bauman 1987, 141–2, 146). Unlike Gellner, who always insisted that rationalistic objective knowledge constantly transcends the limitations of its culture, Bauman argues against this normative model of scientific knowledge and claims that the crisis of modernity has been caused precisely by its scientific achievements and success. The crisis of modernity's political and philosophical illusions has been caused by a commitment to fully materialise and implement them in modern society. Modernity thus evokes the popular picture of the snake eating its tail (Bauman 1993, 209–17) – it continues to exist and reproduce itself by destroying its very foundations. The sociology of postmodernity aims at analysing these processes of destructive continuity and possible discontinuities in the systems of economy, science, politics and education or culture. It aims at understanding the historical period of modernity in which Ulrich – the hero of Robert Musil's novel *The Man without Qualities* – has become 'the man without bonds' (Bauman 2003, vii).

One can take Bauman's recent treatises on liquid modernity, lives, love, etc. as studies of the snake of our modernity biting its tail. Liquid modernity is both a symptom of modernity's crisis and a window of opportunity to respond to it. It is both a threat and challenge. Bauman describes our liquid modernity as a novel phase in the history of modernity and, inspired by Gramsci's notion of reality as something flexible and fluid (Bauman 1992, 206) and more recent theories of postmodernity, employs *The Communist Manifesto's* revolutionary vision of 'melting the solids' of modern society (Bauman 2000, 2–4). The modern spirit of revolution and social change melts tradition and other burdens of history which should not stand in its way and challenge its ambitions.

However, Bauman emphasises that this early modern adoration of the fluidity of revolutionary time destroying the solids of the timeless past was far from a glorification of the anti-essentialist world of modernity inspiring conversational, tolerant and hermeneutically constituted politics. Contrary to this ethos of late modernity, early modern calls for melting the solids were:

> not in order to do away with the solids once and for all and make the brave new world free of them for ever, but to clear the site for *new and improved solids*; to replace the inherited set of deficient and defective solids with another set, which was much improved and preferably perfect, and for that reason no longer alterable (Bauman 2000, 3).

The pre-modern solids were to be replaced by the modern solids which could last and be trusted due to the historical and instrumental reason. Traditions of the past were to be washed away by the melting emancipatory power of reason.

Bauman had already commented on this vision of modernity in his book *Legislators and Interpreters* (1987) in which he also emphasised that for Marx, the intended outcome of melting the solids was a new social organisation subjected to a purposeful design, routinization and rational supervision (Bauman 1987, 112). The vision was part of Enlightenment ideology according to which people as rational individuals actually make society through rational government (Bauman 1992, 10). However, the present state of liquid modernity has emerged as a continuation of this call for melting the solids, this time the modern solids of social and scientific rationality. The snake has bitten its tail and, apart from the process of delegitimising reason, the call for melting the solid has become the solidly governing imperative of life in liquid modernity.

Liquid modernity signifies the end of the Panopticon-based modern power era which needed to control territory and was bound by the mutual engagement of the powerful and those subject to their power. Liquid power effectively avoids territorial confinement with its illusion of social order and stability. The techniques of liquid power are:

> escape, slippage, elision and avoidance, the effective rejection of any territorial confinement with its cumbersome corollaries of order-building, order-maintenance and the responsibility for the consequences of it all as well as of the necessity to bear their costs (Bauman 2000, 11).

Instead of the art of surveillance, liquid power is defined by the art of escape and disengagement from all forms of social responsibility. Liquidity marks the disintegration of social networks and institutions of collective action such as the state and democratic party politics. The current rigidity of social systems consists of the paradoxically stable imperative to get rid of all social bonds and networks that may prevent the processes of the ever-growing liquidity of modern society. It is the world of 'togetherness dismantled' (Bauman 2003, 119).

The liquid art of escape transforms into the politics of fear, uncertainty and common anxiety. Safety policy becomes a dominant form of political discourse and deliberation in the risk-prone liquid society. The population's perpetual demand for public safety feeds on the perpetual supply of liquid uncertainty and its political manipulation and abuse. Bauman uses Crozier's definition of domination as the possibility of keeping one's own actions unbound, uncertain and unpredictable while stripping those dominated of their ability to control their moves. He notes that:

> Nothing has changed in this respect with the passage from heavy to light modernity. But the frame has filled with a new content; more precisely, the pursuit of the 'closeness to the source of uncertainty' has narrowed down to, and focused on, one objective – instantaneity. People who move and act faster, who come nearest to the momentariness of movement, are now people who rule. And it is the people who cannot move as quickly and more conspicuously yet the category of people who cannot at will leave their place at all, who are ruled. … The contemporary battle of domination is waged between forces armed, respectively, with the weapons of acceleration and procrastination (2000, 119–20).

According to Bauman, this 'lightness of being' is generally seductive and we all increasingly live our lives as 'instant lives' (Bauman 2000, 123–9). Uncertainty and insecurity call for the renewal of bonds and feelings of togetherness.

In the liquid modern condition, the political call for the recreation of community is a symptom of the deep political crisis of the public space and democratic debate. The political crisis of liquid modern society is caused by the dismantling of modern democratic institutions of the state. The solidity of the modern democratic state's institutions, originally guaranteed by the identity of the political nation, is being flushed away under the pressure of other political identities imagined and grounded in religious, linguistic, cultural, territorial or ethnic and gender differences (Bauman 2002, 11). The common destiny – this precondition of democratic politics and civil society – has melted away.

Nevertheless, the current political crisis should not be treated just as yet another ideological battle between modern liberalism and communitarianism. The revival of identity politics and various forms of ethnically and culturally defined communitarianisms should, rather, be perceived as a rational response to the political crisis. Community-based identity politics searches for bonds and solid indisputable foundations in social settings which promote unbounded politics and life-style. The right to a communal exclusivity, bonds, boundaries and separation is nothing but a call for defending and constituting something missing in liquid modern society. In this context, Bauman strengthens his argument by quoting Eric Hobsbawm's remark that 'never was the word "community" used more indiscriminately and emptily than in the decades when communities in the sociological sense became hard to find in real life' (Hobsbawm 1994, 428; quoted in Bauman 2000, 171). The absence of solid social ground and security makes all these promises of life in homogeneous and unproblematic community very attractive, socially rational, and politically explosive.

Liquid modernity as a political and critical challenge

Behind the futile, yet very dangerous political search for a perfect community lies the crisis of democratic community and citizenship. Liquid uncertainty is the prime root of political inhibition (Bauman 2002, 70–6). After the demise of the nation state, there seems to be no space for democratic community, its practices and ethos. Political trust has no firm ground which could assume public commitments and responsibilities. The crisis of political institutions is part of the more general social crisis of emancipation and liberation. Bauman quotes Marcuse to remind us that 'we are facing liberation from a society where liberation is apparently without a mass basis' (Marcuse 1968; quoted in Bauman 2000, 16).

The process of individualization is an aspect of the history of modernization which used to be automatically associated with the image of the linear development of individual liberation, emancipation, autonomy, and self-assertion of all members of modern society. In early modernity, the process used to be perceived as the individual's struggle against the forces of tradition and prejudice. The emancipated individual used to be considered a person aware of the fact that her identity was a task for which she was responsible and towards which she must constantly work to preserve her individual autonomy and freedom. In liquid modernity, however, the process of individualization takes new forms derived from increasing promises of individual fulfilment, happiness and satisfaction, with no prospect of their ever being achieved in the individual's life. Individuality and the imperative of self-assertion and self-satisfaction determine institutional and communication networks but, at the same time, they are not the subject of the individual's own choice. As Bauman comments: 'Let there be no mistake: now, as before – in the fluid and light as much as in the solid and heavy stage of modernity – individualization is a fate not a choice' (Bauman 2000, 34). One of main contradictions of liquid modernity, therefore, is a growing gap between the individual as a self-asserted and self-created member of modern society and the individual as a member of society assigned to act individually without ever having any choice other than to act in the prescribed way. It seems that the first collective pressure of liquid society is to act according to individual interest.

The paradox of individualization is recognized by all living their lives in liquid modernity, from single mothers and unemployed workers to top managers, politicians, and even social scientists. It generates an unprecedented number of opportunities for self-creation and self-satisfaction together with troubles and anxieties arising from the need to cope with and materialise these choices. Bauman says that:

> The yawning gap between the right of self-assertion and the capacity to control the social settings which render such self-assertion feasible or unrealistic seems to be the main contradiction of fluid modernity – one that, through trial and error, critical reflection and bold experimentation, we would need collectively to learn to tackle collectively (Bauman 2000, 38).

According to Bauman, the dissolution of the common public sphere and collectively shared and pursued institutions is one of the greatest risks of liquid modernity. Individuals do not necessarily have anything in common. When they come together and meet they may act entirely separately and pursue their individual interests irrespective of common needs and collective interests. Bauman quotes Alexis de Tocqueville's warning against the political indifference of the individual which 'is the citizen's worst enemy' (Bauman 2000, 36). In contrast to the private or privatised individual, the citizen always seeks personal welfare within the boundaries of the polity's common, democratically formulated and shared interests.

The disintegration of civic culture, indeed, is a negative consequence of the process of liquid individualization. Instead of democratic deliberations and conflict-resolutions, current 'democratic' politics is the politics of particularised and fragmented egoisms unified by the atmosphere of fear. The public disappears under the pressure of fragmented private interests, individualised lives and liquid emotions insufficient for the revitalisation of common bonds. State agencies, including the army and police, are too burdensome and expensive and are therefore being replaced by more flexible and mobile private agencies. Policing the global village requires devolving jurisdiction to local agencies while stripping the nation state of its democratic legitimate power. The common public sphere is increasingly replaced by more and more sophisticated techniques of surveillance feeding on the politics and culture of fear and personal anxiety, as if the main political interest were to keep the squares and streets safe and free from suspicious strangers of all kinds.

According to Bauman, individuals need to re-engage in the public space of democratic politics if they are to regain some control over their choices and possibilities of self-assertion. The current gap between individuality as a fate and as a choice has been caused by the abandonment of the *agora* – the public space where individual and particular problems and interests are transformed into public matters and policies (Bauman 2002, 50, 75). Bauman explores possible ways of revitalising civic bonds and democratic *agora*-based politics and associates the chance of human emancipation with the revitalisation of critical theory in the society of individuals. Liquid modernity is the state of uncertainty caused by the loss of social ends and dominated by the unnerving question of what one can actually do. In the past, critical theory's first job was to protect the individual against all kinds of social exploitation and collective pressure. In liquid modernity, the opposite is called for: the prime danger is not public space colonising the private sphere, but the private sphere's colonisation of the public domain. The oppressive rule of tradition or the modern bureaucratic and omnipresent state has been replaced by the advancing pressures of individualised interests, pursuits and fears. According to Bauman:

> The task is now to defend the vanishing public realm, or rather to refurnish and repopulate the public space fast emptying owing to the desertion on both sides: the exit of the 'interested citizen', and the escape of real power into the territory which, for all that the extant democratic institutions are able to accomplish, can only be described as an 'outer space' (Bauman 2000, 39).

The only chance of bridging the individualization gaps and resolving the fateful pressures of liquid modernity is to revitalise civic skills and various forms of civic engagement including the control of the powerful who are always ready to escape and avoid their social and political responsibilities in liquid modernity.

The advent of individualized life-politics based on 'an ideology of intimacy' transmuting political issues into psychological ones (Sennett 1974, 259; quoted in Bauman 2003, 31) has been contributing to the politics of uncertainty and our fear of those threatening to invade our private spaces (strangers, immigrants, juveniles, etc.). If human emancipation – this first goal of critical theory – still means anything in liquid modernity, it means reconnecting the two aspects of individual life: the real prospects of individuals' lives and their chance of choosing particular forms and actions of self-assertion and self-fulfilment (Bauman 2000, 40–1). Current liquid life-politics following only individualised interests and the tribal demands of different communities must be replaced by the pursuit of a public politics of engaged citizens.

In the past, critical theorists successfully argued that individual interests, desires and intimations needed to be protected against the unholy alliance of legislative reason and the modern political legislator. Human emancipation depended upon the protection of the personal domain against the totalitarian tendencies of modernity. Now, however, Bauman argues, individual liberty depends upon the critical ability to defend the public sphere, the democratic deliberative basis of political power, and the civic skills of individuals in transcending their communitarian bonds, various forms of postmodern tribalism, and life-politics based on the vague and uncertain concept of happiness (Bauman 2002, 121–57).

Social theory needs to revitalise the early modern concept of politics as the ongoing critique of reality instead of presenting its seemingly objective descriptions. Politics is an open-ended and self-reflexive process of transcending the present social condition by collective action, and social theory needs to be part of it. Close to Derrida's understanding of justice as opening up for the refounding of law and politics (Derrida 1992, 27), Bauman concludes that:

> The model of justice pursued by any form of politics is, after all, not *gegeben* but *aufgegeben*, always a step ahead of the status quo. Justice is a task looming in the yet-unknown future, a task which itself needs yet to be posited, faced and confronted, prompted by present suffering condemned as unjust (Bauman 2002, 56).

According to Bauman, the civic democratic ethos subsequently depends on the Aristotelian model of citizenship, that is, on the mutual conditionality of the autonomy of society and the autonomy of its members who need both the ability to select issues to be confronted and the belief that it is within their power to deal with these issues and remove present injustices.

***

This volume of essays opens with Zygmunt Bauman's chapter on uncertainty and the politics of fear as one of the most important features of liquid modernity. Bauman argues that liquid modernity is an era without any grand theories or political ideas, and is characterised by a new 'legitimation formula' of the politics of fear and safety which is responsible for the erosion of civil liberties and human rights. The production of a 'state of emergency' is facilitated by growing fears about personal safety and calls for the containment of 'the human waste' – immigrants, criminals, asylum-seekers, etc. The nation state is impotent in protecting its citizens against the vagaries of the global market élites and subsequently can legitimise its power only by incessant warnings against terrorist and other social threats. It takes repressive measures to tackle those threats and thus 'protects' the safety of an increasingly uncertain and insecure public.

The period of uncertainty is equally marked by the absence of solidarity with the weak who are marginalised and whose rights deteriorate as a result of the legitimation formula of fear and public safety. Bauman characteristically employs a sociological perspective and a semi-journalistic argument to launch a scathing attack on currently dominant political clichés, media images, and the imagined fears deriving from the public and private anxieties of the liquid modern society that is obsessed by its privatised wealth and safety and ever more cynical about its public welfare.

The next part of the book consists of three primarily theoretical essays drawing on central concepts in Bauman's recent writings. While Anton Schütz provides a complex analysis of *liquidity* in the philosophical, social and legal theoretical context, Pablo Ghetti examines the world of *waste* and combines Bauman's theoretical notions with a deconstructionist approach. Finally, Andreas Philippopoulos-Mihalopoulos engages in the analysis of *fear* and its counterpart – fear of fear – to suggest the emergence of 'the lawscape'.

Schütz opens by pointing to the internal paradoxes of Bauman's concept of liquid modernity and its methodological function of a calculated theoretical question mark effectively ruling out any 'solid theory of liquid society'. Its main mobilizing effect is arguably the description of human and social misery. Liquidity blurs social boundaries, laws, and distinctions and thus unlocks the blurred politics and rhetoric of 'collateral damage' inflicted on those marginalized already before the damaging action was taken. 'The human waste' is an intrinsic part of the very notion of collateral damage. Using the theoretically inspiring comparison with Luhmann's general social theory of autopoietic systems, Schütz highlights the *Lebenswelt*-sensitivity in Bauman's semantics of liquidity. It seems that liquid modern society still fights back against the undesired consequences of its liquidity and aims at securing the minimum solidity and shared meaning necessary for its persistence. However, this quest for solidity is ambiguous as illustrated by what Schütz calls the 'corporate Leninists' of the leading globalized business élite. The social distribution of liquidity and solidity remains in the hands of the powerful leaders. The leadership's solid knowledge and 'truth' subsequently need to be confronted by a sociological knowledge evolving from within liquid society – knowledge that is neither a definitive event, nor a general theory of liquid modernity.

Pablo Ghetti emphasises the political tone of Bauman's social theory, especially when describing the dismantling of togetherness and solidarity in our increasingly interdependent world. The globalized era of interdependence is contrasted with the intrinsic logic of the independence of all sovereign power and existing empires. Drawing on Bauman's book, *Wasted Lives: Modernity and its Outcasts* (2004a), and works by Jean-Luc Nancy, Jacques Derrida and Giorgio Agamben, Ghetti shows that the waste is a by-product of modernity and its belief that the world as it is can – or, indeed, should – be changed. The possibility of order relies on the simplification of the world's complexity and sameness. Waste may be produced by modern technology and economic growth but its naming is always subject to the political processes of exclusion and subordination. Confronting the waste of liquid modernity, Bauman calls for solidarity of purpose; the term is examined by Ghetti for its original Latin meaning (*solidare* – to make solid, or weld together) and radicalized, with the help of Nancy's philosophy, as an absolute solidarity of sharing out different senses of the world.

Andreas Philippopoulos-Mihalopoulos takes two key concepts – liquidity and fear – and, using many examples and illustration from philosophy, social theory, literature and art, toys with them to locate fear in liquid society. He shows that the beginnings and ends of fear are liquid and highlights Bauman's paradox of liquid fear as fear of the end of fearing. Like Bauman, Philippopoulos-Mihalopoulos argues that fear needs to be de-psychologized and perceived as a form of liquid society's self-description initiating the need for solid safety in the liquid world. Furthermore, he introduces the ambitious concept of 'the lawscape' as a fusion and circularity of two epistemic domains – normatively rich law and the dis/orderly city – ridden with conflict, crossings and paradoxes. In the lawscape, the ambivalence and paradoxes of fear are approached in a transdisciplinary manner and linked with cinematographic, architectural, socio-legal and philosophical references.

In the third part of the book, Emilios Christodoulidis and Grazyna Skąpska focus on political and ethical issues in liquid modernity and the interplay between social liquidity and solidity. Christodoulidis focuses on *work*, scrutinizes Bauman's use of Polanyi's classical book *The Great Transformation* (1944), and comes to the conclusion that the discontinuity between solid and liquid modernity is overstated in Bauman's theory. He claims that it is exactly the 'old' solidity of capitalism, including the commodification of labour, that enables the fluidity and flexibility of 'light' liquid capitalism. Christodoulidis subsequently uses Polanyi and Bauman's critical analyses of the world market and globalized capitalism, applies them to societies in economic and political transition such as Poland or South Africa, and looks for the possibilities of resisting the pressures and tensions of the globalized economy.

Grazyna Skąpska also analyses political transitions and their *ethics*, especially different ways of dealing with past human rights abuses and injustices. She contrasts post-communist 'lightness of being', emerging consumer life-style, and the calculated reluctance to address and debate the crimes of Stalinism with the ethical need to face up to and publicly deal with past atrocities. Skąpska calls for a critical public debate presenting difficult truths which would warn against repeating the political crimes of the totalitarian past, challenge the sameness of post-totalitarian popular opinion, and point to an exit from the existing social and political status quo. She is highly critical of the forgetfully liquid post-communist Polish society and calls for its ethical solidification by means of civic virtues combined with the emotions of public shame and guilt.

The fourth part of the book continues to examine the political context of Bauman's social theory of liquid modernity, especially the notions of European identity, political integration, cosmopolitanism, and constitution-making. Jiří Přibáň comments on Bauman's book *Europe: An Unfinished Adventure* (2004b) in order to highlight the modern intellectual tradition of describing Europe as a culture of ambivalence and multiplicities circling around a cosmopolitan ethos. Despite his appreciation of Bauman's criticism of European *legalism*, Přibáň is rather critical of the attempt to legitimize the adventurous integration of Europe by citing its cultural and ethical legacy, and says that the European Union's current politics of depoliticisation is in danger of becoming its own haunting spectre and political disaster. Building a European liquid politics and identity is, indeed, a risky process but it is also needs to be opened up to genuinely democratic options for which cultural traditions, legacies and values cannot be a substitute. Přibáň subsequently argues that European cosmopolitanism is an incessant search for political identity-building confronted, supplemented and expanded by its alternatives.

Drawing on Bauman's critique of ethno-nationalism and other forms of *identity* politics in the era of globalisation, Vito Breda examines the role of constitutional identity, cosmopolitanism, communitarianism and nationalism at a time when the traditional power and sovereignty of the nation state are significantly limited. Breda analyses Habermas's notion of constitutional patriotism, its communitarian and nationalist alternatives in an era of globalisation, and comes to the conclusion that Bauman's ambivalent description of liquid modernity supports the normative project of national identity-building diluted by cultural diversity. The ambivalence of liquid modernity is revealed in the recognition of cultural diversity within the framework of a democratic constitution which successfully challenges the cultural unity of the political nation but also opens a constitutional debate over the role of identity politics in modern constitutional theory.

In the final part of the book, the issues of social policies, integration, identity and immigration are addressed by Pierre Guibentif and David Nelken. Guibentif provides a profound theoretical analysis of the notion of liquidity as a theoretical concept and as a metaphor used in opposition to solidity and 'solid modernity'. According to Guibentif, the metaphorical use of liquid modernity 'infuses the force of common-sense notions into the sociological discourse' while its conceptual use draws descriptive and interpretive force 'from the distance it establishes between these two realms'. Establishing the hermeneutical dynamics of Bauman's notion of liquidity, Guibentif continues by outlining the division of the social world as a project to be created by a *social policy* and the social world as reality 'out there' to be encountered and understood by the agents of that social policy. He subsequently shows that current legislation in the field of social policy involves a number of elements and procedures corresponding to the notion of liquidity despite the constant interplay and combinations of solids and liquids in this field of legal regulation.

Finally, David Nelken takes Bauman's remarks about the civilisational difference between settled and nomadic populations and applies it in the fields of the sociology of identity and an empirical study of immigrants in Italy. Nelken avoids philosophical speculations about the meaning and value of *immigration* and the *integration* of immigrants and, instead, presents empirical research illustrating the plurality of immigrant identities and the various economic interests, status, loyalties, and values of different immigrant groups. He is particularly interested in the practice of cultural navigation which enables individuals to relate fluidly beyond their cultural boundaries without actually integrating into cultures beyond those boundaries. Interviews with some young immigrants in Italy subsequently reveal a fascinating picture of diversity and the highly specific and individualized practice of cultural navigation – the exploring and testing of cultural boundaries.

The volume brings together different theoretical perspectives, criticisms and interpretations of Zygmunt Bauman's sociology of liquid modernity. Some contributors, such as Schütz and Guibentif, rigorously assess Bauman's conceptual and methodological framework while others, such as Philippopoulos-Mihalopoulos and Skąpska, take a more liberal approach and refer to Bauman's work mainly to support their own theoretical concepts and conclusions. Some chapters focus on specific aspects of Bauman's sociology, such as the notion of waste (Ghetti), work (Christodoulidis) or Europe and its cosmopolitanism (Přibáň). And some chapters, such as those by Breda and Nelken, use Bauman's theory as a complementary view contributing to current debates in the sociology, philosophy and politics of identity. Despite this variety of theoretical perspectives, methodologies and pragmatic uses of Bauman's sociology of liquid modernity, all the essays in this book nevertheless share the view that recent changes characterized as 'liquid modernity' and 'liquid society' find their specific reflections within the domain of law and acknowledge the inspirational force of Bauman's recent work for the sociology of law, socio-legal studies, and critical legal science.

References

Bauman, Z. (1987), *Legislators and Interpreters: On Modernity, Post-modernity and Intellectuals* (Ithaca: Cornell University Press).

Bauman, Z. (1989), *Modernity and Holocaust* (Oxford: Blackwell).

Bauman, Z. (1992), *Intimations of Postmodernity* (London: Routledge).

Bauman, Z. (1993), *Postmodern Ethics* (Oxford: Blackwell).

Bauman, Z. (2000), *Liquid Modernity* (Cambridge: Polity).

Bauman, Z. (2001), *The Individualized Society* (Cambridge: Polity).

Bauman, Z. (2002), *Society under Siege* (Cambridge: Polity).

Bauman, Z. (2003), *Liquid Love: On the Frailty of Human Bonds* (Cambridge: Polity).

Bauman, Z. (2004a), *Wasted Lives: Modernity and its Outcasts* (Cambridge: Polity).

Bauman, Z. (2004b), *Europe: An Unfinished Adventure* (Cambridge: Polity).

Bauman, Z. (2005), *Liquid Life* (Cambridge: Polity Press).

Bauman, Z. (2006), *Humanitní vědec v postmoderním světě [A Humanist Scientist in the Postmodern World]* (Prague: Vize 97 Publishing).

Derrida, J. (1992), 'Force of Law: The "Mystical Foundation of Authority"' in D. Cornell et al. (eds.), *Deconstruction and the Possibility of Justice* (London: Routledge) 3–67.

Gadamer, H.G. (2003), *Truth and Method*, 2nd revised edition (London: Continuum).

Gellner, E. (1996), *Conditions of Liberty: Civil Society and Its Rivals* (London: Penguin).

Hobsbawm, E. (1994), *The Age of Extremes: The Short Twentieth Century 1914–1991* (London: Michael Joseph).

Marcuse, H. (1968), 'Liberation from the Affluent Society', in D. Cooper (ed.), *The Dialectics of Liberation* (London: Routledge), 175–92.

Polanyi, K. (1944), *The Great Transformation: The Political and Economic Origin of Our Time* (Boston: Beacon Press).

Sennett, R. (1974), *The Fall of Public Man* (New York: Random House).

PART I
LIQUIDITY, UNCERTAINTY AND FEAR

Chapter 1

Uncertainty and Other Liquid-Modern Fears

Zygmunt Bauman

It has been mostly in Europe and its former dominions, overseas offshoots, branches and sedimentations (as well as in a few other 'developed countries' with a European connection of a *Wahlverwandschaft* rather than *Verwandschaft* kind) that the addiction to fear and the security obsession have made the most spectacular progress in recent years.

In itself, it appears to be a mystery. After all, as Robert Castel rightly points out in his incisive analysis of the current insecurity-fed anxieties, 'we – at least in the developed countries – live undoubtedly in some of the most secure (*sûres*) societies that ever existed' (Castel 2003, 5). And yet, contrary to the 'objective evidence', it is the cosseted and pampered 'we', of all people, who feel more threatened, insecure and frightened, more inclined to panic, and more passionate about everything related to security and safety than people of most other societies on record. This is the puzzle that needs a resolution if the twists and turns of the popular sensitivity to danger and the shifting targets on which that sensitivity tends to be focused are to be comprehended.

With the benefit of hindsight, we may see the 1970s as a decade of not just another transformation but, borrowing Karl Polanyi's famous conception (Polanyi 1944), of the 'Great Transformation Mark Two' and a veritable watershed in modern history. That decade separated the 'glorious thirty years' of the post-war reconstruction, social compact and 'developmental optimism' that accompanied the dismantling of the colonial system and the mushrooming of 'new nations', from the brave new world of erased or punctured boundaries, information deluge, rampant globalization, a consumer feast in the affluent North, and the 'deepening sense of desperation and exclusion in a large part of the rest of the world' arising from 'the spectacle of wealth on the one hand and destitution on the other'(Hall 2001/2).

We have not fathomed as yet the full depth of that great transformation. Not for lack of trying: given the brevity of time distance, all findings and judgements must be (and better be) seen as partial, and all syntheses as provisional. With the passage of time, successive layers of emergent realities come into view, each calling for more radical revision of received beliefs and a further widening of a new, laboriously woven conceptual net. We have not yet got 'to the bottom of things'; even if we had, though, we could not decide with certainty that we had.

One fateful aspect of the said transformation was however revealed relatively early and has been thoroughly documented since: namely, the passage from a 'social state' model of inclusive community to the 'criminal justice', 'penal', or 'crime control', exclusionary state. David Garland, for instance, observes that:

> There has been a marked shift of emphasis from the welfare to the penal modality … The penal mode, as well as becoming more prominent, has become more punitive, more expressive, more security-minded … The welfare mode, as well as becoming more muted, has become more conditional, more offence-centred, more risk conscious …The offenders … are now less likely to be represented in official discourse as socially deprived citizens in need of support. They are depicted instead as culpable, undeserving and somewhat dangerous individuals (Garland 1971, 175).

Loïc Wacquant notes the 'redefinition of the state's mission'; the state 'retreats from the economic arena, asserts the necessity to reduce its social role to the widening and strengthening its penal intervention' (Wacquant 2001).

Ulf Hedetoft dwells on another aspect of the transformation of the last 20–30 years, or perhaps describes the same aspect from a different angle. He notes that 'borders are being redrawn between Us and Them more rigidly than ever before' (Hedetoft 2003, 151–2). Following Andreas and Snyder (Andreas and Snyder 2000), Hedetoft suggests that in addition to becoming more selective, bloated, diversified in their assumed forms, and diffuse, borders turned into what could be called 'asymmetric membranes' that allow exit but 'protect against the unwanted entrance of units from the other side'.

Control measures have been stepped up at external borders but, just as importantly, a tighter visa-issuing regime is imposed in countries of emigration. In 'the South'… [Borders] have diversified, as have border controls, taking place not just at the conventional places but in airports, at embassies and consulates, at asylum centres, and in virtual space in the form of stepped-up collaboration between police and immigration authorities in different countries.

As if to supply immediate evidence for Hedetoft's thesis, the British Prime Minister Tony Blair received Ruud Lubbers, the UN High Commissioner for Refugees, and suggested the establishment of 'safe havens' for prospective asylum seekers *near their homes*, that is, at a safe distance from Britain and other well-off countries that until recently served as their natural destinations. In the typical Newspeak of the current Great Transformation, the then Home Secretary David Blunkett described the topic of Blair/Lubbers's conversation on 10th February 2003 as 'new challenges for developed countries posed by those who used the asylum system as a route to the West' (using that same Newspeak, one could complain, for instance, of the challenge to the settled population by shipwrecked sailors who used the rescue system as a route to dry land).

The most recent round of curbs imposed in Britain on immigration and asylum policies vividly illustrates that shift. As the Home Secretary, Charles Clarke, spelled it out in March 2006:

> migration for work, migration to study is a good thing ... What is wrong is when that system isn't properly policed, and people are coming here who are a burden on the society, and it is that which we intend to drive out … So we will establish a system ... which looks at the skills, talents, abilities of people seeking to come and work in this country, and

ensures that when they come here they have a job and can contribute to the economy of the country.

All other claimants – prospective immigrants with not enough 'brownie points' for professional education nor experience in the kind of services where there is a deficit of home-grown professionals – are to be denied social rights and in due course deported altogether: just as one would, if only one could, proceed with the native 'redundant' population, recently renamed, symptomatically, 'the underclass'. The Prime Minister, as the press reported, hailed the plans, arguing that they would address the public's justifiable concerns about abuse of the immigration and asylum systems. They would, said Tony Blair, ensure that it is 'only people you really need to come in and work that get work permits'.

As always in Tony Blair's public statements, the words must have been rehearsed in focus groups, carefully chosen and weighed, with a view to striking a responsive chord in the mood of the electors. Ostensibly, they are aimed only at the aliens knocking at Britain's door, but they would not amount to a convincing case if they did not chime in with the way 'the population at large', that is, a decisive majority of voters, think about underdogs, or (what, after years of cuts in social provisions, amounts to much the same) about 'welfare recipients' (that is, people who do not just possess, but also use their 'social rights'). Criteria for 'external exclusion' (to deploy Christian Joppke's distinction) are after all brewed and tested at home; they are but applications of the principles arising from domestic practices of 'internal exclusion' (Joppke 2005).

Social rights are now to be offered selectively. They should be given if – and only if – the givers decide that giving them would accord with their interests, not on the grounds of the common humanity of the recipients. And the two sets of people – those who pass the second test and those who would pass the first – do not overlap.

Perhaps the two tendencies signalled here are but two intimately related manifestations of the way politicians pander to (or beef up) ever more obsessive popular concerns with security; perhaps they both stem from the shift of balance between the perpetually present inclusivist and exclusionary systemic inclinations; or perhaps they are mutually unrelated phenomena, each subject to its own logic. It can be shown, however, that whatever their immediate causes, both trends derive from the same root: the global spread of the modern way of life, which by now has reached the furthest limits of the planet, cancelling the division between 'centre' and 'periphery' or more correctly 'modern' (or 'developed') and 'pre-modern' (or 'underdeveloped' or 'backward') forms of life. This division accompanied the early stages of modernity, the phase in which modern transformations were confined to a relatively narrow, through constantly expanding, part of the globe which, for that reason, could use the resulting power differential as a safety valve protecting itself from overheating, and the rest of the planet as a dumping site for the toxic waste of its own continuous modernization. The planet is now full; that means, among other things, that typically modern processes like order-building and economic progress take place in every nook and cranny of the globe and so, everywhere, redundant humans earmarked as 'human waste' are turned out in ever rising volumes, but without 'natural' refuse tips suitable for their storage and potential recycling. The process first spotted by Rosa Luxemburg a century ago (though described by her in mainly economic, rather than explicitly social terms), has reached its ultimate limit.

Rosa Luxemburg, let us recall, suggested that though capitalism 'needs non-capitalist social organizations as the setting for its development', 'it proceeds by assimilating the very condition which alone can ensure its own existence' (Luxemburg 1961, 387, 416). Non-capitalist organizations provide a fertile soil for capitalism: capital feeds on the ruins of such organizations, and although this non-capitalist *milieu* is indispensable for accumulation, the latter proceeds at the expense of this medium, by eating it up.

A snake feeding on its own tail ... Or we could say, referring to a practice invented later, when the distance between tail and stomach had become already dangerously small and efforts to postpone the critical point grew truly desperate, the 'asset stripping' that demands that every new asset be stripped must, sooner or later, exhaust the supply or reduce it below the level required for its own sustenance. At the far (but not that far) end of that practice loom wars which devastate a country, thereby creating a new 'virgin land' open for grazing. On 8 August 2004 (when nosy journalists were safely away exploring beaches or mountain paths), an office of co-ordinator for post-conflict reconstruction and stabilization was created by the White House. It has produced, to date, 5–7-year 'post-conflict' plans for 25 countries (most of which are still unaware that they have been placed on the list of future 'rogue states') and is in the process of signing 'pre-completed' contracts for jobs with the largest – and closest to the White House – corporations. 'Reconstruction', comments Naomi Klein, has been 'revealed as tremendously lucrative' – though not for the natives, who may only expect a new waves of 'privatization and land grabs' likely to be, as before, 'locked in before the local people know what hit them' (Klein 2005).

Rosa Luxemburg envisaged a capitalism dying for lack of food – collapsing through eating up the last meadow of 'otherness' on which it grazed. A hundred years later it seems that the most awesome problem confronting global capitalism is social, not economic. A most fatal – possibly *the* most fatal – result of modernity's global triumph is the acute crisis of the (human) waste-disposal industry, with the volume of human waste outgrowing the extant managerial capacity, and a plausible prospect of modernity (now planetary) choking on its own waste products which it can neither reassimilate nor dispose of.

There are numerous signs of the fast rising toxicity of accumulating waste. The morbid consequences of industrial and household waste for the ecological balance and carrying capacity of the planet have been for some time now a matter of intense concern (though not much action has followed the debates). We have not, however, got anywhere near seeing through and grasping in full the far reaching effects of the growing masses of 'wasted humans' on the political balance and social equilibrium of human planetary coexistence.

***

Loïc Wacquant notes a paradox:

> The same people who fought yesterday with visible success for 'less state' to set free capital and its uses of the labour force, arduously demand today 'more state' to contain and hide

> the deleterious social consequences of the deregulation of employment conditions and the deterioration of social protection for the inferior regions of social space (Wacquant 2001, 40).

Of course, this is everything but a paradox. The apparent change of heart shares in the strict logic of the passage from recycling to the disposal of human waste. The passage was radical enough to need the keen and energetic assistance of state power, and the state obliged.

First, it dismantled the collective insurance against individuals dropping off (temporarily, it was assumed) the productive treadmill – the kind of insurance that made obvious sense to both the left and the right as long as the fall (and thus the assignment to productive waste) was deemed to be temporary and seen as a preliminary and brief stage of recycling ('rehabilitating', returning to active service in the industrial workforce). This quickly lost its 'beyond left and right' support once the prospects of recycling started to look remote and uncertain and the facilities of regular recycling appeared increasingly incapable of accommodating all who had fallen or never risen in the first place.

Second, it designed and built new secure waste-disposal sites – a move certain to command ever growing popular support as the hopes of successful recycling fade, the traditional method of human-waste disposal (through exportation of surplus labour) ceases to be available, and the suspicion of universal disposability spreads wider and deepens as the horrors of 'wasted humans' come home to roost.

The immediate proximity of large and growing agglomerations of 'wasted humans', likely to become durable or permanent, calls for stricter segregationist policies and extraordinary security measures, lest the 'health of society', the 'normal functioning' of the social system, be endangered. The notorious Parsonsian 'tension-management' and 'pattern-maintenance' tasks which each system needs to perform in order to survive are now reduced almost entirely to the strict separation of 'human waste' from the rest of society, its exemption from the legal framework within which the life pursuits of the rest of society are conducted, and its 'neutralization'. 'Human waste' can no longer be removed to distant waste-disposal sites and placed firmly outside the bounds of 'normal life'. It needs therefore to be sealed off in tightly closed containers.

The penal system supplies such containers. In David Garland's succinct and precise summary of the current transformation, prisons which in the era of recycling 'functioned as the deep end of the correctional sector' are today 'conceived much more explicitly as a mechanism of exclusion and control'. The walls, not the things that happen inside them, 'are now seen as the institution's most important and valuable element' (Garland 2001, 177–8). The earlier intention to 'rehabilitate', to 'reform', to 're-educate', and to return the stray sheep to the flock now, at best, attracts occasional lip service – to be countered by an angry chorus, baying for blood, conducted by the leading tabloids, with leading politicians singing the solo parts. Explicitly, the main and perhaps sole purpose of prisons is human waste disposal – a final, definitive disposal. Once rejected, forever rejected. For a former prisoner on parole or on probation, return to society is almost impossible – return to prison almost certain. Instead of easing and guiding the road 'back to the community' for prisoners who served their term of punishment, the function of probation officers is keeping the community safe from the perpetual danger temporarily let loose. 'The interests of convicted offenders, insofar as they are considered at all, are viewed as fundamentally opposed to those of the public' (Garland 2001, 180).

Indeed, offenders tend to be viewed as 'intrinsically evil and wicked', they 'are not like us' – all similarities are purely accidental:

> There can be no mutual intelligibility, no bridge of understanding, no real communication between 'us' and 'them' ... Whether the offender's character is the result of bad genes or of being reared in an anti-social culture, the outcome is the same – a person who is beyond the pale, beyond reform, outside the civil community ... Those who do not or cannot fit in must be excommunicated and forcibly expelled (Garland 2001, 184–5).

In a nutshell, prisons, like so many other social institutions, have moved from the phase of recycling to that of waste disposal. They have been reallocated to the frontline of the battle to resolve the crisis of the waste-disposal industry as a result of the global triumph of modernity and the new fullness of the planet. All waste is potentially poisonous – or at least, being defined as waste, contaminating and disturbing the proper order of things. If recycling is no longer profitable and its chances (in the present-day setting, at any rate) are no longer realistic, the right way to deal with waste is to speed up the process of degradation and decomposition while isolating it as securely as possible from the ordinary human habitat.

> Work, social welfare, and family support used to be the means whereby ex-prisoners were reintegrated into mainstream society. With the decline of these resources, imprisonment has become a longer-term assignment from which individuals have little prospect of returning to an unsupervised freedom ... The prison is used today as a kind of reservation, a quarantine zone in which purportedly dangerous individuals are segregated in the name of public safety (Garland 2001, 178).

Building more prisons, making more offences punishable by imprisonment, the policy of 'zero tolerance', and harsher and longer sentences are all elements of rebuilding the failing and faltering waste-disposal industry on a renewed foundation more in keeping with the new condition of the globalized world.

The *Guardian*'s recent survey (24 January 2003) of the most widely read dailies in Britain, bore the title: 'Press whips up asylum hysteria. Editors dub Britain a gangsters' haven as they make direct links between refugees and terrorists'. While the British Prime Minister uses every public appearance to warn the listeners that an imminent terrorist assault on Britain is certain, though its place and time are uncertainty incarnate, whereas his Home Secretary compares British society to a 'coiled spring' because of its seething and festering asylum-seeker problems, tabloids are quick to link and blend the two warnings into an asylum/terrorist hysteria.

Were there a competition for the best political formula for the new current edition of officially endorsed fear, first prize would probably go to the *Sun*, which offered a most perfect combination – one that, in addition to being eminently easy to ingest, left nothing to guesswork or the imagination: 'We have an open invitation to terrorists to live off our benefits'. Indeed a masterstroke. The novel fear of terrorists merged and cemented with the hatred – already well entrenched, but constantly needing replenishment – of 'spongers'. The crusade against 'welfare scroungers' has acquired a new indomitable weapon.

Whereas the war against *economic* uncertainty has been taken off the agenda by a state that fulminates against ignominious 'welfare dependency' and exhorts individual subjects to individually seek-and-find individual cures for individually suffered existential insecurity, the new brand of officially inspired and whipped up collective fear has been enlisted in the service of the political formula. Concerns with personal safety have been thereby shifted away from the slushy ground of market-promoted *precarité* (onto which the state governments have neither the capacity nor the will to move), onto a safer and much more tele-photogenic area (where the awesome might and steely resolution of the rulers can be, for a time at least, effectively displayed).

Other tabloids promptly fell in line with the *Sun*, hotly contesting priority in unmasking the sinister connection of asylum seekers with terrorist conspiracy (the *Daily Express* reproduced twenty of its old front pages with the triumphant conclusion 'We told you so!'), composing ever new variants of the choral motif and vying for most striking notes and highest pitches (the *Daily Mail* suggested that 'had Hitler come to Britain in 1944 he would have been entitled to asylum'). As Steven Morris, the author of the quoted survey, noted, The *News of the World*:

> placed a column from David Blunkett warning about the myths surrounding refugees and terrorism opposite a report about the asylum seekers who live near the spot where DC Oake died [*shot in the course of arresting immigrant suspects*]

Indeed, no 't' has been left uncrossed, no 'i' undotted. As Fazil Kawani, communications director of the Refugee Council, summed up the overall message: 'These reports give the impression that all asylum seekers are terrorists and criminals'. In a bizarre mixture of clichés drawn from mutually incompatible value universes, the *Sun* (in its editorial of 27 January 2003) expounds:

> This sea of humanity is polluted with terrorism and disease and threatens our way of life … Blair must say *no more now*, revoke the human rights law *now* and lock up all the illegals *now* until they can be checked.

In his thorough study of the genealogy of modern fears (Robert 2001, 35–58; see also Robert and Mucchielli 2002), Philippe Robert found out that from the early years of the twentieth century (that is, by more than a sheer coincidence, from the years when the prospect of 'the social state'(Castel 1995) first appeared on the political horizon), fears of crime began to subside and went on diminishing until the mid-1970s, when, instead, a 'personal safety' panic, focused on the crime apparently brewing in the *banlieues* where immigrant settlers were concentrated, erupted. What did erupt was, however, in Robert's view, merely a 'delayed-action bomb': security concerns were already firmly in place because of a 'double whammy' of a slow yet steady phasing out of collective insurance which the 'social state' used to offer, and the rapid 'deregulation' of the labour market.

In Hans-Jörg Albrecht's view, it is only the link between immigration and the public image of the causes of violence and security that is novel; otherwise, nothing much has changed since the beginning of the modern state, when basic folkloristic images of devils and demons that used to 'soak up' diffuse security fears 'have been transformed into danger and risks' (Albrecht 2002). Demonization has been replaced by the concept and the strategy of 'dangerization'. Political governance, therefore, has become partially dependent on the deviant other and the mobilization of feelings of safety. Political power, and its establishment, as well as its preservation, are today dependent on carefully selected campaign issues, among which safety (and feelings of being unsafe) is paramount.

Immigrants, let us note, are a better fit for the purpose than any other 'issue'. There is a sort of 'elective affinity' between the immigrants – that human waste of distant parts of the globe unloaded onto 'our own backyard' – and the least bearable of our own, home-grown fears. In the times when all places and positions are shaky and no longer reliable, the immigrants are bad news. They exude the faint odour of the waste-disposal tip which in various disguises haunts the nights of the victims and prospective casualties of rising vulnerability. For their detractors and haters they embody – visibly, tangibly, in the flesh – the inarticulate, yet hurtful presentiment of their own disposability. One is tempted to say that were there no immigrants knocking on the door, they would have to be invented. Indeed, they provide the governments with an ideal 'deviant other', a most welcome target for the 'carefully selected' 'campaign issues'.

Stripped of a large part of their sovereign prerogatives and capacities by the globalization forces which they are impotent to resist, let alone to control, governments have no choice but to 'carefully select' targets which they can (conceivably) control and against which they can aim their rhetorical salvos and flex their muscles while being heard and seen to be doing both by their grateful subjects. As Adam Crawford explains:

> 'community safety', in so far as it is concerned with 'quality of life' issues, is saturated with concerns about safety and 'ontological insecurity'. It evokes a 'solution' to crime, incivility and disorder, thus enabling the (local) state to reassert some form of sovereignty. Symbolically, it reaffirms control of a given territory, which is visible and tangible … The current governmental preoccupation with petty crime, disorder and anti-social behaviour reflects a source of 'anxiety' about which something can be done in an otherwise uncertain world (Crawford 2002, 31–2).

And the (national, recast in the age of globalization into local) governments of our days are 'casting about for spheres of activity in which they can assert their sovereignty' (Zedna 2000, 201) and demonstrate in public, convincingly, that they have done so.

Associations may be murderous, particularly if hammered home with dull monotony and deafening loudness. They may also, for the same reasons, become self-evident – no longer calling for proof. Heeding Hume's warning, we may insist that *post hoc* (or *apud hoc*, for that matter) *non est propter hoc*[1] – but then Hume suggested that assuming the opposite is a most common fallacy and one most difficult to eradicate. The association of terrorists with asylum seekers and 'economic migrants' could be over-general, unwarranted or even fanciful, but it had done its job: the figure of the 'asylum seeker', once prompting human compassion and spurring the urge to help, has been sullied and lastingly defiled, and the very idea of 'asylum', once a matter of civil and civilized pride, has been reclassified as a dreadful concoction of shameful naivety and criminal irresponsibility.

As for the 'economic migrants' who have retreated from the headlines to give way to the sinister, poison-brewing and disease-carrying 'asylum-seekers' – even the fact that they embody, as Jelle van Buuren pointed out, everything that the dominant neo-liberal creed holds sacred and promotes as the precepts that should rule the conduct of everyone ('the desire for progress and prosperity, individual responsibility, readiness to take risk etc.') did not help their image (van Buuren 2002). Already accused for years of 'sponging' and sticking to their unprepossessing customs and creeds, they would not now, however hard they tried, be able shake off the wholesale charge of terrorist conspiracy attached to 'people like them' – strangers who have come to stay.

The 'social state', that crowning of the long history of European democracy and until recently its dominant form, is today in retreat. The social state based its legitimacy and rested its demand for the loyalty and obedience of its citizens on the promise to defend them and insure against redundancy, exclusion, and rejection – against the consignment to 'human waste' caused by individual inadequacies or misfortunes, and so brought certainty and security into lives in which chaos and contingency would otherwise rule. If hapless individuals should stumble and fall, there would be someone around ready to help them onto their feet again.

Erratic conditions of employment buffeted by market competition were then, as they continue to be, the major source of uncertainty about the future and insecurity of social standing and self-esteem that haunted the citizens. It was primarily against *that* uncertainty that the *social* state undertook to protect its subjects, by making jobs more secure and the future more assured. For many reasons (among which the globalization of markets and the consequent global redistribution of waste – the twin processes which the sole effective political agencies, nation states, can neither arrest nor even seriously influence – loom larger than most), this is however no longer the case. Contemporary states cannot deliver on the social state's promise and its politicians no longer repeat that promise. Instead, their policies portend a yet more precarious, risk-ridden life calling for a lot of brinkmanship while making consistent life-projects all but impossible. Politicians these days call upon their electors to be 'more flexible' (that is, to brace themselves for yet more insecurity to come).

Under the circumstances, finding a new 'legitimation formula' on which the self-assertion of state authority and the demands of discipline may rest is a most urgent imperative for every government presiding over the dismantling and demise of the social state. Becoming a 'collateral casualty' of economic progress now controlled

1 Meaning, roughly, that if A comes before B (or coincides with B) this does not prove that A and B are related as cause and effect.

by free-floating global economic forces is not something that state government can credibly promise to stave off. But beefing up fears about personal safety threatened by similarly free-floating terrorist conspirators while promising more security guards, a denser net of X-ray machines and close circuit television, more frequent checks, and more pre-emptive strikes and precautionary arrests to protect that safety, look like an expedient alternative.

Unlike the all too tangible and daily experience of insecurity manufactured by the markets, that need no help from political powers other than to be left alone, the seige mentality and the perceived threat to individual bodies and private possessions must be *actively cultivated.* Threats must be painted in the darkest of colours, so that what becomes extraordinary is not *the advent* of the feared apocalypse but, on the contrary, the *non-materialization of threats*, presented to a frightened public as remarkable, a stroke of luck, attributable to the exceptional skills, vigilance, care and good will of state organs. What must be done is done, and to spectacular effect.

Almost daily, and at least once a week, the CIA and FBI warn Americans of the imminent attempts on their safety, putting them in a state of constant security alert and making individual safety the focus of diffuse tensions. The American President keeps reminding his electors that 'it would take one vial, one canister, one crate slipped into this country to bring a day of horror like none we have ever known'. That strategy is eagerly (albeit more modestly – because of a lack of funds rather than will) copied by other governments overseeing the burial of the social state. A new popular demand for a strong state power capable of resuscitating the fading hopes of state-endorsed social protection against consignment to waste, is built on the foundation of *personal* vulnerability and *personal* safety, instead of *social* precariousness and *social* protection.

As in so many other cases, America is again playing a pioneering, pattern-setting role in the development of that new legitimation formula. Little wonder that many a government facing the same task looks toward America with sympathetic anticipation finding in its policies a useful example to follow. Underneath the ostensible and openly aired differences of opinion on the ways to proceed, there seem to be a genuine 'union of minds' between governments, not at all reducible to a momentary coincidence of transient interests; an unwritten, tacit agreement of state-power holders on a common legitimation policy. This is exemplified by the zeal with which the British prime minister, watched with rising interest by other European prime ministers, embraces and imports American novelties related to the production of a 'state of emergency': locking the 'aliens' (euphemistically called 'asylum seekers') in camps, giving 'security considerations' unquestioned priority over human rights, writing off or suspending many human rights that have existed since the time of the Magna Carta and habeas corpus, the 'zero tolerance' policy towards the alleged 'budding criminals', and regularly repeated warnings that *some*where, *some*time, *some* terrorists will most surely strike.

We are all now potential candidates for the role of 'collateral casualties' of a war we did not declare and to which we did not give our consent. When measured against that threat, hammered home as being much more immediate and dramatic, it is hoped that the orthodox fears of social redundancy will be dwarfed and possibly even put to sleep. The news of education or health service problems, the relentless dilapidation of infrastructure and transport facilities, of a further curtailment of social provisions and a further growth in youth unemployment, are thereby relegated to the inside pages of the dailies and banished from public attention and (for a time at least) from the political agenda.

'Collateral damage' was a term specifically invented to denote human waste specific to the new planetary frontier-land conditions created by the impetuous and unrestrained globalization drive which thus far has effectively resisted all attempts at taming and regulation. Currently, fears relating to that variety of modern waste-production seem to overshadow more traditional apprehensions and anxieties relating to waste. Little wonder that they are most eagerly employed in the construction (and, so, also in the attempts at deconstruction) of new planet-wide power hierarchies.

***

Once visited upon the human world, fear acquires its own momentum and developmental logic and needs little attention and hardly any additional investment to grow and spread – unstoppably. In David L. Altheide's words, it is not fear of danger that is most critical, but rather what this fear can expand into, what it can become (Altheide 2003, 19). Social life changes when people live behind walls, hire guards, drive armoured vehicles, carry maces and handguns, and take martial arts classes. The problem is that these activities reaffirm and help produce a sense of disorder that our actions perpetuate.

Fear prompts us to take defensive actions, and taking defensive actions gives immediacy and tangibility to fear. It is our responses that recast the sombre premonitions as daily reality, making the word flesh. Fear has now settled inside, saturating our daily routines; it hardly needs any further stimuli from outside, since the actions it prompts day in, day out supply all the motivation and all the energy it needs to reproduce. Among the mechanisms vying to approximate the dream-model of *perpetuum mobile*, the self-reproduction of the tangle of fear and fear-inspired actions comes closest to claiming pride of place.

It looks as if our fears have become self-perpetuating and self-reinforcing, as if they have acquired momentum of their own, and can go on growing while drawing exclusively on their own resources. That ostensible self-sufficiency is of course but an illusion, just as in the case of numerous other mechanisms claiming the miracle of self-propulsion and self-nourishment. Obviously, the cycle of fear and fear-dictated actions would not roll so smoothly and go on gathering speed, were it not continuing to draw its energy from existential tremors.

The presence of such tremors is not exactly news; existential quakes have accompanied humans throughout their history, as none of the social settings in which humans conduct their life-pursuits have ever offered foolproof insurance against the blows of 'fate' (so called to differentiate them from adversities humans *could* avert, and conveying not so much their peculiar nature as the recognition of human *inability to predict them*, let alone prevent or tame them). By definition, 'fate' strikes without warning and is indifferent to what its victims do or abstain from doing in order to escape its blows. 'Fate' stands for human ignorance and helplessness, and owes its awesome frightening power to those very weaknesses in its victims. And, as the editors of the *Hedgehog Review* wrote in their introduction to the special issue dedicated to fear, 'in the absence of existential comfort' people tend to settle 'for safety, or the pretence of safety' (2003, 5).

The ground on which our life prospects are presumed to rest is admittedly shaky – as are our jobs and the companies that offer them, our partners and networks of friends, the standing we enjoy in wider society, and the self-esteem and self-confidence that come with it. 'Progress', once the most extreme manifestation of radical optimism and a promise of universally shared and lasting happiness, has moved all the way to the opposite, dystopian and fatalistic pole of anticipations: it now stands for the threat of relentless and inescapable change that, instead of auguring peace and respite, portends nothing but continuous crisis and relentless strain. Progress has turned into a sort of endless and uninterrupted game of musical chairs, in which a moment of inattention results in irreversible defeat and irrevocable exclusion. Instead of great expectations and sweet dreams, 'progress' evokes insomnia full of nightmares of 'being left behind' – of missing the train, or falling out of the window of the fast-accelerating vehicle.

Unable to slow down the mind-boggling pace of change, let alone predict and control its direction, we focus on things we can, or believe we can, or are assured that we can, influence: we try to calculate, and minimize the risks that we, or those nearest and dearest to us at the moment, face, uncounted and uncountable dangers which we suspect the opaque world and its uncertain future holds in store. We are engrossed in spying out 'the seven signs of cancer' or 'the five symptoms of depression', or in exorcising the spectre of high blood pressure and high cholesterol level, stress or obesity. In other words, we seek *substitute* targets on which to unload the surplus existential fear that has been denied its natural outlets, and find such makeshift targets in taking elaborate precaution against inhaling someone else's cigarette smoke, ingesting fatty food or 'bad' bacteria (though avidly swilling the liquids promising to contain the 'good' ones), exposure to sun, or unprotected sex. Those of us who can afford it fortify ourselves against all visible and invisible, present or anticipated, known or yet unfamiliar, diffuse but ubiquitous dangers through locking ourselves behind walls, stuffing the approaches to our living quarters with TV cameras, hiring armed guards, driving armoured vehicles (like the notorious SUVs), wearing armoured clothing (like 'big-soled shoes') or taking martial arts classes. 'The problem', to quote Altheide once more, 'is that these activities reaffirm and help produce a sense of disorder that our actions precipitate' (2003, 19). Each extra lock on the front door in response to successive rumours of foreign-looking criminals in cloaks full of daggers, each revision of the diet in response to successive 'food panics', make the world look *more* treacherous and fearsome, and prompt *more* defensive actions – that will, alas, add more vigour to the self-propagating capacity of fear.

A lot of commercial capital can be garnered from insecurity and fear; and it is. 'Advertisers', comments Stephen Graham, 'have been deliberately exploiting widespread fears of catastrophic terrorism, to further increase sales of highly profitable SUVs' (Graham 2004). The gas-guzzling military monsters grossly misnamed 'sport utility vehicles' that already account for 45 per cent of all car sales in the United States, are being enrolled into urban daily life as 'defensive capsules'. The SUV is:

> a signifier of safety that, like the gated communities into which they so often drive, is portrayed in advertisements as being immune to the risky and unpredictable urban life outside … Such vehicles seem to assuage the fear that the urban middle classes feel when moving – or queuing in traffic – in their 'homeland' city (Graham 2004, 186).

Like liquid cash ready for any kind of investment, the capital of fear can be turned to any kind of profit – commercial or political. And it is. Personal safety has become a major, perhaps even *the* major selling point in all sorts of marketing strategies. 'Law and order', increasingly reduced to the promise of personal safety, has become a major, perhaps *the* major selling point in political manifestos and electoral campaigns. The display of threats to personal safety has become a major, perhaps *the* major asset in the mass media ratings war, adding yet more to the success of both the marketing and political uses of fear capital. As Ray Surette puts it, the world as seen on TV resembles 'citizen-sheep' being protected from 'wolves-criminals' by 'sheep dogs-police' (Surette 1992, 43).

The most seminal characteristic of the present-day avatars of fears otherwise familiar to all previously lived varieties of human existence is perhaps the decoupling of actions inspired by fear from the existential tremors that generate that fear. In other words, fear is displaced from the cracks and fissures in the human condition where 'fate' is hatched and incubated, to areas of life largely unconnected with the genuine source of anxiety. No amount of effort invested in those areas is likely to neutralize or block the source, and so it fails to alleviate the anxiety, however earnest and ingenious that effort might be. It is for this reason that the vicious circle of fear and fear-inspired actions rolls on, losing none of its impetus – yet coming no nearer to achieving its ostensible objective.

Let me make explicit what has been implied before: the circle in question has been displaced from the area of security (that is, of self-confidence and self-assurance, or their absence) to that of safety (that is, of being sheltered from, or exposed to, threats to one's own person and its extensions). The first area, progressively stripped of institutional state-supported protections, has been exposed to the vagaries of the market and turned into a playground for global forces beyond the reach of political control and so also beyond the ability of those affected to respond adequately, let alone effectively resist. The communally endorsed insurance policies against individual misfortunes, which in the course of the last century came to be known collectively as the social (welfare) state, are now being wholly or partly withdrawn and cut below the level needed to validate and sustain the confidence of security. It is no longer hoped, let alone trusted, that extant institutions embodying the original promise will survive further and imminent cuts. With the state-built and state-serviced defences against existential tremors progressively dismantled, and arrangements for collective self-defence, like trade unions and other instruments for collective bargaining, increasingly disempowered by the pressures of market competition that erodes the solidarity of the weak, it is now left to individuals to seek, find and practice individual solutions to socially produced troubles, and to do all that through individual, solitary actions while equipped with tools and resources patently inadequate to the task.

The messages coming from the sites of political power exhort more flexibility as the sole cure for already unbearable insecurity – and so paint the prospects of yet more uncertainty, yet more privatization of troubles, yet more loneliness and impotence in individual struggles for security – and indeed more uncertainty. They promise no hope of collective foundations of existential security, and so offer no incitement to solidarity actions; instead, they encourage the listeners to focus on their individual survival in a fragmented and atomized, and so increasingly uncertain and unpredictable world.

The retreat of the state from the function on which, for the better part of a century, its claims to legitimation were founded, throws the issue of legitimation again wide open. A new consensus on citizenship ('constitutional patriotism', to deploy Jürgen Habermas's term) cannot be built now, as it used to be built not so long ago, on the assurances of constitutional protection against the vagaries of the market that play havoc with social standing and sap the rights to social esteem and personal dignity. The integrity of the political body in its currently most common form of a nation-state is in trouble, unless alternative legitimation is sought.

In the light of what has been discussed before, it is not at all surprising that an alternative legitimation of state authority and another formula for the benefits of dutiful citizenship is currently sought in the state's promise to protect its citizens against the dangers to *personal safety*. The spectre of social degradation, against which the social state swore to insure its citizens, is being replaced by the threats of a released paedophile, of a serial killer, obtrusive beggar, mugger, stalker, poisoner, terrorist – or better still, by all such threats rolled into one in the figure of an illegal immigrant – against whom the security state promises to defend its subjects.

In October 2004, BBC2 broadcast a documentary series under the title 'The Power of Nightmares: The Rise of the Politics of Fear'. Adam Curtis, the writer and producer of the series and one of the most acclaimed makers of serious television programmes in Britain, pointed out that while global terrorism is undoubtedly an all too real danger continually reproduced inside the 'no-man's land' of global wilderness, a good deal, if not most, of its officially estimated threat:

> is a fantasy that has been exaggerated and distorted by politicians. It is a dark illusion that has spread unquestioned through governments around the world, the security services, and the international media.

It is not too difficult to trace the reasons for the rapid and spectacular rise of that illusion:

> In an age when all the grand ideas have lost credibility, fear of a phantom enemy is all the politicians have left to maintain their power.

Numerous signals of the imminent shift in state-power legitimation to that of the 'security state' (or, more correctly, the 'personal safety' state) could be spotted well before 11 September – even if people needed, as it appears, the shock of the falling Manhattan towers reproduced in slow motion for months on end on millions of TV screens, for the news to sink and be absorbed, and for the politicians to reharness popular existential anxieties to the new political formula. The presidential battle between Jacques Chirac and Lionel Jospin took a form of a public auction, with two political leaders vying to outstrip each other in promising yet more flexing of muscles in the war against crime, leading to more severe legislation and imaginative punishments for juvenile or grown-up delinquents and the alien and alienating 'strangers in our midst'. When George W. Bush used toughness in the 'war against terror' in his fight to repulse the challenge of his contender, and when the British leader of the opposition attempted to unsettle the 'New Labour' government by focusing the diffuse existential anxieties arising from deregulated labour markets on the threats presented by Gypsy travellers and homeless immigrants, the seeds of fear they sowed fell onto already well prepared soil.

It was not a mere coincidence (according to Hugues Lagrange) that the most spectacular 'safety panics' and the loudest alarms about rising criminality, coupled with ostentatiously tough actions by governments, and manifested, among other things, in the rapidly rising prison population ('substitution of a prison state for the social state'), have occurred since the mid-1960s in the countries with the least developed social services (like Spain, Portugal or Greece), and in countries (like the United States and Britain) where social provisions were being drastically reduced (Lagrange 2004, 2–3). No research conducted up to the year 2000 showed a significant correlation between severity of penal policy and the volume of criminal offences, though most studies did discover a strong negative correlation between 'the carceral push' and 'the proportion of market-independent social provisions' on the one side and 'the percentage of GDP diverted to such provisions' on the other. All in all, the new focus on crime and on dangers threatening the physical safety of individuals and their property has been shown beyond reasonable doubt to be intimately related to 'the mood of precariousness', and to follow closely the pace of economic deregulation and of the related substitution of individual self-responsibility for social solidarity.

'There are no terrifying new monsters. It's drawing the poison of the fear' – observed Adam Curtis. Fear is there, saturating daily human existence as deregulation reaches deep into its foundations and the defensive bastions of civil society fall apart. Fear is there – and drawing on its seemingly inexhaustible and self-reproducing supplies in order to rebuild depleted political capital is a temptation many a politician finds difficult to resist. And the strategy of capitalizing on fear is also well entrenched – indeed, it is a tradition reaching back into the early years of the neo-liberal assault on the social state.

Long before September 11th, surrendering to that temptation while drawing on its redoubtable benefits were already well-rehearsed and tested. In a study poignantly and aptly called 'The Terrorist, Friend of Power', Victor Grotowicz analysed the uses to which the government of the German Federal Republic put the terrorist outrages perpetrated by the RAF (Red Army Faction) (Grotowicz 2000). He found that whereas in 1976 only 7 per cent of German citizens considered personal safety to be a paramount political issue, two years later a considerable majority of Germans viewed it as much more important than the fight against unemployment and inflation. During those two years the nation watched on their TV screens the photo-opportune exploits of rapidly swelling police and secret service forces and listened to the ever bolder auction bids of their politicians promising ever tougher measures in the all-out war against the terrorists. Grotowicz found as well that, whereas the liberal spirit of the original emphasis of the German constitution on individual freedoms had been surreptitiously replaced with previously resented state authoritarianism (and Helmut Schmidt publicly thanked the lawyers for abstaining from testing whether the new Bundestag resolutions conformed to constitutional law), the new legislation played mostly into the hands of the terrorists, enhancing their public visibility and stature well beyond the limits they could conceivably have attained on their own. Indeed, the common conclusion of the researchers was that the violent reactions of the forces of law and order had added enormously to the terrorists' fame. One could only suspect that the ostensible function of the new, ostentatiously stern and merciless policies, with the declared aim of eradicating the terrorist threat, played second fiddle to their hidden purpose, which was to shift the grounds of the state authority from the area it neither could nor intended to effectively control, to another area – in which its power and determination to act could be spectacularly demonstrated, to almost unanimous public applause. The most evident result of the anti-terrorist campaign was the rapid increase in the fear saturating society; as to the terrorists, the campaign's declared target, it brought them closer than they could otherwise have dreamt of to their own target of weakening democracy-sustaining values. (We may add that the eventual falling apart of the RAF and its disappearance from German life was not brought about by the repressive police actions; it was due to the changed social conditions, no longer fertile ground for the terrorist *Weltanschauung* and its practices.)

Exactly the same may be said of the sad story of Northern-Irish terrorism, obviously kept alive and boosted in large measure by the harsh military response of the British; its ultimate collapse could be ascribed to the Irish economic miracle and to 'metal fatigue' rather than to anything the British Army did or was capable of doing.

Not much has changed since. As the most recent experience shows (in the words of Michael Meacher), the endemic ineffectiveness, or even outright counterproductivity of military actions against modern forms of terrorism continue to be the rule: 'Despite the "war on terror", over the past two years ... al-Qaida seems to have been more effective than in the two years before 9/11' (Meacher 2004). Adam Curtis goes a step further, suggesting that al-Qaida barely existed at all except as a vague and diffuse idea about 'cleansing a corrupt world through religious violence', and started life as an artefact of lawyers' action; it did not even have a name 'until early 2001, when the American government decided to prosecute Bin Laden in his absence and had to use anti-Mafia laws that required the existence of a named criminal organization'.

Given the nature of contemporary terrorism, the very notion of the 'war on terror' is, jarringly, a *contradictio in adiecto*. Modern weapons, conceived and developed in the era of territorial invasions and conquests, are singularly unfit to locate, strike and destroy the extra-territorial, endemically elusive and eminently mobile targets, minute squads or just individuals travelling light, who disappear from the place of assault as rapidly and inconspicuously as they arrive, leaving behind few if any traces. Given the nature of the modern weapons at the disposal of the military, responses to such terrorist acts must be as awkward as shaving with an axe, clumsy and fuzzy, spilling over a much wider area than the one affected by the terrorist outrage, and causing more 'collateral casualties', a greater volume of 'collateral damage', and so also more terror, than the terrorists could possibly produce on their own with the weapons at their disposal. (The 'war on terrorism', declared after the terrorist assault on the World Trade towers, has already caused many more 'collateral victims' among the innocents than the outrage to which it was a response.) This circumstance is, to be sure, an integral part of the terrorists' design and the principal source of their strength, which much exceeds the power of their numbers and arms.

Unlike their declared enemies, the terrorists need not feel constrained by the limited resources they themselves command. When working out their strategic designs and tactical plans, they may include among their assets the expected and well-nigh certain reactions of the 'enemy', which are bound to magnify considerably the intended impact of their own atrocity. If the purpose of the terrorists is to spread terror among the enemy population, the enemy army and police will certainly ensure that the end is achieved to a far greater degree than anything the terrorists themselves could achieve through their own capacity.

Indeed, one can only repeat after Meacher: more often than not, and most certainly after 11 September, we seem to be 'playing Bin Laden's game'. This is, as Meacher rightly insists, a lethally flawed policy. Furthermore, agreeing to play Bin Laden's game is even less forgivable for not being motivated by the intention of eradicating the terrorist scourge, following instead an altogether different logic from the one which such an intention would inspire and justify.

Meacher accuses the governments in charge of the 'war on terrorism' with an unwillingness to contemplate what lies behind the hatred:

> why scores of young people are prepared to blow themselves up, why 19 highly educated young men were ready to destroy themselves and thousands of others in the 9/11 hijackings, and why resistance [in Iraq] is growing despite the likelihood of insurgents being killed (Meacher 2004).

Instead of pausing for this sort of contemplation, governments act (and in all probability, some of them, notably the United States, are set on continuing in the same style – as the appointment of John R. Bolton of 'no such thing as the United Nations' fame as US Ambassador to the UN vividly testifies). And whereas a thought not followed by action would be admittedly ineffective, thoughtless action proves just as toothless – as well as causing a huge increase in moral corruption and human suffering. As Maurice Druon pointed out, 'before launching its war on Iraq, the American government had but four (intelligence supplying) agents, who moreover were all double agents' (Druon 2004). Americans started the war assured 'that American troops would be welcome as liberators, with open arms and flowers'. But, to quote from Meacher once more:

> the death of more than 10,000 civilians, with 20,000 injured and even higher Iraqi military casualties, is exacerbated, one year on, by the failure to deliver key public services, … rampant unemployment and a gratuitously heavy-handed US military (Meacher 2004).

Terrorist forces would hardly buckle under such blows; on the contrary, they draw and replenish their strength precisely from the clumsiness and prodigality of their adversary. Excess characterizes not only the explicitly anti-terrorist operations;

it is also a conspicuous feature of the alerts and warnings addressed at their own populations by the anti-terrorist coalition. As Deborah Orr observed a year ago:

> many flights are intercepted, yet are never found to have been actually under threat … The tanks and troops were stationed outside Heathrow, even though they eventually withdrew without finding anything at all (Orr 2004).

Or take the case of the 'ricin factory' discovery, publicly and vociferously announced in 2003 and immediately

> trumpeted as 'powerful evidence of the continued terrorist threat', although in the end, the germ warfare factory at Porton Down couldn't prove that any ricin had ever been in the flat touted as a significant terrorist base (Campbell 2005).

Indeed, as Duncan Campbell reported from the courts where the alleged 'ricin conspirators' were judged, the only document on which the case was based was already at an early stage proved to be an 'exact copy of pages on an internet site in Palo Alto, California' (Campbell 2005). No link to Kabul or Al-Qaida could be found, and the prosecution felt obliged to drop the charge. This did not stop Home Secretary David Blunkett from announcing two weeks later that 'Al Qaida and the international network is seen to be, and will be demonstrated through the courts over months to come, actually on our doorstep and threatening our lives'; in the United States, Colin Powell used the 'London ricin ring' as a proof that 'Iraq and Osama Bin-Laden were supporting and directing terrorist poison cells throughout Europe'. All in all, although 500 people had been held under the new terrorist laws up to the beginning of February 2004, only two have been convicted.

Orr points out that, in the face of such inanities, the hypothesis of powerful trade interests being instrumental in fanning up the terrorist scare must acquire at least some credibility. Ample data show such suspicion to be credible. There are indications that the 'war on terror' has increased considerably, instead of combating, the world-wide proliferation of small weapons: the authors of an Amnesty International and Oxfam joint report estimate that half a million people are killed each year by small weapons, 'the real weapons of mass destruction' (Bowcott and Norton-Taylor 2003). The profits which American producers and traders of 'self-defence stuff and gadgets' make from popular fears which in turn are strengthened and magnified by the very ubiquity and high visibility of such stuff and gadgets, have been also amply documented. All the same, it needs to be repeated that the staple and most massive product of the war waged against terrorists accused of sowing fear has, thus far, been fear itself.

Another highly visible product of that war has been the far-reaching constraints imposed on personal freedoms – some of them unheard of since the times of the Magna Carta. Conor Gearty, professor of human rights law at the London School of Economics, lists a long inventory of laws limiting human liberties which have been passed already in Britain under the rubric of 'anti-terrorist legislation', only to agree with numerous other worried commentators that it is by no means certain whether 'our civil liberties will still be here when we seek to pass them on to our children' (Gearty 2004). The British judiciary has so far complied with the governmental policy that 'there is no alternative to repression' – and so, as Gearty concludes, 'only liberal idealists' and other similarly gullible well-wishers may 'expect the judicial branch to lead society' in the defence of civil liberties in this 'time of crisis'.

The stories about the sinister activities inside the Guantánamo camp or Abu-Ghraib prison, cut off not only from visitors but from any national or international law, and of the gradual but relentless descent into inhumanity of men and women appointed to perpetrate or supervise that lawlessness, have been widely enough publicised not to need repeating here. What is less often mooted, however, is that the demons that surfaced in those remote places may only be particularly extreme, radical and impudent, wild and reckless specimens of a larger family of lemures that haunt the attics and cellars of our homes down here – in the world where, to quote Attali:

> individualism triumphs. No one, or almost no one believes that changing life of others is of any relevance to his or her own life. No one, or almost no one, believes that voting can change his or her condition, and, a fortiori, the condition of the world (Attali 2004).

A world, in other words, in which each individual is left on his or her own while individuals are tools of each other's promotion.

Solitary life may be joyous and is likely to be busy – but it is bound to be risky and fearful as well. In such a world, there are not many rocks left on which struggling individuals can build their hopes of rescue and on which they can rely in case of personal failure: human bonds are comfortably loose, but for that same reason frightfully unreliable, and solidarity is as difficult to practise as its benefits, and even more so its moral virtues, are difficult to comprehend.

The new individualism, the fading of human bonds and the wilting of solidarity are the other side of the globalization coin. In its present, purely negative form, globalization is a parasitic and predatory process, feeding on the potency sucked out of the bodies of nation states and their subjects. To quote Attali once again, nations organized into states

> lose their influence on the general direction of things and forfeit in the process of globalization all the means they would need to orient their destiny and resist the numerous forms their fears may take (Attali, 2004).

Society is no longer protected by the state, or at least, it is unlikely to trust the protection on offer; it is now exposed to the rapacity of forces it does not control and no longer hopes or intends to recapture and subdue. It is for that reason in the first place that state governments struggling day in, day out to weather the current storms, stumble from one ad-hoc crisis-management campaign and one set of emergency measures to another, dreaming of nothing more than staying in power after the next election but otherwise devoid of far-sighted programmes or ambitions, not to mention visions of a radical resolution to the nation's recurrent problems. 'Open' and increasingly defenceless on both sides, the nation state loses its might, now evaporating into the global space, and its political acumen and dexterity, now increasingly relegated to the sphere of individual 'life politics' and 'devolved' to individual men and women. Whatever might and politics still attached to the state and its organs dwindles gradually to a volume sufficient perhaps to serve a large police precinct. The reduced state can hardly manage to be anything other than a security state.

Having leaked from a society forcefully laid open by the pressure of globalizing forces, power and politics drift ever further in opposite directions. The problem, and the awesome task that will in all probability be the current century's paramount challenge, is reconciling power and politics. The reunion of the separated partners inside the domicile of the nation-state is perhaps the least likely outcome.

On a negatively globalized planet, all the most fundamental problems – the meta-problems conditioning the tackling of all other problems – are *global*, and being global they admit of no local solutions; there are not, and cannot be, local solutions to globally originated and globally invigorated problems. The reunion of power and politics may be achieved, if at all, at the planetary level. As Benjamin R. Barber poignantly put it:

> no American child will feel safe in bed if in Karachi or Baghdad children don't feel safe in theirs. Europeans won't boast much longer of their freedoms if people in other parts of the world remain deprived and humiliated (Barber 2004).

No longer can democracy and freedom be assured in one country or even in a group of countries; defending these in a world saturated with injustice and populated by billions of humans denied human dignity would inevitably corrupt the very values they are meant to defend. The future of democracy and freedom can be made secure on a planetary scale – or not at all.

Fear is arguably the most sinister of demons nesting in the open societies of our time. But it is the insecurity of the present and uncertainty about the future that hatch and breed the most awesome and least bearable of our fears. That insecurity and uncertainty, in its turn, is born of the sense of impotence: we seem to be no longer in control, whether individually, severally or collectively – and to make things still worse, we lack the tools that could elevate politics to the level where power has already settled, and so enable us to recover and retake control over the forces that shape our shared condition while determining the range of our possibilities and the limits to our freedom to choose: control which has now slipped or has been torn out of our hands. The demon of fear will not be exorcised until we find (or more precisely *construct*) such tools.

References

Albrecht, H.-J. (2002), 'Immigration, crime and safety', in A. Crawford (ed.), *Crime and Insecurity: The Governance of Safety in Europe* (Uffculme: Willan Publishing), 159–85.

Altheide, D.L. (2003), 'Mass Media, Crime, and the Discourse of Fear', *Hedgehog Review* 5:3, 9–25.

Andreas, P. and Snyder, T. (2000), *The Wall around the West* (Lanham MD: Rowman and Littlefield).

Attali, J. (2004), *La voie humaine* (Paris: Fayard).

Barber, B.R. (2004), In conversation with Artur Domosławski, *Gazeta Wyborcza*, 24–6 December, 19–20.

Beckett, A. (2004), 'The Making of the Terror Myth', *Guardian*, G2, 15 October, 2–3.

Bowcott, O. and Norton-Taylor, R. (2003), 'War on terror fuels small arms trade', *Guardian*, 10 October, 19.

Campbell, D. (2005), 'The ricin ring that never was', *Guardian*, 14 April.

Castel, R. (1995), *Métamorphoses de la question sociale; une chronique du salariat* (Paris: Fayard).

Castel, R. (2003), *L'insécurité sociale: Qu'est-ce qu'être protégé?* (Paris: Seuil).

Crawford, A. (2002), 'The governance of crime and insecurity in an anxious age: the trans-European and the local', in A. Crawford (ed.), *Crime and Insecurity: The Governance of Safety in Europe* (Uffculme: Willan Publishing), 27–51.

Druon, M. (2004), 'Les stratèges aveugles', *Le Figaro*, 18 November, 13.

'Fear Itself' (2003), Editorial introduction, *Hedgehog Review* 5:3, 5–8.

Garland, D. (2001), *The Culture of Control: Crime and Social Order in Contemporary Society* (Oxford: Oxford University Press).

Gearty, C. (2004), 'Cry Freedom', *Guardian*, G2, 3 December, 9.

Graham, S. (2004), 'Postmortem City: Towards an urban geopolitics', *City* 8:2, 165–96.

Grotowicz, V. (2000), *Terrorism in Western Europe: In the Name of the Nation and the Good Cause* (Warsaw: PWN).

Hall, S. (2001/2), 'Out of a Clear Blue Sky', *Soundings*, Winter, 9–15.

Hedetoft, U. (2003), *The Global Turn: National Encounters with the World* (Aalborg: AUP).

Joppke, C. (2005), 'Exclusion in the Liberal State: The Case of Immigration and Citizenship Policy', *European Journal of Social Theory* 8:1, 43–61.

Klein, N. (2005), 'Allure of the blank slate', *Guardian*, 18 April.

Lagrange, H. (2003), *Demandes de sécurité* (Paris: Seuil).

Luxemburg, R. (1961), *The Accumulation of Capital* (tr. A. Schwarzschild) (London: Routledge).

Meacher, M. (2004), 'Playing Bin Laden's Game', *Guardian*, 11 May, 21.

Orr, D. (2004), 'A relentless diet of false alarms and terror hype', *Independent*, 3 February, 33.

Polanyi, K. (1944), *The Great Transformation: The Political and Economic Origins of Our Time* (New York: Reinhart).

Robert, P. (2002), *Entretien avec Philippe Robert*, 'Une généalogie de l'insécurité contemporaine', in *Esprit*, December, pp. 35–58.

Robert, P. and Mucchielli, L. (2002), *Crime et unsecurité; l'état de savoirs* (Paris: La Découverte).

Surette, R. (1992), *Media, Crime and Criminal Justice* (Pacific Grove, Cal.: Brooks-Cole).

Van Buuren, J. (2002), 'Le droit d'asile refoulé à la frontière', *Manière de Voir*, March–April, 76–80.

Wacquant, L. (2001), 'Comment la "tolérance zéro" vint à l'Europe', *Manière de Voir*, March–April.

Zedner, L. (2000), 'The Pursuit of Security', in T. Hope and R. Sparks (eds.), *Crime, Risk and Insecurity* (London: Routledge).

PART II
THEORIZING LIQUID MODERNITY

Chapter 2

How *aufarbeiten* 'Liquid Society'? Zygmunt Bauman's Wager

Anton Schütz

Sociological navigation in liquid society

Bauman nowhere claims that introducing the semantics of *liquidity* into the phenomenological account of life in contemporary Western society and its theoretical study is a groundbreaking innovation. He carefully avoids arguing that any defining authoritative body of doctrine, any specific outline of political action, or, even less, any coupling of political doctrine *and* political action, underlies his liquidity terminology. Nonetheless, he uses it as his lead-concept[1] and compassing denominator for the vast gamut of early twenty-first-century social evolutions and societal microevolutions studied in his recent writing (Bauman 2000; Bauman 2003; Bauman 2005). I shall argue that this is of the essence of what Bauman does in his work, that the reference to *liquidity*, in the various connections in which it appears in Bauman's text, has the precise methodological function of an explicit, calculated question mark, and that Bauman's later books are innovative precisely by dint of allowing such an open reference in and using it as the matrix of the action at work in his writing. Liquidity, in Bauman, is emphatically not the sign or summary of some over-arching conception. It is the name of the point at which sociological theory fails to offer, *succeeds* in failing to offer, the epistemologically satisfying thing, the infinitely coveted but inexorably unavailable model, a solid theory of liquid society. The myth of a pre-established conjugality between a power of effective implementation naturally releasing a discourse of justification, which in turn provides the power device with the required amount of plausible efficiency, that self-fulfilling saga of a coincidence between action and doctrine, government and goal, power and competence, is silently suspended in Bauman's text. An underlying scepticism, a probable disillusionment, a 'negative politology' perhaps – all in rather blatant opposition to a picture of postmodernity that used to be very common only some twenty years ago, some aspects of which are to be found in Bauman's own previous writing (for instance, Bauman 1997) – shape his portrayal of twenty-first-century postmodern society. Bauman describes postmodernity no longer as the mere *matter of writing* which the two last decades of the twentieth century have been

1 The present study especially refers, within the astonishing output from 2000 onwards, to the publications thematically dedicated to the liquidity topic. Together, they constitute what can be understood as a pioneering twenty-first-century social-critical history of the present.

overly pleased to see in it, no longer as an ever only hermeneutically adumbrated *Ding an sich*, but as a matter of painstakingly revealed real life conditions – as a landscape of failed projects of governance and ruins of politico-social rationality. As the most immediate result of this change of perspective, postmodernity loses the major propaganda virtue to which a large part of its short and irrelevant, but global triumph can be attributed without hesitation: that of a cheerleading category. The colours have faded and darkened, and as a consequence, a number of earlier, both modern and even pre-modern standards, moralistic, patriotic, and confessional, that had since long been discarded or at least banned from visibility, are allowed to emerge again, and enjoy, if not public, at least media-wide rehabilitation.

Seen from that angle, the society Bauman approaches in his liquid-related publications is arguably no longer of the postmodern species. If there is, nonetheless, one absolutely traditional category that looms large in Bauman, it is no doubt that of *misery*. Liquid society is the society of a whole gamut of newly emerging types of misery. There are diverse special or *uneigentlich* types, but largely the new misery is of the ordinary sort, and obvious to the unimpaired eye. Abandoned by the agencies of wealth and power, silenced by the self-authenticating, self-denying interventions of the media, new misery, clad in society-wide misrecognition – recognised, that is, only as a 'threat to safety' – is the predominant aspect of the evolution unfolded in Bauman's studies. This evolution leads society from an earlier and eminently wishful self-representation, the multicultural narrative of the melting-pot (itself already a 'liquid'-related metaphor), to its less edifying present sequel. The uncanny story of the present geo-social encounter with the liquid theme unfolds against the new horizon of such unmasterable challenges and impossible missions as how to uphold unjustifiable boundaries, for instance, by controlling uncontrollable migration flows. A long list of claims, notions, and values, all of immemorial standing, including community, equality, solidarity, indeed 'social behaviour' (the normative category without which the newly discovered syndrome of 'anti-social behaviour' makes no sense), are in the process of being made redundant, casually and unspectacularly. This is not a matter of political will, but of situation-imposed factors – factors which, abandoned by political will, indeed precisely by dint of the cunning move of unplugging them from the forces underlying political choice, are allowed to operate as *necessities*. Necessity is only amenable to severely reduced, if not purely nominal, Orwellian newspeak versions of law and politics: *necessitas non habet legem*. The resulting regime can and has been described as that of bare, biopolitical or more exactly non-political, housekeeping, a management (Legendre 1983)[2] or an *oikonomia*[3] working as infra-legal decision-making routines, except that under

2 On the topic of management and its understanding, much of the extensive list of studies and 'lessons' published by Pierre Legendre from the 1960s onwards is still hugely instructive today. Legendre was the first author to shift the focus of the study of power from the paradigm of bureaucracy to that of management.

3 On the politico-conceptual history of *oikonomia* and related notions, on its paradigmatic status in Western governance, see Agamben (2007). Such routines were practised as a matter of course and dealt with *sub verbo* '*oikonomia*' (or in Latin '*dispositio*'). They tend to make early church history look like a textbook for the study of post-modern administration.

conditions of permanent necessity, of normal exception, the infra-legality is, in fact, upgraded into diverse degrees of meta-legality (Agamben 2006). And conditions of permanent necessity are doubtlessly provided by the fact that the new *oikonomia* here at stake appears as definitively deprived of any *oikos*, and that the horizon of the new management is essentially unmanageable. We are thus confronted with a situation in which the auspicious notions of economy, of economic rationality, of management, turn into euphemisms for the programming of exceptional and very generally sacrificial measures and the routines of their implementation. The semantics of liquid/liquidity provides Bauman with a vocabulary sufficiently eloquent to name and analyse the unfettering of the limits of *ad hoc* action thus vindicated, without detouring into academic terminology – as it is the case for a whole range of authors who ground their analyses in partly related notions such as *contingency* and *differentiation.*

Bauman, to be sure, does not even say, in so many words, that the liquid-modern social world is based on the ruin of the mythical machinery of mutual confirmation and reciprocal reproduction between political structures endowed with implementation power and justificatory discourses capable of conjuring up legitimate grounds, or that it was this successful partnership that, in its prosperous times, constituted the basic equipment of solid modernity, and endowed it with sustainable conditions of governance. Yet the picture he paints leaves no doubt about the elementary level at which the transition towards the type of regime he calls 'liquid' undercuts the very possibility of 'regime' or sustainable governance (Bauman 2000, 166ff.). While the liquifying of social relationships entails a tremendous increase in the range, intensity and immediacy of powerlessness in individual lives and their exposure to power, giving rise to innumerable new and unaccounted for forms of enslavements and quasi-enslavements, we see equally uncanny but entirely different changes in the identity of the power resources that fuel these new dependency relationships. Power tends to come less and less in the familiar guise of factually possessed and 'enjoyed' chances of effective and visible domination, and more and more in the bewildering attire of a naked *fait accompli* unaccompanied by any interpretable penumbra or significant resonance, as a *factum brutum* without agent, without action, even without precisely identifiable enjoyment (let alone claims of responsibility upon which law is founded). The process of substituting a liquid Leviathan for a solid Leviathan (or alternatively, a liquid Behemoth for a solid Leviathan) entails, in other words, both an explosion of subjection, and an implosion of mastery.

Fait accompli, 'collateral damage'

On the one hand, a new Western 'New Economic Policy', answering global challenges (as did Lenin's older Soviet NEP – which, of course, responded to a thoroughly different set of global challenges), programmes an unending sequence of austerity packages, imposes all-time highs of deprivation and new poverty, erases the very reference which through Western time immemorial had served politics as its heading and horizon. This reference is none other than the quest for a good life, coupled with the assumption that society possesses in its political institutions a range of enabling tools fitted to that task. These tools are delicate, they are always potentially aggravating, they need an increasing amount of care and control, yet in principle these tools have been effective with regard to implementing and continuing the quest for a good life, both for the Polis and the individual. This kind of quest had survived, under very diverse overarching power economies – for example, the period of the conquest and pacification policy of imperial Rome, the competition between Popes and Emperors, the era of the divine right of kings, and even, indisputably, Soviet-type one-party rule (each of them, to be sure, polluted, paralysed, denaturalized by its own intimate kind of corruption). With liquid modernity, something genuinely new appears. One of the merits of Bauman's historiographic fine-tuning of the 'liquid' concept is that it helps to isolate a 'liquid substance' which, on the one hand, fits a widespread pattern of current experience, and on the other hand, sets it off from earlier programmatic steps towards a purely functional (in that limited sense, equally *liquid*) self-definition of modern society as liberated from its solid (traditional) fetters. Bauman is perfectly aware that such earlier appearances of liquid and liquidation are commonplace at earlier stages of modernity. Jeremy Bentham's appeal to pain and happiness as regulators for human behaviour provides a clear case in point. The evolutions of contemporary society noted by Bauman underline no longer the topicality of the quest of a good life, but the remnants of its failure: alienation, self-alienation, proletarisation, finally – with Agamben's suggested shorthand of *legitimate negligibility become man*, the *homo sacer* (Agamben 1998).[4] More optimistic outlooks do exist: an example not mentioned by Bauman is the claim that the 'Empire' is every day more exposed to the challenge of the 'multitudes' – an overly confident prophecy which, in view of the growing silence and *désengagement* of those multitudes, proves every day more clearly that it is, regrettably, but a raving *rêverie*.

On the other hand, the relationship between action and outcome no longer corresponds to the rational confidence in a strategy of goal-achievement or programme-realization. This relationship, in its current state, is on the contrary most perfectly understood by (an appropriately broadened and qualified version of) the concept of a *fait accompli*. Specifically I shall focus here on 'collateral damage'. Some violent deaths are regretted *in specie*, 'but' – the 'but' never fails to follow the apology, invariably *in the same sentence* – at the same time reasserted as unavoidable *in genere*. The notion, which has circulated for more than twenty years now, is a mode of the civil explanation of military causality.[5] 'Collateral damage', the *species*,

4 Archaic in origin, yet massively contemporary in its application, the notion of the *homo sacer* – which, as far as I can see, has not yet been analysed from this viewpoint – intersects with, or at least covers, as a sub-set of its semantics, a series of earlier themes of theological, philosophical or politico-economical background. They include, most prominently, 'alienation' and 'proletariat'.

5 The presence of military modes and models in the underlying structure of political and even cultural history – rather than merely 'strategic' ones, as the current euphemism has it – has been ground-breakingly analysed in terms of dispositive (Foucault 1983). For the interplay of intended and unintended effects, collateral damages and collateral benefits, and their location within the general architecture of governance and administration see Agamben (2006).

and 'fait accompli', the *genus*, both spell out the general conditions of contingent or liquid life in so far as both pertain to the genre *happening* – in the original, strong sense of to 'happen' which stipulates that the happening be unanticipated, or devoid of a pre-existing plan of action, but furthermore, that it be unanticipatable as well.[6] The form of happening or *fait accompli* in general, of 'collateral damage' in particular, should be understood as a signal and a manifestation of deep modifications in the understanding of politics. Most decisively, the declaration of 'collateral damage' after a military intervention can take on, in certain circumstances, an important share of the role which, only a century ago, was fulfilled by the declaration of war *before* a military intervention. At a first level, embarrassingly, in spite or perhaps in virtue of the wide, history-shaping, geo-political task it is given, the language game of 'collateral damage' can be perfectly analysed in typical old-style neurotic family communication. The expression of one's official *regretting* of one's own damaging action is meant to 'conceal' – which is to say, to more effectively reveal – one's more than official *reproof* of the *other* person's *previous* action. At the same time, it serves to notify to the other person the possibility of equally 'collateral', thus equally regrettable *future* damages in case of further instances of misbehaviour or non-compliance.

But there is more to it than that casual *chef d'oeuvre* of the art of the double-bind, and this has to do with Bauman's distinction solid/liquid. 'Liquid' refers not only to a change in relation to elements, masses, and metaphorically to the quasi-material conditions known to sociologists as 'social tissue' or even 'social bond'. It points most relevantly to lines and laws, to boundaries, thresholds, distinctions. By becoming liquid, they become blurred. The expression 'collateral damage' thus epitomizes the view that military action can entail, apart from its intended or major effects, also diverse minor and regrettable ones. This, at least, is the small contribution the formula collateral damage offers on the explicit level. Not explicitly said, only tacitly and urgently submitted to silent-submissive acceptance, is the underlying claim that the intended effect, the action itself, is unquestionably commendable. The action is collateral to the extent to which it is the unintended concomitancy of an intended principal action. If intended, is the latter not beneficial as well?[7] The blurring effect takes place in the silence imposed by the sombre quid pro quo the formula invites. That casualty x, destruction y, are *not* to be understood as a *success* of our military campaign is what we make clear by the apologies we offer, and by

6 'To come about by "hap" or chance' (*Compact Oxford English Dictionary* 1985, s.v. 'to happen').

7 At least, the fact of accepting the offered apologies for the collateral part seems certainly to give rise to a presumption that, by the same token, one also endorses the main, intended part. The negative complexity at work in the modern notion of collateral damage sets it apart from the earlier concept of a collateral *benefit*. In his *On Providence*, Alexander of Aphrodisias, writing at the turn of the third century AD, explains that the Ninth Sphere exerts its providence over the world accidentally rather than deliberately. He chooses as his example of such unintended care the man who, although he has never given a thought to the idea of nourishing the mice and lizards, cockroaches and ants living in his house, nonetheless factually provides for their sustenance – by intentionally providing for that of his family (Thillet 2003, 67).

acknowledging and endorsing, *urbi et orbi*, our duty of offering apologies. These unintended, only factually inflicted casualties and destructions are thus admittedly regrettable. The policy, however, which not only has regrettably caused these casualties and destructions but may also continue to cause, equally regrettably, further such casualties and destructions, is the other side of the apology.

What is blurred in the very notion of 'collateral damage' is nothing less fundamental than the distinction between being and action. According to this distinction, which is an old and in a concept-historical perspective quite resilient distinction, whatever happens happens to a being, for instance a person, and not to an action, for instance, a military campaign.[8] Only beings can perform as legal subjects and indeed as historic subjects, as in law only beings (although not only persons) can come forward with claims, be confronted with claims, and so on. This is what the notion of 'collateral damage' takes issue with. In view of the damage's 'collateral' status, mostly decipherable as a euphemistic hint to the status of the damage's *victims* and their marginal status before the damage, the damaging action itself – which is after all part of a larger and historically relevant policy – steps in as the damage's actual, intelligible subject. The narrative of the collateral damage presents us with an *action* that has become the *victim* of *its own unintended effect*. It indeed suggests that the *action* would be treated unjustly if it were made liable for its own (the *action's* own) unintended effects.

Another instance of a blurred or strained language game can be taken from the recent evolution of ordinary language, or more precisely from what happens when academic language dresses up as ordinary language. Take the notion 'out there'. Every university teacher knows the formula as an irreplaceable pedagogico-epistemological enabling device and short-hand way of summarizing the minimal requirements for any lecture theatre communication to achieve the difficult task: the task of taking into account, and integrating into its own routine, its own decentered position. The teacher who refers to an outside opens up what would otherwise always threaten to be a strictly ritual separation. Still around after many years of demolition (or, perhaps, 'deconstruction'), the formula is currently undergoing a deep transformation. Much like a historic town-house renovation, a radical change of function (of context and referent) is taking place under a conserved façade (in this case, of 'meaning'). Until now, the idea of referring to an 'out there' was to expose a claim to a (potentially perilous) *other side*. It served as measure and test for anything taught, claimed, said, believed, inside the walls of the cosy classroom. In its new shape, whatever is introduced as an outside presents itself *eo ipso* and *as well* as *another inside*, another equally outside-exposed entity, or in Luhmannian lingo, another system in the system's environment. 'Out there' thus refers now to *positions* located *within* a larger common ('global') communication process. As a consequence, 'out there' is no longer open to whoever claims or wishes to be there; instead, certain minimal requirements must be satisfied. The distinction between in

8 A *threefold* distinction of any specific 'matter of law', according to whether it pertains to persons, things, or actions, has played an important role throughout the entire post-history of Roman Law, and can be traced back to a phrase of the second-century AD Roman lawyer Gaius's genre-pioneering work 'Institutiones' (De Zulueta 1946, 4).

here and out there itself, thus enters the era of selective exposure. It becomes itself subject to a split into *two* 'out there*s*': a lawful out there that includes all items and actors one can and has to count upon, the good society of respectable others, and a second, lawless out there – the universe of the legitimate negligibility of mere life, predestined to the techniques of *fait accompli*. The victims of future collateral damage will not be recruited amongst the participants in the amicable exchange of feed-ins and feed-backs, but among preselected candidates for destructive action later-to-be-regretted, a threshold populace of uninvited fairies and uncooperative rogues (and, generally, people who don't get their act together).

It is tempting to discover in the vicissitudes of the out there, the splitting of its referent into an internal, treatable one, integrated into the machinery of communication and decision-making, and an external one, which embodies its other side and whose exclusion only provides the machinery with its identity and profile, a version of the problem which self-referential and autopoietic thinking had been looking into throughout the last two or three decades of the twentieth century. There is, Luhmann teaches, one thing that 'systems' cannot do: act outside themselves (Luhmann 1995, 455ff.). The working of systems supposes that they can communicate about their environment, never with their environment. The notion of 'operative closure', the standard autopoietic version of the system's riposte to the onslaught of its environment, points with increased accuracy to the process of de-realization which affects the second and lawless outside which has been stripped of its referential function (Luhmann 1995, 447).[9] *This* outside is now irrelevant, the first, *relevant* outside being plugged into the system – upgraded to the level of an ultimate testing ground of all internally selected chances and risks. Now, 'operative closure' is an ill-famed term. One might well ask why. One might ask whether the best way of indicating one's disagreement with an object is to avoid a term that designates it with precision. However, the enigma of the term's disreputableness dissipates as soon as one looks closely enough, and with required sociological *désinvolture*, at its genesis. The token critical legal or social academic has had to bear much disappointment in his or her life, through the last 20 or 30 years, without budging – is it not obvious, almost natural, in these conditions, that a term like Luhmann's 'operative closure' should present a uniquely welcome and affordable occasion for reasserting one's unbroken integrity, in the tone of august indignation here allowed? This being said, it is to be feared that the closure-issue offers an embarrassingly rich harvest of occasions for the second-order-observation of the postmodern legal academy. Feared indeed, for, supposing that under such observation a certain set of fundamental values turns out to be eminently compatible with the sociable task of taking sides and showing to which bunch one belongs, eminently incompatible with the task of understanding society, a fault-line opens up which would clearly paralyse the reference to the academy, to scholarly ideology as such.

9 On some politico-historical implications, see Balke (1998, 130ff.).

The current restoration of the solid: 'leadership'

Has Luhmann's 'frivolously intellectualist' acknowledging of contingency, and the constraints that flow from it, a differently structured, yet comparable respondent in Bauman's foregrounding of a new general *liquid* social condition? Here is the difference: while Bauman's concern is related to the vicissitudes of *Lebenswelt*, Luhmann's is to how decision-making processes can *subtract* themselves from *Lebenswelt*.[10] And here is Luhmann's answer: by means of functional differentiation. 'Draw a distinction!' (Luhmann 1997, 60) Heeding this injunction pays off by reducing complexity, by making situations manageable. Yet the operation has its price. Here is how Bauman calculates this price: 'Between the overall order of things and the volatile individual agencies, vehicles and stratagems of purposeful action, there is a perpetually widening gap with no bridge in sight.' The price is, in other words, an emerging fault line. The paradoxical genesis of this fault line consists in the fact that it

> has not been achieved through dictatorial rule, subordination, oppression, enslavement [or] the colonization of the private sphere by the 'system', [but] results, on the contrary, from the radical melting of the fetters and manacles rightly or wrongly suspected of limiting the individual freedom to choose and to act.

And Bauman concludes:

> *Rigidity of order is the artifact and sediment of the human agent's freedom* [. . .], the product of "releasing the brakes", [of] deregulation, liberalization, "flexibilization", increased fluidity (Bauman 2000, 5; his italics).

What is remarkable here is that the new fluidity – an innovation hatched within the *Lebenswelt* – favours, once obtained and implemented, capacities of decision-making and line-drawing that create a new type of rigidity which succeeds liquidated *Lebenswelt*. Autopoiesis is an enabling device for trouble-shooting. But trouble-shooting 'helps' the maintenance of *Lebenswelt* only at the price of endowing it with a second-order framework that must relativize the *Lebenswelt* and, in the end, replace it. It is not surprising then, that, every time the undistinguished outside *Lebenswelt* shows up in system communication (which, incidentally, happens rarely enough) the result is by no means irritation, but embarrassment – unmitigated indifference or stunned silence. System theorists know why. They know that social systems are machines in the service of decision making, agencies for the drawing of lines, sites of production for *faits accomplis*. Systems know nothing; they only do. All that counts for them is that which 'makes a difference' when fed into decision-making routines.

---

10 *Lebenswelt* is, in autopoietic terms, related to a blockage of system differentiation (Luhmann 1996, 20ff.). The list of irreconcilable discrepancies between Bauman and Luhmann includes, of course, the topic of justice, conceived by the first along Husserlian and Levinassian lines (Bauman 1997) as the gift of an outside and by the second as a condition of functionally defined recursive operations (Luhmann 2004).

If authors like Bauman – although the plural strikes one as clearly inappropriate – seem to be prevented from embracing autopoiesis, the reason is perhaps less the 'anti-humanism' inherent in autopoiesis than their own deep-seated agnosticism and allergy to any semblance of overly ambitious claims of social theory. Putting one's bets on the semantics of 'liquid' means, in any case, making the opposite choice – the choice of a sociological deontology which rules out not only vertical, structural, or 'solid-addicted' approaches, but highly abstract theory architectures *per se*. Bauman's focus on what actually affects people's lives focuses on the directly *Lebenswelt*-sensitive. The focus includes what is today possibly the most difficult and uncanny of all liquid-society related issues – an issue situated more importantly within the *lebensweltlich* than the systemic territory. At stake here is a society still trying to fight back (or at least, claiming to do so) against its intrinsic drift towards increasing deregulation and liquidity. Such a society will aim at *restoring minimal levels of solidity*. This restoration offers the second, equally vital unit that, together with the functional or trouble-shooting unit, forms the bipartite historical machine at its present state. For, in spite of all the discrepancy between autopoiesis with its predominant focus on administration and management, decision and differentiation, and the life-world-centred analysis given in Bauman, a closer observation shows that both approaches turn around the same topic – modernity's trend to liquidity in Bauman, modernity's curse of transforming whatever it touches into a matter of contingency, its 'Midas-touch', in Luhmann (1998, 44ff.). Before both, constituting the other pole of the bipolar, manic-depressive machinery realized in full society size, we find a directly opposed trend – a process of restoration of the spectacular, the representative and its mediatised glory. The aperçus and aphorisms collected under the title *The society of the spectacle* by no doubt the most gifted member of the French 68 movement, Guy Debord, are a good introduction to the complex of representation through the mass-media, and of the restoration of the solid by means of the new glory of the spectacle (Debord 1977). The spectacle as Debord understands it is the infinite repetition of an empty yet visible shape, a disfigured and deformed but nonetheless solid, even eminently meaningful form, itself the object of a programmed dependency relationship to which the public remains prisoner. Debord's theory of an inflation of society with (fake) solid shapes offers an instructive supplement to the liquidity- or contingency-centred accounts. Most importantly, both strands taken together illustrate how the modernity/postmodernity debate turns on an issue of *form* or *shape* – the question to which both references, that to the liquid as well as that to the spectacular, give their divergent answers. It should be remembered that the stakes of another famous conflict would equally respond to this description. In eighth-century Byzantium, the debate turned on the form and amount of veneration a worshipper would be both expected and authorised to offer a visible (material) sculpture.[11] Today the visible-meaningful is placed at the crossroads of a double series of, on the one hand, *aphanisis*, subtraction, becoming liquid, becoming contingent, and on the other hand its inflation by use as a resource for resolidifying society. As the linguist

11 For an introduction to Byzantine iconoclasm, see Grabar (1979), for images as a problem of *oikonomia*, see Mondzain (1996).

Roman Jakobson has pointed out, a 'shape', ideally, is always a 'sound'[12] shape – a source for the shaped object, of its structure, coherence, solidity, and even 'health' (Jakobson and Waugh 1987). A large group of analysts of modernity (or, for some, postmodernity) tend to locate its distinctive feature in the disappearance of, or the separation from, precisely such a soundness-endowing, presumptively normative, and in any case solidly identifiable, apparent shape. Their model is that of a '*Fluß ohne Ufer*',[13] of a process without extra-processual, of a story without trans-historic elements, a reduction of 'substance' to 'function' – and, further, to systems, media, codes, networks. A tendency towards an annihilation of the spectacle. Both Bauman's *liquid* and Luhmann's *contingent* belong to this strand. In a renewed, although not entirely farcical *Gigantomachia* around the old issue of *Darstellbarkeit*, we find Guy Debord among the (much smaller) group of authors identifying the modern within a totalitarianism of the spectacle. The distinctive feature of the society they describe lies in a certain *positive* (in the sense, exclusively, of 'firmly laid down') status of the solid, visible, identity-endowing elements.

It is not easy to imagine a debate between Bauman and Debord. Precisely that which is common to both, the horror provoked by one specific – for Bauman, liquid, for Debord, spectacular – aspect of society, is what lets their positions appear incompatible. For an observer, this is an instructive disagreement. That liquidity's mounting tide should *not* provoke compensatory phenomena would defy sociological good sense. And indeed, the suggestion that the movement towards liquid society involves a counter-movement towards a *société de spectacle* seems to be perfectly in tune with the urgent, sometimes prurient new demands for compensation/overcompensation for lost stocks of solidity. As an outstandingly spectacular – and specifically questionable – instance of this tendency of replenishing solidity against the onslaught of the liquid, I choose the current infatuation with 'leadership' within the academic environment. That 'leadership' should be considered an overriding criterion in academic recruitment policy is today the subject of a rapidly growing consensus. The consensus fits into a highly selective agenda: that of people in charge of performance maximisation, and who are generally struggling with increasingly disappointing levels of compliance. There is, on the one hand, that most telling fact of language: ' leadership' is English for '*Führertum*'. If one feels uneasy with '*Führertum*', it is clearly word-magic to believe that 'leadership' can be endorsed without posing exactly the same problems. Yet the new appeal of 'leadership', with its trail of 'Leadership Academy' foundations, effects on educational, scientific, and employment policies, views of 'leadership' capacities as deserving priority over intellectual ones, and so on – strikes one too for another reason altogether. It is a revocation of the new frontiers of organisational rationality settled many decades ago under the name of a 'managerial revolution'. It proclaims a return to the times *before* James Burnham and all those who have managed, throughout the twentieth century, to separate efficiency-related capacities from merely power-related ones (Burnham

12 The pun in 'sound' obviously adds a supplementary dimension to what I am looking for in the present context.

13 'River Without Banks', the title of Hans Henny Jahnn's novel, *Fluß ohne Ufer*, written 1934–46.

1941). It heralds a regressive turn. Yet, once again, the recrudescence of 'solidity' it exemplifies fails to contradict the diagnosis of the tendency toward liquidity. All too evidently, it bears the hallmark of an imperious trouble-shooting urgency, and signifies a despair-generated, hasty, and probably inadequate response. It conjures up a type of situation in which collective cluelessness compensates for this by donning the insignia of competence, pursuing, in order to make up for its inefficiency, a particularly jealous politics of unanimous consensus. If this is so, it would suggest that the large historical dynamic is liquidation, and would declassify resolidification as a series of punctuating movements. The period observed by Bauman, the first decade of the third millennium AD, coincides with a moment in geo-economic history that sees *industry* and *discipline* (two terms whose Latin radicals share the fact of pointing to individual work performance and work motivation) change their geographic distribution in important respects. A good way of understanding this is offered by the term 'post-colonialism'. The term stipulates (even if few users of the term seem to have noticed it), a world severed from colonialism. But even the most modest portrayal of the geo-economic situation has difficulty fitting into this frame. While studies that call themselves 'post-colonial' loom large in one sphere, cultural inegalitarianism looms at least equally large in another sphere. In an age in which most toys given to Western children, and a large portion of objects in daily use, are made in China, the age of 'killing one's mandarin' is over.[14] What we are only starting to understand is the cost side of this unequal distribution. The globalisation of the labour market globalises the global market-dependence of the workforce and, in turn, also the understanding of the full extent to which the workforce generally is market dependent. As an insuperable example of liquidation and liquefaction, it moves, in a historically unprecedented way, the Marxian notion of the 'reserve army' and its dramatic impact right back to the top of the agenda. Globalisation is among the processes which are increasing liquidity and contingency. Regressive resolidification is, and clearly will be, increasingly demanded to provide the conditions required for this advance.

---

14 Balzac's *Old Goriot* contains the following exchange, which perfectly summarizes, far beyond the usual level of human rights debates, a much discussed dilemma relating to the recognition of other cultures: 'Have you read Rousseau? – Yes. – You remember the passage where he asks his reader what he would do if he could get rich by killing, in China, by a mere act of his will, an old mandarin, without leaving Paris? – Yes. – Well, I am on my thirty-third mandarin (…)' (Balzac 1960, 101; translation modified). There are two respects in which the figure of the *mandarin* matches its double role as a perfect crime victim and as a natural-providential resource for the purpose of replenishing Western budgets: as a *Chinese*, but even more decisively as a Chinese *dignitary*, that is to say, as the possessor of status, a position of power and wealth that, unlike cognate Western positions, is derived from sources unconnected to effectively legitimising virtues and values, which are to be found solely in Christianity or the Enlightenment. The Mandarin is thus stripped bare of any redeeming features.

'Marx's doctrine is all-powerful because it is true'[15]

If the self-enabling success myth of a relationship between sufficient quantities of governmental power and sufficient levels of justificatory plausibility has survived the twentieth century, it is severely inadequate at the dawn of the twenty-first. This double-faced myth is obscured by fog, much like the fortress of Valhalla in now outdated stage-settings of Wagner – except that, here, the fog is not the hallmark of an excessive density, but rather the cumulative and recurrent result of the countless denials and disclaimers that constitute today's negative society. Bauman's engagement with this emergent negative *polis* focuses on the self-enabling myth at the moment of its demise and uses the notion of a liquid social reality. The notion's paradigmatic rank is partly concealed by Bauman's genuinly 'old European' modesty and his manifest dislike for ultimate, *ne-varietur* formulations. In these conditions, the best strategy might consist in a forced encounter with an appositely frontal version of the myth. Perhaps its most uncompromising formulation is Lenin's well-known maxim 'Marx's doctrine is all-powerful because it is true'. I suggest that Lenin's inimitably self-confident encapsulation of revolutionary politics offers a perfect contrast to Bauman's always only tentative approaches to the 'liquid' theme. In his sentence, and well beyond his presumed intentions, Lenin concisely summarizes the attitude of combined care for truth *and* power underlying the philosophical as well as theological account dominant in the West since time almost immemorial – at least for numerous centuries. Of the 'theory' he chooses, he predicates, first, its 'power', then its 'truth', and last – but not least – an internal order between both, a causal rank and file. It is truth that gives rise to power, not the other way round. Power – in Lenin's energetic wording even limitless, omnipotent power – is suspended on truth. According to Lenin, politics, the practice Lenin is dealing with, is not a magical practice, but a power-generation device that transforms *truth* – itself, by Lenin's intervention freed from the suspicion of being nothing but a frivolous exercise undertaken for its own sake and ennobled into a valuable resource – into the commodity of exercisable power. Without it, politics could not advance. The force of his sentence establishes Lenin as modernity's principal law-giver in respect of the inescapable conjugality of knowledge and power – up to the twenty-first century.

In my context, the point of invoking Lenin's phrase is clearly not his or Marx's political agenda, nor is it the fate of Russia or Eastern Europe. That Bauman does not fit into Leninism is equally unsurprising. Instead, the point is: not being a Leninist is today not so trivial after all. Looking closely, *non-Leninists* form a minority today, as exclusive as it is small, and Lenin's phrase about Marx's theory explains why. In order to make it fit the early twenty-first century, all one needs to do is replace 'Marx's doctrine', currently inaccurate, with a *currently accurate* substitute, from one of the currently fittest isms, from neo-darwinism to post-neo-theology. It is true that even if these theories are free from certain of Marx's idiosyncrasies – his disturbing lack of discipline, inclination to speak his mind, and regrettable weakness for 'humanism' – they appear just as woolly as his. Yet, the hold they exert over their audiences has

15 V.I. Lenin, 'Three Sources and Three Components of Marxism' first published in 3 *Prosvescenie* (1913), compare Lenin (1971, 70).

much more to do with Lenin, Lenin the epistemological legislator, the Lenin that pays homage to what, in theory, is 'true' and, therefore, 'all-powerful'. There is in this homage a strategy of solid adaptation to liquid conditions, and this is why it fits so brilliantly with leadership positions in the economic, political, scientific field today. These positions are predicated on maintaining minimal solidity levels – and in this respect, they are served by a theory of the 'all-powerful-because-true' brand. Theories that ordain the conditions in which leadership, success, and power become attainable, whether of the limitless or a less divine sort, offer an almost irresistible solid alternative to the general liquid and precarious situation. No doubt, their recipes fail to promise an alternative to the general liquid regime, but they succeed in formulating exceptions. One example in particular: leadership must be defended, and leadership, and its spectacle, is available under solidity conditions alone. So much for the exception; the rule can be located in the generalisation of liquidity and contingency. Phenomenologically, the most striking difference between dealing with liquid and solid matter consists in the fact that liquid conditions subvert, not causality, but the possibility of causal attribution. Melting, thawing, liquifying, and the precariousness they give rise to, are a technique in the hands of solid leadership. Extreme – extremely unequal – distributions of solid and liquid are a choice tool in the hands of the new breed of what might be called corporate Leninists.

Today's corporate Leninists are in search of still exploitable resources of solidity – they are constantly looking for sources or standards of what can be promoted as 'organisationally meaningful', as a functioning behaviour-motivating machine. A liquified body does not respond, whether we are dealing with individual, social, legal, or electoral bodies. How did liquidation happen? Historically, liquidation/liquefaction's genesis is technological, scientific, and elitist. It can be traced back, for instance, to the avenues of the power-knowledge campaigns fundamental to social modernity – to the 'tech-know-logies' investigated by Foucault, which created the ground for the sciences of population, statistics, police. The new body of quantitatively approached humankind can be understood both as the agency and the theatre of long-standing warfare, with two successive and opposite campaigns, first (throughout the centuries at stake in Foucault's modernity studies) a triumphal conquest by liquidity, then, closer to ourselves, the long reconquest by the forces of solidity, even if it is clear that all solidity thus obtained is bound to be of a weak and phoney kind, the type of solidity accessible to a *société de spectacle*. What is striking in the process that leads to its emergence is its perfect illustration of the idea that each new factual instance of 'liquid society' is compensated by a new illusionary instance of solidification. At least equally striking is that both concepts, liquidity/contingency *and* solidity/spectacularity, are absent or quasi-absent from current academic-sociological discussion. Debord was involved in sectarian politics and lived and died as an outsider; but the fact that his sociological insights have never been claimed by professional sociology casts a cruelly symptomatic light on the distance that marks off the past half-century of sociology from the preceding one. Only many years *after* retiring from a university career has Bauman, who writes as a sociologist, endeavoured to engage insistently and on a wider scale with the liquid topic.

If a strategy could be identified in the efforts made to re-endow liquid society with solid patterns, it would no doubt take the form of a *pro domo* argument for the sake of power and politics, of politics (corporate politics, rather than politics embodied in what, for now, is still called the political system) understood as the solid centre of liquid society. One way of expressing it would be the phrase: protect politics! Or: politics needs to be defended! Foucault's famously ironic title from 1976, 'Society needs to be defended!' (Foucault, 2004) needs updating. If *society* in the 1970s already represented, to Foucault's sharply political eye, the waste land of a spent and compromised promise, it has taken thirty more years to transform *politics* from the single effectively precious realm of action (which undoubtedly it has remained, in Foucault's eyes) into a further presumptive beneficiary of an appeal to come to its defence. Bauman's sociology of the liquid age markedly abstains from a defensive stance with respect to either society *or* politics – not because of any illusions he would cherish as to the new liquidity-induced powerlessness of politics. His biography shows that Bauman has seen solid politics in action, especially before leaving Warsaw in 1968. Bauman's encounter with East European mid twentieth-century official *party* Leninism might well act as a potent lifelong antidote in his later exposure to Western twenty-first-century style market-and-management Leninism. Surprisingly, what Leninism's 'politics-defensive' formulation boils down to, in our age, is a new stage in *depoliticisation*. 'True' and 'all-powerful' are fused into the quietistic totality-immanence that fits the liquidity of lives – a neo-Leninist programme without revolution, of a reformed Leninist economy in the guise of the new, radicalised programme of socialism in not even a single country.

Continuing and discontinuing education

'Fluidity', or 'liquidity' not only describe the overall tendency of a dynamic that can be identified with the *longue durée* of social modernity. They also refer specifically to an experience of novelty, of transformation characteristic of a much more restrained period. One of Bauman's personal choices, which are really his greatest lessons, can be analysed in terms of a distinction between two types or modes of newness: whether it is part of an experience of what is *effectively novel* or, on the contrary, part of a strategy, or programme that presents itself as *professedly innovative* (Bauman 2000, 2). His view is shaped by a preference for the ultimate, capillary feature – for the consumer over the producer, for the effect over the act, for the experience over the operation, for the provisional *aperçu* over the theoretical summary. Bauman's writing style is in that sense close to the sensuous apprehension of thought heralded by T.S. Eliot – closer to Montaigne than to Pascal, to Simmel than to Weber.[16] The society portrayed in his liquidity studies tends to liquidate experience; sacrificing regulation, it loses experience. A certain swap of positions cannot be overlooked. Deregulation is a strategy, or purpose-rational measure, that refers to a precise politico-economical agenda. In his recent study of the specificity of Europe's stance

16 The distance that separates the *freigeschrieben* style of Bauman's post-retirement writing from the scholarly sociological manner of his earlier work can be gauged by looking at Bauman (1973), (1976), (1976a), (1978), (1982).

and predicament in this evolution (Bauman 2004), he identifies this historical moment as that of a 'deregulation-cum-individualisation mark two [which Europe] undergoes, this time, not by its own choice, but succumbing to the pressure of global forces it can no longer control or hope to check'. This process he sets apart from a 'first bout of deregulation-cum-individualization, at the moment when the kinship and neighbourly bonds between people, apparently eternal or at least present since time immemorial, tightly tied into community and corporation knots, were loosened or broken' (Bauman 2004, 98ff.).

Bauman's mature style is the crossing of rare narrative abilities with an unrepentant use of the legacy of more than a century of sociological theory, a legacy of labyrinthine complication and richness, today itself subject to the fate of liquidity and liquidation – not in the form of material annihilation as theoretical waste, but rather, though unhappily with a rather similar outcome, in being permanently disposed of by incorporation into the new *limbo* provided by the new information-technologies. Today, the coexistence of society and information enters a new domain – a new, demand-side, economy. The old theological term of *limbo* is the apposite reference here; it correctly depicts the giant waste disposal sites constituted by our digital network storage devices, where an incalculable mass of information, although in principle retrievable at any moment, is factually trashed. The 'second bout' of modernisation described by Bauman's recent and current work, the process of liquefaction, the triumph of the fluid over the structured, in no way distract him from realizing that there is at least one viewpoint from which the case of a society whose rigid aspects and solid elements are the process of melting away is, strictly speaking, as old as society *tout court*. This viewpoint is that of sociology, a science predicated on the capacity of positing society as an object of autonomous study and discourse. The fact that such a position, such a discipline or observatory, should have found *within* society – at least since the birth of the idea that society and/or humankind could be understood as appropriate objects of scientific investigation[17] – a set of conditions of possibility, an 'eco-niche' sufficient for its continued culture and survival, embodies an improbable feature of the Western history of knowledge, a cultural one-off or anomaly. It cuts the entire history of today globalised Western society in half: a past time of latency, and a time still to come of 'revelation', not in the apocalyptic religious sense, but in that of social/societal agencies of self-thematisation. One cannot emphasize enough the historical originality, and ensuing precariousness, of the existence of such agencies. For a comparative appraisal, the example of law is instructive. Take the adage that 'law is the oldest social science'. The venerable equation, accompanied by a (decisive) interrogation mark, serves as the title of a collection of sophisticated clarifications of law's specificity in the context of modern society (Murphy 1997). Yet, law's function or performance, in the widest sense, is to give rise to rules. Its underlying action, or gesture, is thus a defensive or normative gesture, a 'rule-biased' gesture. Whatever this is, science it is not. The cognitive approach takes into account, reports, analyses, explains. Of course – as has been argued many thousands of times – any legal decision's appropriateness does

17 The notion that the history of a knowledge corresponding to this description extends, in fact, even further into the past, is outlined in Schütz (2005).

depend on factual knowledge. *That* knowledge, however, far from subjecting *society* to its investigative enterprise, remains ancillary to the situational horizon involved in the process of legal decision making. This is why the 'history of English law is not written' (Maitland 1911). It is also why all attempts at defending a continuum hypothesis between legal, or 'jurisprudential', or even 'socio-legal' views, on the one hand, and, on the other hand, the sociological view, are doomed to failure, and why law is *not* a social science: it is not an agency of societal 'self-revelation' or self-thematisation.

If, to avoid cross-contamination, the task of the modern social sciences requires careful separation from the immemorial sciences of law, the next urgent question to ask is where is the cut-off point, especially considering Bauman's recent work, in its suspension at the semantics of liquidity. Throughout its initial latency period, which lasted as long as its objectification as an object *sui generis* has not been achieved, society deigned to describe itself as a 'great chain of being' and thus remained hidden under the mask of an ungraspable collection, a miraculous coordination of 'things'. Yet, to think of this long-standing earlier state as being 'conservative' would be anachronistic. The notions conservative, conservatism offer a response to the problem of progress or intended change in time, and are thus no less than these confined to a very recent past. The only correct expression or distinctive denominator of a society during the protracted period during which the phenomenon of society refused to be conceived of under such categories of change or non-change (so that their existence as societies remains unseen, they are perceived as reigns, realms, bodies, orders) is the reference to its *perfection*. Perfection and latency form one couple. They are overthrown and abolished at once – in the moment in which the inherent perfection of a pre-society order is no longer plausible. Society is born, has acquired a status when it has become clear that *it* (rather than some specific group of actors) is the origin of the really existing trouble it is suffering from. One can also tell the story the other way round. The self-thematisation of society starts exactly at the moment at which society's mandala is no longer woven out of such ingredients as structure, preservation, identity, fixed essences but, instead, out of self-transformation, mobility, fluidity, liquidity. We have to familiarize ourselves with the fact that liquid society has its predecessors in the realm of knowledge and discourse, in the early and pre-history of the 'social sciences' (used here in the widest possible sense, the galaxy of authors factually or potentially in the scope of Foucault's *sub verbo* 'Police') understood as a testing site of liquefaction; the meltdown of the frozen or solid ingredients of society itself starts there, and will take a long time to be grasped in the shape of massive, undeniable empirical results. Those investigated by Bauman are amongst them. The *entrée en scène* of the social sciences, that is to say, the history of societies endowing themselves with such an institutionalised agency or vanguard of self-observation and self-reflection, induces some of its latest and most radical effects only at the moment of liquid modernity. Even if we leave to whom it concerns – the historians – the problem of finding the correct, at least the optimal or appropriate threshold dates, and even if it is true that Bauman himself is quite careful in his claims to novelty when defining the coming-into-being of the 'liquid' way of societal existence, a tendency towards becoming liquid prevails, not for years or decades, but for as long as modernity is reckoned to have existed. On the other hand, there is the notion, repeatedly pointed out by Bauman, that a new type of totality, perhaps a new general economy of moving towards the liquid, on the contrary started only very recently. Accordingly, the appropriate time-brackets for 'liquidity' are provided neither by the long history of post-war Europe, nor by the growing post-1970 awareness of modernity as a contingent, improbable phenomenon. It is even less possible to interpret liquid modernity as a necessary 'evolutionary universal', in Parsons's terms. Liquid modernity is an episode within an episode: a second-order event that replaces residual solid references with liquid flows interacting with liquid flows.

The sustainability of the solid has been the focus of the social sciences ever since the 'melting pot'. Does 'liquidity' fit social change? Amidst the decline of references to nation state, sovereignty, and so on, which pertain to a mechanics of solids, can it replenish available order? Or has order been an infatuation with solidity right from the start? If so, what exactly do we lose in giving it up – in subjecting the last remaining 'solid' items to the liquid flow? But how was liquidity successfully foreclosed, circumvented in the first place? Has legal history in the West, by giving rise to cascades of revolutions – interpretive, legislational, managerial – chosen a special trajectory, a strategy of self-rarefaction or self-defeat (Legendre 1988)? Or, is it, on the contrary, the case that society began to be a self-critical object by subjecting itself to instituted forms of law-dependent decision making – to interpretation? Does enforcing/implementing interpretations and decisions repeat the amazing prehistorical step towards the plasticity of carving and sculpting? Is liquidity, then, liquidity unfettered, liquidity mark two, imperilling precisely these achievements?

One has to consider, if liquid replaces solid, that it is equally true not only that solid had already replaced liquid earlier on, but that it is precisely this first substitution that figures as the unique founding event – from the biblical separation of earth and sea to the successful draining of the Zuijdersee, literally and as a metaphor. The metaphor is well known in the social history of psychoanalysis – see Thomas Mann's famous laudatio from 1930, later taken up by Freud (Mann 1936). Historically, another front at which the liquid/solid antagonism has been played out, a metaphorical, yet significant one, is related to steel and industrial production of solids through melting procedures.[18] Still another is provided by current 'plastic' interpretations of the sign-trace-graph-complex (Malabou 1996; 2004).

Within the 'humanities', the last decades have witnessed diverse trends – linguistic, rhetoric, hermeneutic, iconic. Is it now liquidity's turn? Can the liquid be construed as the general notion underlying Nietzsche and the growth of the desert? Is it involved in the biblical promise, made to Isaac, of progeny, again 'like sand'? A concept has its *limits*, the limits of its meaning, its referent, its context. The limits concerned here are those of its capacity to control, specify, fine-tune what the concept conceives or helps to conceive. The limits of a concept are understood as limits to the concept's ability to set out its limits – comprising devices for eluding, fending off, or discouraging any abuse liable to make it useless. This is not 'paradoxical'; rather,

18 This includes the twentieth-century infatuation with *steel*: Jünger and Marinetti *contra* Péguy who exposes steel as material of prostitution that slavishly embraces any form whatsoever.

it epitomizes the wisdom of a conceptualist common-sense: does the concept still hold on to something, or is it free-wheeling? The limits restricting the sociological reference to 'liquidity', a term which has its perfectly obvious localised standing in scientific discourse as a term in physics, are concerned – in perfect agreement with this wisdom – not with any reductionist peril, but with the semantic Pandora's box opened up by transplanting it from its non-human science background to its human science application. Liquidity, in physics, refers to a momentary condition, a status quo, a real or realised state inscribed somewhere on a large scale of possible states. The 'quo' in 'status quo' says it all: it stipulates that the present 'state' *could* give way to *another* state, including, for instance, an earlier state of its own, a *status quo ante*. The notion of *restitutio in integrum*, on the contrary, is predicated on solidity. The possibility of recovering an earlier state, conditions of perfect reversibility generally, thus directly refer to the markers liquid, solid. The same remark is true of private law. In principle, you can claim back whatever someone, without appropriate grounds, has taken from you. Moreover, the notion of a possible *restitutio in integrum* of the unjustly disadvantaged claimant, by way of imposing restitution on the perpetrator of the disadvantage, has been given fundamental importance in English private law doctrine (Birks 1985). In physics, what has changed into liquid, can generally change back to solid, and conversely. These instances of reversibility, of a potential return fare included in every one-way action, are, however, clearly exceptions to evolution's habitual way of proceeding. While human institutions, although under variable, uncertain and quite limiting conditions, do in principle allow for earlier states to be restored, evolution has generally no inbuilt tendency towards restoration or restitution, grants no remedy to those afflicted by disadvantages, does not involve any means for the return of an earlier state. Dispositives of restitution are reversions – 'negevolutionary phenomena', as they might also be called in remembrance of those *negentropic* phenomena of which there was so much talk in times when people worried about entropy and energy rather than, as in ours, about evolution and ecology. Evolution is situated *without* the precinct in which the principle of restitution prevails, in which, under certain conditions and within strict limits, *restitutio in integrum* imposes its reign. The question of whether Bauman's sociological reference to the *tendency* towards liquidity involves or, on the contrary, excludes reversibility is a difficult one: both the metaphor's physicalist (Ur-)meaning, and the modality and medium of societal becoming unquestionably suppose the possibility of the pendulum travelling to its furthest extent, then swinging backwards. This is, however, not the only possible understanding. Liquidity might as well be thought of as dissolving shapes, forms, structures. To the extent to which this is the case, it is difficult to avoid having to take liquidation as a definitive event. In diagnosing the passage toward *generalised* liquidity, the sociologist would then have to be seen as teaching that the path leading back into the earlier (solid) state is cut off. This proclamation echoes through Bauman's argument even if he leaves the question in suspense; it is not part of the semantic 'home-rule' of the 'liquid' terminology, no matter whether used technically or metaphorically. Rather, a society will see the doors through which it entered its current state close behind it in case it allows liquidity to affect, to liquidate, to dissolve, its self-programming devices. A wide arch spans Max Weber's solid 'iron cage' (Weber 1958; 1994) and Zygmunt Bauman's 'liquid modernity', 'liquid society', 'liquid love'. Any attempt even to name the authors who have participated in the debate between Weber and Bauman would be beyond the scope of this chapter. Yet one can scarcely deny the commonality of topic between the two authors, even if Bauman does not seem to have considered the connection. The passage from solid exceptions to liquid totalities should be seen as one of the formulas which try to depict a loss of freedom no longer accompanied, let alone compensated for, by comparable gains in terms of possibilities elsewhere.[19]

References

Agamben, G. (1998), *Homo Sacer: Sovereign Power and Bare Life* (Stanford: Stanford University Press).

Agamben, G. (2006), *Che cos'è un dispositivo?* (Milano: Feltrinelli).

Agamben, G. (2007), *Il Regno e la Gloria: Per une genealogia teologica dell'economia e dell'governo* (Vicenza: Neri Pozza).

Balke, F. (1998), *Der Staat nach seinem Ende: Die Versuchung Carl Schmitts* (Munich: Fink).

Balzac, H. (1960), *Old Goriot*, tr. by E. Marriage. (London: Everyman).

Bauman, Z. (1973), *Culture as Praxis* (London: Routledge and Kegan).

Bauman, Z. (1976), *Socialism: The Active Utopia* (New York: Holmes and Meier).

Bauman, Z. (1976a), *Towards a Critical Sociology: An Essay on Common-Sense and Emancipation* (London: Routledge and Kegan).

Bauman, Z. (1978), *Hermeneutics and Social Science: Approaches to Understanding* (London: Hutchinson).

Bauman, Z. (1982), *Memories of Class: The Pre-history and After-life of Class* (London: Routledge and Kegan).

Bauman, Z. (1997), *Postmodernity and its Discontents* (London: Polity Press).

Bauman, Z. (2000), *Liquid Modernity* (Cambridge: Polity Press).

Bauman, Z. (2003), *Liquid Love: On the Frailty of Human Bonds* (Cambridge: Polity Press).

Bauman, Z. (2004), *Europe – An Unfinished Adventure* (Cambridge: Polity Press).

Bauman, Z. (2005), *Liquid Life* (Cambridge: Polity Press).

Birks, P. (1985), *An Introduction to the Law of Restitution* (Oxford: Clarendon Press).

19 While no equivalent of the term 'iron cage' can be found in Max Weber's article 'Wahlrecht und Demokratie', it is noteworthy that Weber's own term, the exalted '*ehernes Gehäuse*' – which continues to pose formidable problems to translators (compare its rendering as 'brazen', even: 'rigid', 'casing' [!] in the most recent Cambridge edition, which on this point barely represents progress) – can be seen as perfectly consistent with Bauman's reference to the polarity of solid versus liquid. Contrary to the assumptions traditionally connected with the 'iron cage', Weber's point has little to do with later cinematographic fantasies of the straitjacket, and even less with a reference to a 'piece of machinery'. He credits *professional ethics* with the precious deed of having established a solid framework of economic action. His primary quest is how to prevent this painfully acquired solidity from being either jeopardized by or subjected to monopoly.

Burnham, J. (1941), *The Managerial Revolution: What is Happening in the World?* (New York: John Day Company).

Compact Oxford English Dictionary (1985) (Oxford: Oxford University Press).

Debord, G. (1977), *The Society of the Spectacle* (London: Black and Red).

De Zulueta, F. (1946), *The Institutes of Gaius, Part I* (Oxford: Clarendon Press).

Foucault, M. (1983), *The Will To Knowledge: History of Sexuality*, vol.1 (New York: Routledge).

Foucault, M. (2004), *Society must be defended: Lectures at the Collège de France 1975–76* (London: Penguin).

Grabar, A. (1979), *Les voies de la création en iconographie chrétienne, Antiquité et Moyen Age* (Paris: Flammarion).

Jahnn, H., (2001), *Fluß ohne Ufer* (Berlin: Hoffmann and Campe).

Jakobson, R. and Waugh, L. (1987), *The Sound Shape of Language* (Berlin: Mouton-De Gruyter).

Legendre, P. (1983), *L'Empire de la vérité: Introduction aux espaces dogmatiques industriels (Leçons, vol. II)* (Paris: Fayard).

Legendre, P. (1988), *Le désir politique de dieu: etude sur les montages de l'Etat et du droit (Leçons, vol. VII)* (Paris: Fayard).

Lenin, V.I., (1971), *Karl Marx et sa doctrine* (Paris: Editions sociales).

Luhmann, N. (1995), *Social Systems* (Stanford: Stanford University Press).

Luhmann, N. (1996), *Die neuzeitlichen Wissenschaften und die Phänomenologie* (Wien: Picus-Verlag).

Luhmann, N. (1997), *Die Gesellschaft der Gesellschaft* (Frankfurt: Suhrkamp).

Luhmann, N. (1998), *Observations of Modernity* (Stanford: Stanford University Press).

Luhmann, N. (2004), *Law as a Social System* (Oxford: Oxford University Press).

Maitland, F. (1911),'Why the History of English Law is Not Written', in H. Fisher (ed.), *Collected Papers*, vol.1 (Cambridge: Cambridge University Press), 480–97.

Malabou, C. (1996), *L'avenir de Hegel: Plasticité, temporalité, dialectique* (Paris: Vrin).

Malabou, C. (2004), *La plasticité au soir de l'écriture: dialectique, destruction, deconstruction* (Paris: Scheer).

Mann, T. (1936), *Freud und die Zukunft* (Wien: Bermann-Fischer Verlag).

Mondzain, M.-J. (1996), *Image, icône, économie: Les sources byzantines de l'imaginaire contemporain* (Paris: Seuil).

Murphy, W. (1997), *The Oldest Social Science? Configurations of Law and Modernity* (Oxford: Oxford University Press).

Schütz, A. (2005), 'A genealogy of legal critique', *Law and Critique* 14, 91–112.

Thillet, P. (ed.) (2003), *Alexandre d'Aphrodisias: Sur la Providence* (Paris: Verdier).

Weber, M. (1958), *Gesammelte Politische Schriften* (Tübingen: J.C.B. Mohr).

Weber, M. (1994), *Political Writing*, P. Lassman and R. Speirs (eds.) (Cambridge: Cambridge University Press).

Chapter 3

World and Waste, or the Law of Liquidity[1]

Pablo S. Ghetti

Is there a political tone in sociology? Is there a political tone in liquidity? Bauman's particular tone does not privilege 'the political' as such, yet it is inscribed in a certain tradition that, in its privileging of 'the social', opens up and sets the tone for 'the political' – for a space of political articulations, and more than that, a space for the public in which the roots of sociability, being-with itself, gain generative significance.[2] An inescapable law of sociability, embodied and concealed in all manifestations of the juridical law, is required and invoked.[3] It is invoked at a moment when the world is threatened, when the 'world is full' (Bauman 2002, 11; 2004, 5). The liquid and modern world most conspicuously begets the non-world, the waste that threatens from within the order and the progress of the world. But let me set the tone of my concerns through Bauman's own words in *Society under Siege*:

> Sooner or later, served daily with the evidence of our interdependence, we will have to realize that no one can claim the earth, or any part of the earth as their own indivisible property . . . Reforging solidarity of fate into solidarity of purpose and action is one in which the verdict of 'there is no alternative', so often abused in the case of other choices, can be legitimately pronounced. Either we draw proper conclusions from our global interdependence and turn it to the benefit of all, or it will turn itself, with our overt and tacit support, into a catastrophe after which few if any people will be around to count the merits and demerits of anyone of the conflicting ways of life . . . The choice . . . is between common humanity and solidarity of mutual destruction (Bauman 2002, 16–7).[4]

---

1 I am indebted to Peter Fitzpatrick for commenting on an earlier draft, and to the lively discussions at the workshop on Liquidity and its Law held at the Cardiff Law School.

2 Bauman argues for the necessity of a return to the public sphere, to a sphere of the public in its own right. His account of it does seem to envisage a certain republican tradition, but such a thought that is from the outset caught by the modern experience of liquidity cannot so simply return to a 'republican' past, particularly if this past is contained, foundational and originary. I prefer to see this as a republican 'detour' of Bauman's – that means rearranging and disturbing republicanism itself (Bauman 2000, 176–81).

3 The question of the juridical law will be addressed later. For the moment it is important to understand that the juridical (Derrida 2005, 444) is but one manifestation, albeit powerful and violent, of a more fundamental law of sociability, the pursuit of which guides this text.

4 Notice the cover illustration of Bauman's book – by Bernd Mellmann – of the city of Cologne at night under the 'siege' or 'threat' of a monstrous wave. Global warming is probably the initial inspiration of the photographic illustration, but it fits neatly with all the paranoid concerns and real threats of our time.

Bauman's theory of liquidity (and, with it, a certain hyperactive modernity) heralds an unbearable condition of dispersion, speed, and laceration. Yet, it seems that we are propelled to think, act, unite, and find our ever-resisting togetherness by means of realizing the possibility of our imminent and common destruction. There seems to be only one way of warding off the end, and this is by reforging a solidarity of purpose as no one can ever inherit the earth alone, or claim absolute ownership of any of its parts – this ownership always eludes whoever claims it. But this is precisely what all sovereign power, sovereign systems of power, and empires have done. It is possible to envisage an empire that would organize the appropriation of the earth, a system of land appropriation.[5] Rather than favouring solidarity, a collective escape from catastrophe might well engender more Empire, more allegiance to Empire – if, of course, in the time of liquidity, the link between protection and duty is still in place, and nothing seems to deny this archaic solidity. Here lies the great paradox of liquidity: the more liquid, the more fearful, hence the more explosively communitarian (Schmitt 1997, 34; Bauman 2000, 200–1). With the current development of techniques and technologies of control, and the ongoing international administration of fear, this risk is ever more palpable – even if it is still only a risk, that is, even if it is possible to conceive of a certain administration of liquidity in which such risk is always warded off by an incredible efficiency in the erasure of social spaces, in the incredible solidity of the underlying, individualist grounds of liquidity. This is what Bauman aptly calls Big Brother Mark 2.[6]

However, the aim of this essay is not to uncover the misery of the apocalyptic tone of sociology – entangled in liquidity, solidity, and destruction – but to amplify and further advance the most challenging feature of liquidity, in its aporetic appeal and account of solidity, namely, Bauman's law and his wager on sociability through an encounter with the question of waste. Not that Bauman proposes a return to

---

5 Indeed, in global terms we will have to be able to deal with a delimiting and appropriating power that scarcely respects solidarity – and not only in terms of the new rise of Empire. The organization of the international system is departing from the hopes and promises of multilateral institutions (based on the formal equality of nation states), and moving towards a more directly power-based balance amongst great blocs, or between a less than all-powerful Empire and a small number of significant mediators (Schmitt 2003, 354–5; Mouffe 2005, 115–20).

6 In the question and evolving notion of emancipation, the problem of the totalitarian Big Brother is crucial. In his *Liquid Modernity*, Bauman emphasises the poverty of a critical theory that still revolves around the critique of the totalitarian drive of modernity towards a mass society tantamount to the model of Orwell's *1984*. Rather than offering room for a private, independent life-world, as opposed to its colonization by autopoietic subsystems, it would be necessary to invest today in a new foundation of the public sphere, eminently threatened by the proliferation of a monadic subjectivity – self-reflexive to the extreme, hence entirely alien to social reflection. That implies that the public sphere should be construed beyond its dependence on the private one. In books such as *Society under Siege*, *Wasted Lives*, and *Liquid Love*, it seems that what was more or less implicit in previous works is now overtly exposed, namely, that there is an underlying solidity, or rigidity in liquidity that binds people to the chains of their own auto-satisfaction and private life conditions (Bauman 2002, 66–70; 2003, 46–7; 2004, 131–3).

all-encompassing instantiations of sociability: on the contrary,[7] his shift towards solidarity or commonality conceals the secret of a contingent and rare 'forging' ('reforging solidarity', one wasted repeatedly but not avowed as such) that dwells at the undecidable spacing of being-with, both in singularity and in commonality (Nancy 2000a).

For that, a treatment of the problem of waste is needed – a problem that can both disclose this radical spacing of sociability, and point out its very concealment and near annihilation. It requires an elaboration of the questions of world and globalisation, developed towards an understanding of the incommensurable and vanishing point of sociability, of being-together, which appear already in Bauman's account of waste; for an exposition of being-together that touches its most radical point, I refer to Jacques Derrida and Jean-Luc Nancy. In this chapter, I first elaborate on the intimacy between world and waste, and then expand on the modern drive that discloses this intimacy, in its manifestation as either 'order' or 'progress'. The centrality of waste production there determined has thus to be assessed in terms of the nature of production and creation themselves and their relation to the theory of value in the following section. The challenge of the theory of value today, steeped in waste, subsequently requires a careful account of its complexity, especially with regard to the very creation of waste, which should involve not only waste's misery, but also the opportunities for different uses of creation inherent in waste. In the final section, the opportunities of waste lead to a reassessment of the nature of the liquidity that brings waste to the fore – at the restless core of liquidity lies an almost unbreakable law, whose common enjoyment discloses what is inherent in waste.

The world of waste in progress

The question of world destruction has always been raised by a certain Marxist tradition – this eschatology is perhaps intrinsic to Marx's own work (Derrida 1994, 89).[8] Rosa Luxemburg's motto 'socialism or barbarism' represented a challenge to the Second International's economicist belief in the inexorability of communism. Even though she did convey a strong messianic message that involved the real destruction of the world, the interesting aspect of the motto – which must be seen in the context of a Europe torn apart by the Great War – was that destruction and barbarism were already in play.[9] It is radical in that it shows that capitalism is already a proto-barbarism – even if this word today is quite unhelpful and misleading.

7 Another feature of the apocalyptic tone, now with Dantean colours: 'Abandon all hope of totality, future as well as past, you who enter the world of fluid modernity' (Bauman 2000, 22).

8 For the question of what the apocalyptic tone entails, especially in terms of its lack of destination and divisible sending, delaying, and complication of time, see Derrida, 1993, 152–9).

9 See Bauman's evocation of Luxemburg in this volume. For an example of Luxemburg's countless accounts of capitalism's ever-present violence and destructiveness, see Luxemburg, 2003, 350–1. The question could be expanded to Bauman's constant references to Hannah Arendt, mentioned in relation to the question of common humanity (Bauman 2003, 17) and of

Today, more than ever, it can be said that the end has already occurred – the end of a particular way of organizing the world, and the appropriation of the space of the earth. The world of the nation state's predominant rule is over (Derrida 2003a, 137–51; Bauman 2000, 185–92).[10] The conditions for its reproduction no longer subsist. Other claims with many variables – imperial, transnational, and regional – are already in dispute. The world is gone, Jacques Derrida stated recently, and this is the opportunity for the manifestation and creation of other forms of coexistence. With Paul Célan's verse, 'the world is gone, I must bear you' (*Die Welt ist fort, ich muss dich tragen*), Derrida insists that it is that sort of sociability, the heteronomous law of otherness, which appears when the world is disorganized, suspended (Derrida 2003a, 213; 2003b). This radical otherness, nevertheless, is swiftly contained, and a label is immediately attached to the other. The fall of the wall meant immediately the rise of a label, 'rogue', as Derrida called it recently; it was a time of rogue states – replaced later by other terms that represent other, parallel, interests, such as failed states. But it is not by chance that the world in self-deconstruction appeals to roguishness – to its own wasted products. Roguishness dwells at the core of the creation of the world, and even more at the very reproduction of globalisation, at the revolving drive of globalisation. For Derrida, roguish is he who is sovereign and names the rogue.[11]

Zygmunt Bauman is perfectly aware of the logic of sovereign roguishness. This logic finds expression in his concept of 'wasted lives' under the conditions of modernity. The whole question of waste is tackled in his book *Wasted Lives: Modernity and its Outcasts* (2004). Waste appears as a by-product of two different grammars of modernization. They maintain a certain alliance, even though their impetuses are different. These two grammars are that of order building, and that of

great significance for some of the leaders of the journal *Socialisme ou Barbarie*, (inspired by Luxemburg's motto), especially Claude Lefort (1986, 59–72).

10 For an account of this question in legal theory terms, see Arnaud (2003, 183–270). See, also, Fitzpatrick (2001, 212–15), so as to realize how this transnational aspect of legality – such as that encapsulated in the 'global' reach of human rights and rule of law – can also operate in imperial terms, albeit now of a renewed type. Fitzpatrick's work also contributes here in indicating how the nation states, if not focal points for the construction of extraverted identities and social structures (mainly national ones), are still very significant: 'small but potent – the hidden fist' (Fitzpatrick 2001, 214), they are the entities that have to repeat, convince, and enforce this global motto: 'there is no alternative' (Bauman 2002, 68).

11 I cannot go into the details of Derrida's analyses of this expression, 'rogues', in French, *voyous*, and all that it entails and encompasses. In brief, it portrays, on the one hand, those who live on the streets, who have no definite status, who are excluded, banned – initially 'outlaws', those who lived beyond the borders of the city. It also evokes one who suffers the apparatus of the medieval wheel (*le roué*). On the other hand, *voyou* is attributed to someone possessing a daunting power, because of its indifference to rules, structures, or normative standards of conduct. An uncertain etymology relates it to the *loup-garou*, the werewolf (Derrida 2003a, 102). Ultimately, in its second meaning, the rogue is not far from the sovereign, who stands above a certain order, and is even more of a rogue – to the extent that it claims to be 'just', 'fair', apt to 'save' (saving is here rather displaced towards salutation, welcoming, *salut*) (160–1).

economic progress. I now analyse these two grammars, which are compatible, as shall shortly be shown, with Bauman's understanding of liquidity.

On the side of order building one finds basically human design, will and purpose that discard everything that is unnecessary, so that order, beauty or harmony can arise. In modern art (Bauman's example is Renaissance art), waste is the wrapping that conceals the form that design projects. Modernity here is a defiance of sameness, and it means difference and designed change: 'the modern mind was born together with the idea that the world can be changed. Modernity is about rejecting the world as it has been so far and the resolution to change it' (Bauman 2004, 23). Such a design, though, has also to be seen as realistic: it cannot change at whim, and must consider the conditions of change. In order to master change, design needs thus to simplify the world's complexity, the world's excess. Distinguishing what is essential from the accidental, the needful from the unneeded, is a craft. In this way, order always calls upon disorder. In the non-human world, there is neither order nor disorder. It is human mind that introduces both, always conjured up together. Moreover, this is how Bauman sees the work of Giorgio Agamben, and Schmitt's concept of sovereignty – they disclose the perpetual emergency of modernity. However, here all initiative lies with the rule; the exception does not arise by itself, but always through design.[12]

It is on the level of Bauman's discussion of economic growth that waste loses its political nature and becomes a mere technical or economic problem – the technical problem of a surplus population, unnecessary or actually a hindrance to economic growth. Economic growth, or progress itself understood as an unquenchable drive towards novelty and creation, one that destroys anything that stands in the way of the new, and the new itself must give way, whenever it stagnates. No one issues a command, no one draws the line in advance, and no one bears responsibility. The process is all the more dramatic when it is a question of populations who age, lose productivity, who have not acquired enough skills to compete, or even, in some cases, who do not share the whimsical wish to consume:

> Surplus population is one more variety of human waste. Unlike *homini sacri* . . . the victims of order building designs, they (surplus population) are not legitimate targets, exempted from the protection of law . . . They are rather ... unplanned 'colateral casualties' of economic progress (Bauman 2004, 39).

The two aspects of waste are articulated in many ways. Bauman is well aware that for those who suffer from the exclusion, or subordinate inclusion of modernity, there is not much difference between the political or the economic mode (Bauman 2004, 40). Furthermore, these two grammars of sovereignty and of progress are interdependent in Bauman's work. The tanks of liquid capitalist grammar advance over the lawns of sovereign might. As in all progress, though, it leaves waste behind – refugees,

12 Bauman does not acknowledge the distinction between the works of Schmitt and Agamben. Both take the exception into account, but Schmitt, on the one hand, wanted to inscribe the exception into the norm, to contain it in the sphere of law; Agamben, with Benjamin, on the other hand, seeks the true exception, or the exception to the exception (Agamben 2005, 52–64).

migrants, *sans papiers*, rogues, criminals[13] – and since the traditional exercise of power over a territory is ever more limited, the order-building sovereigns can only wield their might over that waste; personal safety issues outweigh social security, so that the complexity of chaos, and risk may still be contained by the simplicity of order, albeit merely of a symbolic sort (see, Bauman in this volume).

Another site of the alliance between sovereignty and progress is what I call the power to name the waste. This question is already implicit in Bauman's work. Waste may be produced by economic growth, but it is always named as such by political processes of exclusion or subordination. In the so-called society of producers, one finds a reserve labour force; in a society of consumers, some people are merely redundant, of no use, disposable (Bauman 2004, 34–46). But the move from one to another is always a political decision. This political decision however is never merely an expression of a power from above; on the contrary, it is pervasive, socially pervasive, and figural, politically sedimented, ingrained in every micro-instantiation of power (Guattari and Rolnik 1999).

Therefore, even if governmental authorities do not directly admit responsibility for naming the waste, when this 'responsibility' is attributed to anonymous, technical and economic reasons, the fact persists, nonetheless, that everyone has to adhere to this technical legitimacy. Everyone is implicated in naming the 'rogue', even more so, if one considers that governing (and also sovereignty) currently imports necessarily diffuse mechanisms that involve the ever-focal instantiation of power, encapsulated by the logic of governance (Arnaud 2003, 330–56; Fitzpatrick 2001, 184–8). When there was an army of reserve labour (society of producers), the decision not to hire people and leave them in a state of life-threatening suspension could be attributed to those who owned the means of production of life in society – the worker is only implicated in the exclusion process on a second-order reference, by virtue of his own alienation. In a time of redundant labour, though, the non-consumer, the rogue is produced by a constant and pervasive process of exclusion and inclusion: exclusion, for such wasted lives are indeed deprived of the goods, welfare and safety that the consumer enjoys, but also inclusion because they epitomize everything that the consumer abhors, so that this non-consumer belongs to the internal logic of the society that produces it.

Indeed, this inclusion of the flawed consumer can be tracked down to the very social fabric of consumerism. From need, to desire, and now to whim, to whimsical consumerism, a certain production of subjectivity is crucial (Deleuze and Guattari 1983, 15–17; Guattari and Rolnik 1999, 25–65). In this way, if consumption, consumption's expectations, credit and speed drive the system as never before, then the production and administration of subjectivity are more important than ever. What else is best able to cater for this production than the culture of safety that we are now witnessing – excessive bodily, emotional, and medical safety (Bauman 2004, 54)? The culture of safety itself is predicated on the existence of a threat, which must be real enough to serve as a normalizing counter-example – one that requires

13 Through the work of Sandro Mezzadra, one realizes that the 'waste' is itself active and its actions are not fully determined or controlled by the imperatives of order or movement of progress. The author interprets migrations as social movements (Mezzadra 2004).

each one to decide to exclude (and exclude oneself as well, but we will return to this shortly) by asymmetrically including the 'other' – who in spite of having failed the ultimate goal of consumption, is always exposed to the consumerist drive and subjective fabrication of liquid modernity (for asymmetric integrations, see Neves 2001, 262–3).

The value of waste

This pervasive decision-making that transcends the borders of the economic and the political discloses the problem of the co-originary nature of order and progress. To realize that, though, in all its implications, we will need to turn to two other theorists of globalisation, who have pondered globalisation, and the question of the world, exactly in that junction of order and progress, sovereignty and capitalism. I refer to Jean-Luc Nancy and to Jacques Derrida. The treatment of these authors here is necessarily restricted, indicating that contemporary social theory needs to develop further the issues that Bauman has raised. Incidentally, a certain incommensurable deconstruction and liquidity can both be traced back to a radical and hyperbolic type of Marxism – of which more later (Lacoue-Labarthe 2004, 28–52; Heidegger 2004, 72–5).

For Nancy, globalisation is accumulation; it is the technical and economic accumulation that takes place in the sphere of the globe, not of the world. Globe is related to glomus, agglomeration. This constant insistence of the globe on returning to itself for the sake of itself erases the world, and its sense, value and dignity. As in the work of Jacques Derrida, world represents the affirmation of a universalist tradition, mainly the Greek-Roman, and Jewish-Christian Mediterranean world (Derrida 2002a, 374). One of its most famous expressions is what has been known for the last fifty years or so as human rights. Rights, value, or dignity, however, are nothing but masks, figures, spectral impressions that convey the iterability and creativity that lie already in value itself – not as a concept of value, but in every concrete and social production of value. But for Nancy, so that value can be created, one requires precisely a radicality that surmounts the value of value, or the sense in the creation of value. One requires something incommensurable. When, nonetheless, all social goods are commodified (in Bauman's words, when 'the world is full'), when the commodity-form rules absolutely, there is no space for any actual creation of value (actual infinity) – only for an ever 'possible' insistence (infinite possibility) on the form of value, which today appears rather as waste (Nancy 2002, 29). Especially in a time of whimsical consumerism and unyielding social change, use-value itself, once structurally necessary for the composition of the commodity (since labour can only really be labour if it is also useful) is vanishing, and all that remains is the general equivalence and autonomy of money.[14]

Let us briefly pursue this issue more carefully with Marx:

---

14 Evidently, some sort of 'voiding' has always been there – this was the great thesis of Derrida (1994), but the challenge of our time is to think how much the system touches the emptiness of waste itself, and in doing so, how much it requires the void, equalizing the world. In this particular sense, one of the tasks of this thought is to seek the true waste, or the waste of waste.

> Finally, nothing can be a value without being an object of utility. If the thing is useless, so is the labour contained in it; the labour does not count as labour, and therefore creates no value (Marx 1976, 131).

Note that the creation of value in Marx's work requires a space of utility that itself points already to a direction of the production of value – in the classic analysis of the capitalist mode of production, the production of value still has a sense anchored in the fulfilment of needs, ultimately derived from the existence of material needs, and the fact that humans are actually in pursuit of this fulfilment. There are ontological problems here (the problem of ontology even), particularly in elevating humanity to the exclusive entitlement to the production of value – take the distinction between living labour and dead labour, for instance. Yet, there are tensions in Marx's work that allow room for further developments more compatible with the current post-essentialist requirements of theory. Take the distinction between constant capital and variable capital: it conveys a certain contingency and relativity in the distinction between living and dead labour. It is not for their ontological differences that they should be understood separately in the capitalist mode of production, but because of the different dynamics of interaction that they entail. In addition, the less commented upon distinction between fixed capital and circulating capital already blurs the distinction between human and inhuman, where the labour force and raw materials are grouped together in relative readiness for being used up. Therefore, if we think of commodity formation in the contingent mode, Marx's recourse to use-value is not at all wrong, but use-value today has been, as it were, swallowed up, used up. Human labour – the common denominator for the equivalence of different social products – is no longer human abstract labour, as in the abstraction of concrete labour, always directed by a sense of utility and need. All utility and need are already colonized by equivalence, which implies that nothing is actually useful, everything is waste. Strictly speaking, in Marxian terms, all labour today is wasted labour.

Nonetheless, at the time of the erasure – or, at least, the radical concealment – of the actual creation of value, the opportunity for plural creation of value is even greater. For this radical concealment sometimes also conceals the sense of the capitalist production of value itself, as an appropriation of the stance of appropriation, or appropriation of possessive individualism in its combination of the satisfaction of material needs and sovereign mastery.[15] Thus, what capitalism conceals today are material needs themselves (perhaps, in Freudian language, the reality principle) but also, increasingly, the drive of a desire for mastery, and all that it entails in terms of self-assertion, identity, and questioning; all that tends to remain is the formality of a pleasure principle deprived of its material and desiring basis. This is precisely the nature of the consumerist whim, lacking in need, lacking in desire. It is still a system of appropriation, and possessive individualism is not dead either, but the existence

15 As to the question of appropriation in modern political philosophy, see Balibar (2002, 299–317), who shows how Derrida represents another moment in political philosophy when, with and beyond Marx, expropriation is not simply expropriated, when this expropriation of expropriation does not turn into an appropriation of appropriation – pure appropriation without haunting or mystery – but into expropriation of every appropriation, ex-appropriation.

of whimsical consumerism is the apex of formality – pure formal appropriation (Bauman 2000, 72–90; 2002, 180–200).

This appropriation is, hence, mediated by capitalist equivalence, but is now a bit more difficult to grasp. What is the purpose of an assessment of labour – the measure of such equivalence – such as in the work of Nancy, and Marx himself, if all it creates is waste, and if consumers consume themselves in consuming, or waste themselves in wasting? What is important is that there is creation; the creation of waste is still creation – and necessarily creation if, in consumption, it means also self-creation. Furthermore, the waste that is created is – and this is almost unbearable – plural, and more plural than ever: anything can happen within the realm of waste.[16] Perhaps one should not use the term equivalence for what is disseminated by the labour of the general creation of waste, for nothing is of equal value any more but, rather, of equal waste.

Yet, as creative as it is in its dissemination of equal-waste (rather than equivalence), waste-labour (rather than abstract-labour) generally creates nothing less than subjectivity. The subject of consumption is created differently each time – but this creation still obeys the formal sense of appropriation – and this rough symmetry (amongst those self-mastering the waste, rather than those dumped in it) is, as always, crucial for the continued existence of independent decision-making poles of 'economic' action. The creation of a subject of flawed consumption, instead, obeys nothing other than the very lack of formal sense, that is, the sense of consumption's negative definition. This latter creation hints thus at the conditions of reproduction of the system of formal appropriation. The production of equal-waste, like the production of equivalence, always required and still requires a space of difference, or chaos, or an order of a different type – in the past either a space of untainted utility or other modes of production so that the movement of equivalence can operate as a movement.[17]

Modernization is always on the move, as Bauman puts it, but now it appears at a liquid speed so thrilling that it allows no re-embedding of the disembedded (Bauman 2000, 32–4).[18] This continuous disembedding, however, requires something

16 The point here is that the creation of waste unleashes more than equivalence (or the very appropriative sense of this waste-like equivalence) can handle. There is freedom outside the borders of the walled-up cities, and normally it is not at all a pleasant one. The creative chaos that waste unveils, though, one that was always there, might be of significance for re-thinking social and political action. This ludic – rather than subjective – freedom (Derrida 2003a) according to which anything happens, however, produces also a variety of waste, of wasted lives that are almost incommunicable to each other, their experiences of life in waste are rigorously untranslatable. It is still conceivable that a theory of translations of social movements (Santos 2000) coupled with a theory of translation that takes into account the experience of the untranslatable (Campos 1992), could offer an interesting response to this challenge.

17 As in the work of Deleuze and Guattari, production requires anti-production. The latter is a 'surface over which the forces and agents of production are distributed' (Deleuze and Guattari 1983, 10).

18 Here the Deleuzo-Guattarian influence is again remarkable. One cannot fail to recognize here the triad territorialization, deterritorialization, and reterritorialization. Yet, on the level of a society that dwells at the transient time, without ever repositioning itself, or

concrete, solid, or at least alien to itself, so that it may continue. That is how one should understand the somewhat smooth alliance of capital, multiculturalism, and conservatism. It is not really a case of sustaining sound multiculturalism or conservatism, but they do offer some momentary and provisional relief, as liquid and ever disembedding modernity reveals also a counter-embedding (not a stabilization, or re-embedding of the 'network' itself, but a rough and stable structure solely for the purpose of maintaining a general and successful instability). Yet, the destructive necessity of this 'otherness' appears more clearly in the treatment of refugees and asylum seekers, and 'rogues' of all sorts. This destruction also manifests itself in the naming of 'other' cultures, as if globalisation had not taken place, and as if any opposition to the West had not taken place from within a modern logic. The West wastes the waste that the West itself has created, and in doing so, it wastes itself.

The world of general equal-wasting, as predicament and opportunity, rules over the whole world. Only one form rules and contains the brilliance of incommensurable or absolute labour – and there might rest the alliance of monotheism and capital (Nancy 2003, 37–46; 2002, 28–9; 2005, 27–46). The incommensurable becomes the incommensurable appropriative drive coupled with an incommensurable fear of anything that might threaten from within the instability of this liquid wasting-consumption. All value must end in appropriation. It indeed ends, for the world of full appropriation, when the whole world is conquered, has to start to reappropriate itself in an auto-immune fashion, and all that it produces is the un-world. It loses its capacity to produce the world, and it now secretes itself, lacerates itself in creating the un-world, the waste, or what Nancy calls the *immonde* – meaning both dirty, or filthy, but also non-world (Nancy 2002, 16).[19] What is most difficult to grasp, though, is the opportunity of waste, justice waiting in waste.[20]

---

repositioning (re-positing, or resting . . .) so speedily that one cannot grasp its position, on this level one should recall Deleuze's account of a society of control in its differentiation vis-à-vis a society of discipline (Deleuze 1997, 179).

19 For the question of the un-world, see also the illustrative *De Immundo* (Clair 2004). Clair shows how much modern art has been pervaded in the last sixty years by the question of dirt, filthiness, and the extent to which this question is predicated upon a certain retreat of the sense of the world as order. Yet, this filthiness is for him also a function of anal sexuality, as opposed to genital sexuality, and hence, in Freudian terms, a reminiscence of first infancy. The artist who evokes and consecrates his/her own excrement actually epitomizes a time of total individuals living in totalitarian conditions – Hitler is here the *super artist* of (post)modernity. If I do see the relevance of his analyses, especially in so far as they propose a critique of the cynicism of the art world with respect to the un-world, I have reservations with regard to the conflation of leftovers and evil. Furthermore, I approach very carefully Nancy's conception of the *immonde*, especially in so far as it seems constituted by a negative death drive – whereas it is precisely a 'glimpse' beyond the mere principles that the death drive reveals. In so doing, the death drive points out to what is also different from itself, yet inextricable from it: auto-immunity, aporia, and justice.

20 Certainly, justice waits for nothing, it is urgent, but the waste shelters something oblique in its active passivity, in its resisting plurality. It nurtures, caters and cares for justice in a mode of penetrating and trespassing – waste waits on justice. Each time shredded, crumbled, justice happens, but the waste waits on, serves, and provides for justice. Here one would have to pursue the profound resonances between waste and desolation, abandonment, devastation,

Labour of (self) exposure

The crucial point lies exactly at the juncture where the waster is wasted. Note that wasting here is not only 'negative', but also a condition of the general lack of given, predetermined value produced by the self-fulfilment of the world. However, waste is asymmetrically created – both asymmetry and creation are relevant here. Even if this creation, as creation, is always plural, it does create or 'forge' subjectivity on primarily two different and interdependent levels, namely, the waste of liquidity and the waste within liquidity. The waste of liquidity is epitomized by the integrated consumer who tends to disintegrate himself, and the waste in liquidity is epitomized by the flawed consumer who has never been flawless. To be sure, self-disintegration and original flaw are twin 'forgeries', but they do portray two consequences of equal-wasting that are given asymmetric positions in the contemporary world.

More than ever, this old-modern asymmetric relationship, now in liquid modernity, when the world is full, operates directly against the world itself, in a process that Jacques Derrida called auto-immunity (2003a, 59–71). This labour of auto-immunity can start to show us how to move away from equal-waste, and waste-labour towards absolute labour and value. The asymmetric poles of subjectivity referred to above were created in the world as un-world. Each contains, with different intensities, two sorts of auto-immunities. The first is absolute immunity; the second is auto-immunity *stricto sensu* (one that should be, though, compatible with a curvature, as we shall see shortly). The first means the cessation of contact, or immunity as pure salvation, distinction, elevation, distance, and cleanness – hence a radical persistence in the *autos*, by itself and for itself. The second represents, more than that, an actual sapping of the self-assurance and certainty of this very self by means of a radical affirmation of the self, that is, a suspension of the very conditions of reproduction of the self – an immunity operating against the *autos* itself. The predominance of the second over the first is taking place gradually with still unforeseen consequences. Despite this, the challenge of thought in our time is to extricate the creative moment of liberation from the *autos*, ferreting out the excess from the *autos*. This moment of excess, this pure value, not yet appropriated by the system of production of waste – yet glimpsed at by our understanding of it – is what Jean-Luc Nancy has been trying to portray and expose.

For Nancy, creative brilliance exceeds its own value, it accumulates its own value and there lies the origin of capital, of its primary accumulation:

> What precedes capital is richness as spark or brilliance (*éclat*) . . . Capital converts the spark in productive accumulation of a richness defined by its own (re)productivity: doing that, it transforms the spark in undefined process of a sense always to come, or always lost, mixed up with enrichment (Nancy 2002, 48).

---

and especially with the Latin noun *vastus*, and the verbs, *vacare* and *vastare* (be empty, and to 'make' desert). Ultimately one should look at the intertwinement between all figures and intensities of the waste in/of/as desert, and how they enjoy a fruitful relationship with the experience of justice (Derrida 1996; 2002b).

This growth or progress nourished by the incommensurable conceals its own rare and unique origin: it creates itself out of the nothingness as in the image of the spark, but the spark itself obfuscates the emptiness, the void that it requires. In due course, what Nancy conveys is that the 'essence' of accumulation (and of globalisation as this unending glomus that is self-accumulating, but formal, undefined, and predominantly inactual) is not accumulation, or, that the essence of production is not self-referential reproduction; rather, it is an incommensurable labour of coexistences in the world.

Yet, how can we understand that incommensurable richness of sense, or to use Marx's term, value itself? For Nancy, this value arises from coexistence, being-with in separation, coupled with the mundane, or abandoned character of the world. The mundane requires a faith in the world, a faith in the world of coexistence, a faith as a praxis or effectivity of coexistence – praxis or effectivity of the void, not knowledge of it (Nancy 2005). It is here, in the singular-common experience of the world, that sense is created – not potential, but actual experience – and where the world itself is not given but each time recreated by faith. This experience requires, for Nancy, an actual exposure of each one, each time to the secret value that brings, or welds the world together, the value of value, and the value of creation (Nancy 2000b, 31; 2002, 21, and also, obliquely, Bauman 2003, 56). But in welding together the world of coexistences, the experience one finds is that of 'extortion' – since the creation of value of each one is each time appropriated, generally equated as waste, and concealed within an interdependent and flexible 'network' of spaces and spheres of production and consumption (and production of consumption). This extortion has always been there in the self-reproduction of capital, but it is one that now finds its pinnacle in the production of radically extorted, wasted lives (Nancy 1993, 153; 2002, 60).

Labour is still fundamental for the reproduction of this 'system' of appropriation – and the current working and life conditions of the labour-force in fast-growing economies bear witness to this. The value of labour is that which is extorted, that which Marx called value itself (something that Nancy calls absolute value):

> Absolute value is in fact humanity incorporated in work by labour as human labour. It is hence humanity in producing itself by producing objects (or else . . . creating itself insofar as producing itself) (Nancy 2002, 27).

In Marx this simple actuality of value can be seen at work here:

> I do not divide *value*, into use-value and exchange-value as antitheses into which the abstraction 'value' splits up, rather I divide the *concrete social form* [*konkrete gesellschaftliche Gestalt*] of the labour-product; the '*commodity*' is, on the one hand, use-value, and on the other hand, 'value', not exchange value, since the mere form of appearance is not its own content (Marx 1996, 242).

The content of value is not its purity, if there is such content, it is always already extorted – an actuality in play, but tamed by the self-reproduction of capital that denies the very experience of the enjoyment of value. Exposing what already *becomes* is to postulate an ever-changing self-creation of coexistences, of singularities in action, in praxis. This exposure implies enjoyment (*jouissance*) of a free and common spacing of self-creation – enjoyment of the plurality of worlds, of values, or, better, senses of the world. An enjoyment that can only be thought at the height of its impossibility: it can never take place as a stable, final, definite relation, it is neither a final synthesis nor a return to a primeval indistinctness, but it happens as *experience* (Nancy 2001, 45; 2002, 42–6).[21]

The law of liquidity

How can one now envisage this experience of enjoyment, not of waste, but of a singular-common creation of value in a time of waste, a time of non-world? How can one conceive of enjoyment in waste, a justice of enjoyment inherent in waste? In order to do so, first I need to assess the question of the contours of creative coexistence, within the mundane limits of both liquidity and solidity. Second, I have to consider the extent to which coexistence in waste points out to a law of sharing that threatens from within any law of closure, whose model is first of all that of the juridical or sovereign law.

There is, in considering coexistences in the world, a certain necessity for that solidarity of which Bauman speaks – and perhaps, in a certain sense, for the purpose of warding off the worst, if it is already happening, and even if the act of warding off the worst is not easily extricable from the worst itself (Derrida 2002b, 257). Bauman claimed it was necessary to think beyond the obvious solidarity of fate towards the promotion and exercise of solidarity of purpose. Again, the problem is that the solidarity of fate is not simply a given. It must itself be created. This is the only critique that Nancy levels at Marx, and perhaps it is valid for Bauman as well, the sense of the world is not given, it can only be sensed and created in the plurality of worlds. That should be the case if we are not to be re-inscribed in the totalising, global appropriation characteristic of liquidity. Solidarity itself is a problematic term: its contemporary meaning is derived from the Latin verb *solidare*, which means to make solid, or weld together. If there is solidarity of fate today, it unfortunately also means a solidity of fate, the solidity of individual appropriation and consumption.

21 Our whole predicament depends on an understanding of the enjoyment of freedom. What do we mean by freedom here? Do we mean a spacing of enjoyment in its proximity to being, indebted to and fulfilled by the working-trauma of Being? Then we would still be in the realm of Heidegger's philosophy. Our attempt is to conceive of this enjoyment in its radical impossibility, hence not as an ever-present opening to possibility (Heidegger 2001, 364), nor as salvation from or surpassing of ('*überwinden*') man's *Heimatlosigkeit*, the absence of homeland (Heidegger 1998). For Heidegger, the mournful joy ('*trauernde Freude*', Heidegger 2004, 86) of this absence and its 'poverty' can raise man above his misery towards salvation. In our account of the enjoyment of freedom, there should be nothing preserved, sacred; rather, freedom discloses the trace, the accidental, the playful senselessness of coexistence. If there might be something mystical here, though, in the sense of mystical fruition – in this very acquiescence of playfulness – it is still nothing set apart, distinct, superior, preserved, or sacred . . .

Yet, there is in Bauman's work a persistent faith in common humanity[22] – against all odds and all duly sombre social analyses. The necessity to rethink democracy beyond and below the level of the nation state, and towards the exercise of critique and checking against transnational or imperial spheres of power, is all cogent (Bauman 2007). However, the waste, the un-world created by modern liquidity is not a matter of insignificant and well-contained outcasts; it dwells at the heart of richness (Bauman 2004, 44). In this way, the end of the world, the worst in many ways, has already arrived. With Bauman, it is time to address it, to face up to it. In the laceration of the world, in the incompleteness of empire, there is always opportunity for political change. The non-world is always an opportunity for a new world.

Every change or shift, as these terms have been understood in modern conceptualisations, implies the attainment of a new position; the new world tends to invoke the completeness of the world, whereas the challenge of thought today is an understanding of the new world in which the trace of the un-world is exposed and free. And even if the current sense of a shift is obviously to be thought and created in interaction, mundane and contingent transactions amongst different experiences of extortion and the constraint of the liquid economy of waste, the only chance for a shift lies in the exposure of such transactions that already take place in producing waste.[23] These coexisting transactions are not strictly economic, political or juridical. Yet, they obey a law, a law that dwells at the border of these tangential 'worlds'. It is this basic law that provides for radical freedom and sociability, and it is this basic law that Bauman has sought to bring to fruition in many of his recent writings. Defining it, though, is not attainable by theorising, but an attempt to *address* it is found in Derrida's work:

> prior to all *determined* law, *qua* natural law or positive law, but not prior to law *in general*. For the heteronomic and dissymmetrical curving of a law of originary sociability is also a law, perhaps the very essence of law [l'essence même de *la loi*]. (Derrida 1997, 231)

The law of originary sociability has few parameters, but Derrida understood it against the background of what he termed the juridical law, the model for all 'determined law'. In the intricacy of both natural law and positive law, Derrida strives against the sense of every pure definition of law, against the stricture of the law, its mathematical architecture, and its reserved sovereignty – his references in this respect are mainly Kant and Schmitt. Beyond Kant's stricture of the law, defined by constraint and symmetric enforceability – and here Derrida speaks of an essence of law, '*essence du droit*' (2002b, 234) – and beside Schmitt's territorial and autonomous exceptionalism of the legal institution, deconstruction proposes a law of obliqueness (curving), heteronomy, and enlightened dissymmetry. It is oblique

22 I trust that in Bauman's work humanity is a question, and put in question in his references to 'commonality', rather than a definite starting point (Ghetti 2005a, 208–20).

23 These social transactions and de-liberations (Ghetti 2005b, 255–75) should convey the aporia of an incommensurable creation of the world, as the labour of an infinite tracing that still has to endure a posited, finite existence – this labour however is not about business or negotiation (*ne-otium*) as denial of idleness; on the contrary, it is a labour that instils a taste for inconformity, in-operation, and idleness – *desœuvrement* (Derrida and Nancy 2004, 165–200; Nancy 1991; 1993, 161).

because one cannot define it and finally grasp it, one cannot enforce it nor appeal to it directly (for example, in an attempt to found authority on its basis). It is urgent but elusive, and it announces justice, even if this justice is not ultimate, and not ultimately incompatible with the advent of the worst (Derrida 2002b, 237); heteronomic since it is opened, is to come, and is opened to whoever, and whatever comes, playful in trusting the suspending and troubling accident of the *to come* (Derrida 2003a, 35); and dissymmetric in being passive (or beyond mere passivity and activity) and fully indebted to the promise of the *to come*, which comes as having always-already taken place (Derrida 1993, 117–71). This law lacks both territory and enforceability, it has no place, no sovereign mark (or *character*), but it is also inescapable. It cannot ever be transgressed, unless in a mode of concealment, for it is the unlocatable spacing upon which any transaction, any impossible enjoyment happens.

This move, however, should not be seen as a complete reinvention of law, or the contours of law (Derrida 1990, 88): rather, the *law* (*loi* not *droit*) of which he spoke was already in play in legal, political, and religious institutions, even if concealed by the modern closure of systems or sovereignty. In times of liquid waste, of globalisation, times out of joint (Derrida 1994), there is a greater chance for realizing the disjointed nature of this law – with all the risks that have been discussed. Such a law, though, must not be directly equated to liquidity itself, to the liquid, to global appropriative law, or even the law of the sea.

The liquid does resonate with the mythic imagery of the sea and of piracy – if tied, as in Bauman, to the further development of capitalism. The sea represents, in the work of Schmitt (1997, 46), the progress of commercial and industrial powers beyond the comfort of land, and contact with the non-demarcated high seas would inspire a notion of freedom, subjectivity and war unthinkable in the existential space of the land. One would certainly benefit from the exploration of the intimacy between liquid law and the law of the sea – between the liquid radicalisation and 'purification' of a previous impetus, that of the sea itself (Nancy 1993, 85). Nevertheless, both the law of the sea and the liquid law are bound by the fetters of a law of subjectivity and appropriation, and this is precisely what a law of liquidity disrupts – as a law that informs Bauman's appeal to solidarity/commonality.

In the work of Jean-Luc Nancy, this law is called the law of the law, or *nomos*. It is not, as it was in Carl Schmitt's work, primarily a *nomos* of appropriation, as in Schmitt's conflation of *nomos* and *nehmen* (Schmitt 2003, 326). This *nomos* means for Nancy, primarily, sharing (*partage*), but also imports *jouissance*, enjoyment – joy and enjoyment of the shared and creative spacing of the *law*, as *loi* (Nancy 2002, 179). It means sharing out different senses of the world, and different worlds, and passion for sharing and enjoyment of a *praxis* of the world – one that is opportunity and grace (Nancy 2005, 65–87). In his apocalyptic mode, Bauman, I trust, wishes fundamentally to engender another solidarity, more radical than any solid solidarity, an absolute solidarity that by being absolute dissolves the very yoke of liquid individualism and consumption. Such an absolute can only be found in what Jean-Luc Nancy called the absolute law of sharing or, to be more precise, the enjoyment of the absolute law of sharing. It is with this right, the exposed right given by the law of sharing, that Bauman's work requires, albeit inconspicuously, the affirmation of 'the political'.

References

Agamben, G. (2005), *State of Exception* (Chicago: University of Chicago Press).

Arnaud, A-J. (2003), *Critique de la Raison Juridique 2, Gouvernants sans frontières – Entre mondialisation et post-mondialisation* (Paris: L.G.D.J.).

Balibar, E. (2002), '"Possessive Individualism" Reversed, From Locke to Derrida', *Constellations* 9:3, 299–317.

Bauman, Z. (2000), *Liquid Modernity* (Cambridge: Polity Press).

Bauman, Z. (2002), *Society under Siege* (Cambridge: Polity Press).

Bauman, Z. (2003), *Liquid Love – On the Frailty of Human Bonds* (Cambridge: Polity Press).

Bauman, Z. (2004), *Wasted Lives – Modernity and its Outcasts* (Cambridge: Polity Press).

Bauman, Z. (2007), 'Uncertainty and Other Liquid-Modern Fears', in this volume, 17.

Campos, H. (1992), 'Da tradução como Criação e como Crítica' in *Metalinguagem e Outras Metas* (São Paulo: Perspectiva).

Clair, J. (2004), *De Immundo – Apophatisme et apocatastase dans l'art d'aujourd'hui* (Paris: Galilée).

Deleuze, G. (1997), *Negotiations 1972–1990* (New York: Columbia University Press).

Deleuze, G. and Guattari, F. (1983), *Anti-Oedipus* (Minneapolis: University of Minnesota Press).

Derrida, J. (1990), *Du droit à la philosophie* (Paris: Galilée).

Derrida, J. (1993), 'On a Newly Arisen Apocalyptic tone in Philosophy' in P. Fenves, (ed.), *Raising the tone of Philosophy* (Baltimore: The Johns Hopkins University Press), 117–71.

Derrida, J. (1994), *Specters of Marx* (London: Routledge).

Derrida, J. (1996), 'Faith and Knowledge, the Two Sources of "Religion" at the Limits of Reason Alone', in J. Derrida, and G. Vattimo (eds.), *Religion* (Stanford: Stanford University Press), 1–78.

Derrida, J. (1997), *Politics of Friendship* (London: Verso).

Derrida, J. (2002a), *Negotiations, Interventions and Interviews 1971–2001* (Stanford: Stanford University Press).

Derrida, J. (2002b), 'Force of Law – The "Mystical Foundation of Authority"', in G. Anidjar (ed.), *Acts of Religion* (London: Routledge), 230–98.

Derrida, J. (2003a), *Voyous – Deux essais sur la raison* (Paris: Galilée).

Derrida, J. (2003b), *Béliers. Le dialogue ininterrompu, Entre deux infinis, le poème* (Paris: Galilée).

Derrida, J. (2005), 'La bête et le souverain', in M-L. Mallet (ed.), *La démocratie à venir* (Paris: Galilée).

Derrida, J. and Nancy, J-L. (2004), 'Responsabilité – du sens à venir', in F. Guibal and J-C. Martin (ed.), *Sens en tous sens – Autour des travaux de Jean-Luc Nancy* (Paris: Galilée), 165–200.

Fitzpatrick, P. (2001), *Modernism and the Grounds of Law* (Cambridge: Cambridge University Press).

Ghetti, P.S. (2005a), 'From the Posthumous Memoirs of Humanity: "Democracy *to come*"', *Law, Culture and the Humanities* 1:2, 208–20.
Ghetti, P.S. (2005b), 'Laws of Deliberation, From Audaciousness to Prudence … and Back', *Law and Critique* 16:3, 255–75.
Guattari, F. and Rolnik, S. (1999), *Micropolítica – Cartografias do Desejo* (Petrópolis: Vozes).
Heidegger, M. (1998), 'Letter on Humanism' in W. McNeill (ed.), *Pathmarks* (Cambridge: Cambridge University Press), 239–76.
Heidegger, M. (2001), *Fundamental Concepts of Metaphysics: World, Solitude, Finitude* (Indianapolis: Indiana University Press).
Heidegger, M. (2004), *La Pauvreté (Die Armut)* (Strasbourg: Presses Universitaires de Strasbourg).
Lacoue-Labarthe, P. (2004), 'Présentation' in M. Heidegger, *La Pauvreté (Die Armut)* (Strasbourg: Presses Universitaires de Strasbourg).
Lefort, C. (1986), *Essais sur le politique (XIXe–XXe siècles)* (Paris: Éditions du seuil).
Marx, K. (1976), *Capital, vol. I* (Harmondsworth: Penguin Books).
Marx, K. (1996), '"Notes" on Adolph Wagner' in *Later Political Writings* (Cambridge: Cambridge University Press).
Mezzadra, S. (2004), 'The Right to Escape', *Ephemera – Theory and Politics in Organization* 4:3, 267–75.
Mouffe, C. (2005), *On the Political* (London: Routledge).
Nancy, J-L. (1991), *The Inoperative Community* (Minneapolis: Minnesota University Press).
Nancy, J-L. (1993), *The Experience of Freedom* (Stanford: Stanford University Press).
Nancy, J-L. (2000a), *Being Singular Plural* (Stanford: Stanford University Press).
Nancy, J-L. (2000b), *Corpus* (Paris: Métailié).
Nancy, J-L. (2001), *L' 'il y a' du rapport sexuel* (Paris: Galilée).
Nancy, J-L. (2002), *La Création du Monde, ou La Mondialisation* (Paris: Galilée).
Nancy, J-L. (2003), 'Deconstruction of Monotheism', *Postcolonial Studies* 6:1, 36–46.
Nancy, J-L. (2005), *La Déclosion (Déconstruction du christianisme, 1)* (Paris: Galilée).
Neves, M. (2001), 'From Autopoiesis to the Allopoiesis of Law', *Journal of Law and Society* 28:2, 246–64.
Santos, B.S. (2000), *Crítica da Razão Indolente – Contra o Desperdício da Experiência* (São Paulo: Cortez).
Schmitt, C. (1996), *The Leviathan in the State Theory of Thomas Hobbes – Meaning and Failure of a Political Symbol* (Westport, Connecticut: Greenwood Press).
Schmitt, C. (1997), *Land and Sea* (Washington D.C.: Plutarch Press).
Schmitt, C. (2003), *The Nomos of the Earth* (New York: Telos).

Chapter 4

Fear in the Lawscape

Andreas Philippopoulos-Mihalopoulos[1]

Locating the demon

Where is fear located in liquidity? In a flow of liquid communications, observation must also assume analogous amounts of liquid predisposition which will follow the epistemic object in its movement. At the same time, observation must maintain the construction of a certain anchorage with regard to which any distinction is performed. Even in liquidity, the distinction is to remain first in its arbitrariness, stable in its contingency, and operational in its division (Spencer Brown 1979). However, locating fear proves distinctly elusive, with various distinctions exchanging their lacerating crossings and levels of observation, enabling a veritably fluid process of locating and necessarily engaging with an intentional paradox between observed and observer, inside and outside, fear and anxiety, liquidity and rigidity.

Fear pushes into the liquid. It begins and ends in liquidity, where the observer is constantly pushed into a floating *liquet* that leaves the garden of *non-liquet* behind. *Liquet* is an acceptance of the jurisdiction of the distinction between what is to be decided and what not (and further, what has been decided). The absence of *non-liquet* from the fan of probabilities engages the one who distinguishes into a perpetual risk discourse, where projections of present-past into the future are fraught with a forced directionality away from the beginning. But all this simply conceals the fact that there is no original choice: one begins by having already decided, distinguished. *Liquet* opens up more liquid distinctions, but in itself it remains the first, arbitrary and operationalising distinction (that further enables the first crossing). The Edenic wall crosses itself by creating its outer side and showing to the ones inside that the choice has never existed. From the first *liquet* (which in its folds always hides its negation) comes the expulsion to the perpetual *liquet* (every time once) as the liquefied uncertainty, in whose folds fear expands and contracts in panting fluctuations. The liquidity of fear is a direct challenge to social liquidity: fear in liquidity is fear *of* liquidity, and as such it can never be a distinction (it remains on both sides, inside and outside, in liquidity and rigidity). Fear is kicked out of liquidity, because this is the only way in which liquidity can capitalise on fear. But, in its turn, fear always kicks back, rendering its location not just bouncy and fluid but positively 'demonic'.

---

1 I am grateful to Jiří Přibáň for giving me the opportunity to explore my fears, and to the insightful comments of the workshop participants, and especially Anton Schütz, whose words are a perpetual source of inspiration. This text is replete with my grandmother's absence, who died between the title and the text of the section 'Nothing There'.

This is the beginning of the text. But every beginning is preceded by the demon. One of the latter's most famous apparitions is in Goethe's story of *Faust* as revisited in Bulgakov's *The Master and Margarita* (2004). One fine day, Bulgakov's demon appears in the city of Moscow. He creates appropriate chaos, kicks everyone outside the city walls, locks them in a madhouse, and then imperiously flies away, leaving behind a lingering threat of return. The demon has been invited into the city and its text for the great synthesis, where the Master and his beloved Margarita get together again. But the demon has also been invited here, in this very volume, in fact preceding the volume: 'Fear is arguably the most sinister of demons nesting in the open society of our time' writes Bauman in the end of his contribution. Bauman evokes the demon for the great *apo*synthesis of liquidity, the apocalyptic liquefaction of society and its fears. But this Master's Margarita is yet to be found – could it be Society? Globalisation? Community? Utopia? Europe? The Stranger? Love? All the above? The task will be postponed with the pre-announced paradox: for Bauman, fear is both his demon and his Margarita. Leaving open the issues of 'open' 'society' for the purposes of the present chapter (but *contra* Philippopoulos-Mihalopoulos 2007a), I will proceed singularly to the multiplicity of Bauman's demons.

A cameo in David Lynch's *The Lost Highway* reminds us that the devil has the gift of bilocality: here and there, on this and the other end of the telephone line, speaking to you at a party and waiting for you at home. A demonology of fear entails a bifurcation: the location of fear is to be fixed both here and out of here, in the system and its environment, this and that side of the wall, on the boundary and in its shadow, in liquid *liquet*, fiercely riding a temporal slice and simultaneously echoing in both origin and destination. Fear is ambivalent: 'Fear was my cradle…it taught me many a lesson and it whispered into my ears secrets, which I could have never known, were that hateful monster not so faithful a companion of my life' (Seedo 1964, 5, 8). Fear becomes the arches of the bridge spanning the distinction between origin and destination, mother and desire, the difference that always stands 'be-fore' me although having already arrived 'before' me, linking origin and destination in a fold of utopia (Philippopoulos-Mihalopoulos 2006c). Fear doubles up in its intentionality that uroborously links itself to itself: fear *of* fear becomes a faithful companion, always expelled 'before' the city and its law. For there is always a 'before' the city and the law, which, unsurprisingly, returns in this text relentlessly, locating itself 'be-fore' the fluidity of the text's boundaries.

For the boundaries to be escaped, the boundaries will have to be defined. Here, I am bound by and for the *lawscape*, namely the epistemic and ontological combination of the city and the law that is used later in this text as the ideal terrain on which to observe the paradox of fear. Fear is found folded in between law and city, intentionally wedged between their reciprocal kicks, a breath of claustrophobia that leads into the horizon of anxiety (or fear *of* fear), and its further possibilities of escape. The escape from the lawscape is planned along liquid lines: a 'liquid' use of Luhmann's systems theory will be the defining pool of this text, allowing flows from Kierkegaard's theological explorations and Heidegger's venture to the nothing. These are combined with an incipient theory of paradox (whose foundational thoughts can be found in Philippopoulos-Mihalopoulos 2005) that will be raising its two heads regularly throughout the text. The endeavour to locate fear takes place on the internal boundary of the lawscape, and this will be the first stage of the exploration. Fear will be sought, not in its individual apparitions, but between the two sides of the lawscape, namely city and law, as the systemic demon that pulls the two together while disrupting their continuum. Fear always escapes from the lawscape, since neither law nor the city can deal with it – so fear is found expelled in the environment, in the nothing outside identity. However, this is only impressionistic, for the paradoxicality (or bilocality) of fear appears portentously in the fear of fear, which remains within the system as an echo of the ostracisation. The two are linked intentionally, since the pulling power of fear populates the nothing outside and renders it correlative in an always receding horizon of invitation between the sides of the paradox: system and environment, law and city, knowledge and ignorance, observer and observed, liquidity and rigidity.

But before that, a word on my founding inspiration for this piece, namely, Bauman's alluring flirtation with fear. In its 'sinister' form, Bauman's fear appears in most of his recent writings as a capitalisable value of contemporary globalised capitalism. Fear can be produced in order to underscore power structures (Bauman 2004), and it is indeed produced and perpetuated in every conceivable form in order to heighten the perceived need for 'personal safety' (Bauman, this volume), as opposed to the more diffused term 'security' (Bauman 1998, 118). The object of fear may be, amongst a pretty long list, terrorism (Bauman 2005a, 8ff.), crime (Bauman 2006), deregulation (Bauman 2005, 7), strangers (Bauman 2003, 109), globalisation (Bauman 2005b), loss of control (Bauman 2006), even the end of fear itself (Bauman 2004, 93). Fear is paralysing, not just because it 'has settled now inside, saturating our daily routines' (Bauman 2006), not even because it is 'self-perpetuating and self-reinforcing' (Bauman 2006); but because it is a paradox, to which Bauman concedes a special role in the formation of contemporary societal self-description. 'Modern-liquid' fear for Bauman is a stabilising factor of the contemporary hierarchical structure in all its liquidity. Using, after Derrida, the concept of *pharmacon* in its dual meaning as both medicine and poison, Bauman embarks upon a paradoxification of fear: 'we tend to become fear-dependent; we are fear's addicts. We need a dose each day – and as in any addiction worth its name each day we need a larger dose than the day before. What we fear most is an overdose, *and we fear it because we fear the end of fearing it portends.*' (Bauman 2004, 93, added emphasis).

Paradoxification goes further when fear-hunting becomes a utopia in itself (Bauman 2005c). Bauman crosses to the other side of the paradox when he points to the most romantic fact about fear: that when it goes, spontaneity, flexibility, adventure, and the ability to surprise go with it too (Bauman 2005b, 166). Fortunately, Bauman hasn't lost his ability to surprise. He remains one of those rare cases of authorship that manages to excite equally sociologists, media theorists, political commentators, administrators, legal scholars, philosophers, and uncategorisable hybrids like the instant author. And here, perhaps not unduly, the instant author is excited. Bauman's description of fear departs from the solidly sociological, even from the playfully journalistic or the passionately political, and insinuates a paradox that remains operational despite its self-clogging. Fear is seen both as a demon *and* as a Margarita, as the object of tremor and desire in a perfect marriage that goes beyond simple differences between 'existential' and 'modern' fears (Bauman

2006), or indeed 'cosmic' and 'official' fears (Bauman 2004), and initiates thus the very operation of paradox. The source of excitement is not so much that these two antithetical sides of fear are being presented side by side; rather, that the two sides are seen as complementary to each other in their fragmented unity; that indeed, the operation of the paradox of fear is based precisely and solely on the fact that fear *is* a paradox.

Ironically, what Bauman managed to convey in only a couple of phrases will inevitably take me a whole chapter. Thus, I feel obliged to carry on with a few more distinctions and acceptances of *liquet* in order to bring the reader to where I would like – perhaps to the 'madhouse' outside the city, the *ou-topos* outside the *polis*, or the site of mourning where the morning sight will bring an operational paralysis (Rose 1996). For it is only from there, from the *outside*, that an observer can retain her liquid anchorage and painstakingly erect an illusion of observation. But this outside is neither the Cartesian canyon, nor simply the Luhmannian second-order cannon (Luhmann 1998). The outside of the paradox (because it is the paradox that the present observer desires to observe) is nowhere to be found, except perhaps in the intentionality between inside and outside. It is a veritable utopia because it defines itself in constant contradistinction to itself. It refutes its location by sliding in between its apparitions, a Derridean spectre that allows for no respite except for its promise of return. Thus, a paradox is the constant oscillation between the two points of an antithesis. It requires and tolerates no external definition since it is perfectly formulated to define and annul itself simultaneously. Paradoxes are perfection, but just as any perfection, paradoxes are inoperable (Philippopoulos-Mihalopoulos 2005). When confronted with paradoxes, one hides away in the various avenues of deparadoxification, which Luhmann (2004: 64) has enumerated: 'unfolding, making invisible, civilizing, making asymmetrical.' Regardless of their positionings (and those in which they squeeze the observer), they are all emanations of one epistemological gesture: the distinction.

Where is a distinction located in liquidity? The answer would have to take into consideration the intentional link between the observer (the one who makes the distinction) and the distinction itself. But here I wish to go before the distinction, since my object (already a distinction no doubt) is fear, which, I will posit, is not a distinction. Fear can only operate when it is found at its most inoperational, namely, when the paradox of fear (as demon *and* Margarita, as 'before' and 'be-fore', as origin and desire, as mourning and morning, as paralysis and *lysis*) is revealed in all its apotheosis as the circular causality between its two values (demon *because* Margarita, origin *because* desire, and so on), to remain inescapable because of the mutual erasure of the positionings. In that sense, fear can only operate when its paradoxical composition is *not* split into its (individually) operational positionings: it can only operate when inoperative. The initial question of this chapter can now be revisited in a more informed way: fear of liquidity is not to be found in liquidity but in the incestuous intentionality between observer and observed in their desperate attempt to attain a relative rigidity. The link between observer and observed is a contingent rigidity that understands liquidity as the tautology between society and its communicational behaviour (however *outré*, at least at first instance), and on that basis it resists liquidity. When societal self-description coincides with description, and any point of observation is always already included in the coincidence, the only escape is a constructed illusion of rigidity. As such, fear is resistance, and is reborn at every instance of its exclusion. Fear pushes into liquidity by initiating the need for security to be located in the intentional link between observer and observed. Fear of liquidity wraps liquidity (and its fears) as a negative bracketing, at the same time outside and inside, a process of observation and an echo of expulsion. The demonic desire of fear balances on the very boundary between liquidity and rigidity.

It is for all the above that the need to de-psychologise fear becomes relevant.[2] Both observer and observed are systems in the Luhmannian sense, which operate with distinctions, communications, observations, and so on. In what follows, law and the city will be observing each other in an escape game for two. The escape game is the epistemological and ontological plane of the *lawscape*. Fear is to be sought between and outside these two observers, at the same time their demon and desire. But before that, a description of the lawscape.

Escaping lawscape

As the fusion between law and the city, the 'lawscape' can be defined on various levels as both contingent and actual but always paradoxical. The paradox is amply evinced in the way the two have so far avoided being looked at together in any conclusive way. While the discourses of *Law and...* are widely rehearsed and accepted, *Law and the City* is seen as a subset of either the generic 'Law and Geography' movement (Blomley et al. 2001; Holden and Harrison 2003), or the gender or criminological current on cities and personal safety (e.g., Cooper 1998; Moran et al. 2003; Little 1994; Hayward 2004; Virilio 2005). While these are useful positions from which to observe the lawscape, they are not adequate for the kind of study followed here (the beginning of which can be found in Philippopoulos-Mihalopoulos 2007b). The lawscape is not employed here as another contextualised study of law, or indeed as part of the project of space reinstatement, but as an interdigitation of two epistemic domains that remain inoperable, unless one sees them as indistinguishable in their paradoxical (in)operationality. In this sense, the paradox of the lawscape is revealed only as an absence of operationality.

The recent turn of theory to paradoxes, not in the usual attempt to deparadoxify them, but to employ them while accepting their paradoxicality (e.g., Luhmann 1995b; Bateson 1972; Lyotard and Thebaud 1985; Schmitt 1976), encourages the combination between law and city. A more detailed analysis of the specific paradox can start by focusing on the tension between the two, that is, the connection of continuum and difference between law and city, expressed in the conjunction 'and': lawscape is law *and* city brought together in a circular continuum, and kept separate in a distance of *différance* that feeds into the paradox. Continuum first: law and the city can be seen in a connection of reciprocal reflection. Thus, law's

2 Although of course existing studies of fear from a psycho-sociological point of view are valuable beginnings: Bourke (2005), for a gripping cultural-historical argument; Robin (2004), for an applied discussion of Hobbes's, de Tocqueville's and Arendt's analyses of fear.

normative surplus of categorising, naming, organising – in short, distinguishing and deparadoxifying – is manifested in the materiality of the urban dis/order on social, spatial, historical, etc. levels. At the same time, the city is reflected onto the legal internalisation of power struggles, violence in its legitimating use, and production and consumption of capital. The city is revealed, not just as the gaming table of such occurrences, but significantly as the prime avenue of legal internalisation of society, the cognitive domain of the legal system *par excellence*. It is in this way that the city amplifies law's communication with itself: legal communications thunder about in the condensed and intensely regulated urban environment – think of planning restrictions, environmental regulations, zoning, social control, borders between private, public and restricted access areas, pavements, roads, traffic lights, metro barriers, flows of people, headscarves at schools, hoods in shopping malls, power architecture and landscaping, and so on. Likewise, the law understands the city in the way a geometrical 'ruler' would, offering (in)flexibility and (un)reliability, thus guaranteeing that the contingent difference between distance and propinquity will carry on fluctuating.

The circularity between law and the city on these epistemological levels can be observed in a fairly uncomplicated way. What is arguably more complex is the passage from epistemology to ontology. Observed from precisely such a point of crossing, the circularity can be, at least for now, described as an instance of 'structural coupling' (Luhmann 1992), which is a way out of systemic isolation (but not closure) and into a state of simultaneous self-observation. As such, structural coupling requires a certain historicity of reciprocity. The continuum is adapted to conditions of liquidity without significant changes, for it is already coupled with a deferential difference; the very tension between continuum and difference guarantees the relative solidity of observer and observed in conditions of liquidity. The expectation of operationality from a clearly inoperative paradox is what makes the interweaving between law and the city possible (but not operational, even in view of structural coupling). The inoperative paradox remains relevant, precisely on account of its inoperationality. The connection between observed and observer (observer and observer, law and the city, and so on) is one of incestuous interweaving, unobservable except as a second-order construction of structural coupling, that can only resonate within each one of them (observed and observer) as a paradox *accompli*, a complementarity that precedes the need for alterity, a mutual invitation that eschews tracing.

The incommunicable complementarity between law and city – a direct consequence of the self-referential construction of the systems – seems to be the crux of the matter. It is the case that both law and the city, from the arguably limited point of a system's self-description (which, however, does not necessarily distance itself sufficiently from a description) follow an 'egological' (Husserl 1973, 35) spatialisation of their boundaries that accords with the positioning of themselves within the space. The priority of spatialisation brings along a priority of origin, which coincides with the priority of their destination. From a systemic point of view, the destination is none else but the evolutionary perpetuation of the system, to which effect the system will cannibalise, always *malgré soi*, the proximate definitional parameter – in this case, the law or the city. Cannibalisation between systems has the relatively gentile effect of allowing the other to carry on floating about ontologically unchewed. The internalisation of the projected imagery (in the form of palatable ignorance) by the system has little to do with the other system as such, since the only access a system has to its environment (and systems therein) is through an internalised reconstruction ('re-entry'; Luhmann 1993) of the difference between system and environment.

Thus, 'law is everywhere' (Sarat 1990) is not just a descriptive comment on the current state of societal juridification, but, at least for the purposes of this chapter, a veritable expression of law's self-description as a discourse within whose cognitive boundaries the whole horizon can potentially fit. This totalising view has as a consequence some anticipated self-misdescriptions: first, that law is a reliable panacea for society's conflicts; and second, that law's monopoly on normativity allows and calls for blanket-applicability. A way to avoid such totalisation is by counterpoising law to other disciplines – an operational rupture inserted between observer and observed (in other words, the internalised boundary of the difference between system and environment) – that offers precisely the unresolvable paradox between continuum and difference. The issue that arises now is, of course, how the system understands and internalises such a rupture: in other words, how to resist tautology between self-description and description? How to convert descriptions into self-descriptions? How to pass successfully from epistemology to ontology?

Attempts at answering these questions are reserved for the last section of the chapter, after the discussion has touched upon a firmer description of the lawscape, which, in its turn, will offer a firmer grip on the relation between the two sides of the paradox. For, while the epistemological issue has been solved in favour of a somewhat evident circularity, there remains the issue of totemic priority between the two, inevitably cropping up whenever one considers hospitality within boundaries. This too, of course, can be solved through a circularity – perhaps less evident this time – which involves a certain understanding of priority of invitation (Levinas 1981; Derrida 1999). But in so doing, one hits upon the definitional mechanics of the lawscape: the lawscape is neither a simple disciplinary coincidence, nor a facile tautology, difference or rupture between law and city. The lawscape is the ever-receding horizon of prior invitation by the one (the law/the city) to be conditioned by the other (the city/the law). In the invitation, a summons to continuum is protended. But in the priority of the other invitation, the rupture is reinstituted as the inviting distance of an alterity that always precedes. Thus, the continuum is enabled precisely on account of the rupturing effect of the priority of invitation, and the rupture disabled and invited anew with every continuum. City and law eagerly wait for each other to go first, wearily exchanging 'after-yous', while dispassionately meaning 'before you'. The Kafkian invitation is always already there but can never be consumed without being interrupted by its prior invitation: for just as the man from the country spent his whole life waiting before the law's doorkeeper, in the same way the doorkeeper spent his whole life waiting for the man waiting (Kafka 1961). Thus, the paradox of the lawscape is revealed in the interweaving of invitation (to condition) and priority of invitation (as rupture). The 'and' of Law and the City, replaced by 'because', points to an almost allopoietic construction – except that 'allo' cannot be distinguished from 'auto'.

Since the reciprocal invitation comes even before the need to invite, the always-already coupling of the law and city is so obvious that becomes invisibilised. This is the reason for which it appears impossible to be aware of the frequency of the legal presence in the city, and conceptually strenuous to think of law's materiality as formed in its urban grounding. The a priori nature of the interweaving means that there is no easily identified origin, cause or indeed discernible direction of 'irritation'. It also means that the system internalises the priority of alter, not of course as alter, but as a sort of estoppel, logged in the operations of the system. This estoppel does not reveal alterity: if anything, it obtrudes its revelation, it covers up its *substance* but exposes a procedural (non-)understanding of alterity that operates within the system. This procedural estoppel disallows the system from egologically rolling onto the other side of the bed too.

But there is something more to it – or perhaps the present observer fancies seeing something more here (what's the difference?). The 'and' in Law and City has been too quickly swallowed by the elegant 'lawscape' even with the inelegant addition of the estoppel. In a gesture of controlled prestidigitation, any lexical hiccup, any insinuation of tension and a priori ir-rupture were smoothed over by an 'e-scape', the escape of the *e* and the scapegoating of the one terrific thing perched on the boundary between continuum and rupture: the demon of fear. Fear re-emerges in the 'and' that puts together tearings of historicity and strictures of passage, and claims its place in the self-contained syllables of the lawscape. No longer invisibilised, fear is revealed again through its very own bodies of appearance: the violent embrace between the law and the city. Fear reclaims its bilocality, visibilises the rupture between law and city, and throws into relief a boundary that has been kept silent. Only then does fear allow the lawscape to carry on with its internal tension. The escape from the lawscape is a bumpy flight to 'the other side of the air' (*An die Musik*, Rilke 1995, 143).

Fear (of fear)

In Kurosawa's *I Live in Fear*, fear, the city and the law are revealed in their constant tension. The fear of a new nuclear holocaust haunts a man so much that he decides to move to Brazil with all his family. However, the latter do not share his fear, take the case to a family tribunal, manage to declare him 'irresponsible' and finally put him in a mental asylum. The judge from the tribunal comes to visit him and finds a totally deranged man who looks at the setting sun and thinks that it is the earth burning because of a nuclear holocaust. The film's many scenes from busy city streets, constantly crossed by people and trams, turn into an agoraphobic nightmare. The city breeds fear and the only possible reaction is to escape. However, the law guards the limits of the city and immures the man in his urban angst by not allowing him to escape. But nor does it deal with him. Indeed, the law cannot deal with fear: it is deemed irrational, therefore not worthy of protection. The protagonist allows his fear to push him into his own small private holocaust, an act of abandonment to and, at the same time, resistance against his fear: before he is shut in the asylum, the old man puts fire to the family foundry – the family's only source of income – to convince them to move. The fire in the foundry – the means of expelling the fear – is repeated eternally, at the end of every day, in the colours of the sunset seen from his cell window. The demon of his fear revisits him at dusk, and the judge sits by helplessly, wondering why he failed to protect him. What is it that stops the law from dealing with fear?

The answer is multiple. It has to do with internal and external boundaries and projections of ignorance. The law fears a lot of things: it fears doubt, it fears resistance, it fears revolution, it fears the streets and their ghosts, the city and its limits, society and its embrace, the past, the future, justice, utopia. The law fears everything that the city is; but, at the same time, the law 'relies' on the city, 'acknowledges' its continuum, constructs a rigidity between them that resists the surrounding liquidity. The law even fears itself, in that any look in the mirror may reveal mismatches between description and self-description, means and mission, force and stability. But law's fear is never revealed or suppressed in the way psychology would expect: there are no drawers in the system, no hideouts. Instead, it is expelled, pushed out of the law's boundaries, safely folded away in the recesses of the systemic environment, an unwanted, forgotten, noxious quantity of waste, which would otherwise clog the operations of the system. Just as a city must get rid of its waste in order to carry on functioning and not being buried under the sheer horror of its excreta, the law must forget its fear, and, furthermore, forget its forgetting too, in order to erase any trace that may return to haunt it later (Bauman, this volume, as well as 2003 in relation to cities; Philippopoulos-Mihalopoulos 2004).

The city follows the same pattern when it comes to its fears: the city fears the law while inviting it; it fears violence, while relying on it; it fears limitation while exercising it; it fears difference while attracting it. Fear of personal safety – a capitalisable fear *par excellence* (Bauman 2005d) – has brought about precautionary measures that manifest themselves physically through fences and gates, zones and walls, cameras and restricted areas. These measures have replaced the old civic currency of civility, tact, trust, security and so on (Zukin 1995), and have shuttered most illusions of self-determination: the individual's fate is an eagerly constructed area of self-play only when present theory looks back, to the ages of a pre-differentiation, and erects idols of control (Bauman, this volume; Morrisson 1995). The city fears the institutions on which it relies: it fears the depression of stable identity and the impressions of together-in-difference (Young 1990). It also fears the way its urban mapping thematises the world: for the conditions of urban life are the conditions of humanity (Bauman 2005b, 162). Most significantly, the city fears the mapping drawn by its very fear: urban mapping has turned inside out. The city is no longer the safety box that would protect humans from other humans and the wrath of the gods, but a veritable nest of snakes where fear is internalised and bred within the city walls (Ellin 1997). Ironically, there is no longer the need for cities to be circumscribed, since the boundaries have moved inside, piling up layers upon layers of insecurity and setting off what Bauman calls 'the dream-model of *perpetuum mobile*' (this volume). The city lacerates itself by constantly dividing its entrails, distinguishing between inside and outside, safe and unsafe, 'abatement' and 'enhancement' areas (Davis 1998) where the law ploughs the land and gives birth to abysses of fear. There is a map projected over every city, fractally reshaped according to the dreams and nightmares of its citizens, redrawing the legal-urban boundaries according to traumas and failed expectations, and bringing the city face to face with its fear of being something different to its self-description.

City and law deal with their fears in exactly the same way. Their fears are comparable, complementary, and indeed reflected in each other. Just as the law, the city fears itself in that any look in the mirror may reveal mismatches between description and self-description, between slum and utopia, legality and illegality, death and survival. So the city builds its wall and keeps its fear out: 'Fear is a factor that, due to its destabilising influence, is expelled and excluded from society' (de Muynck 2004, 8). The city ostracises its *fleurs du mal* and forgets their forgetting, since it already has enough ghosts haunting its street corners. The man in fear is sent outside the city, to the madhouse where he can indulge his fear without upsetting the urban narcissism. Fear is converted into waste, ostracised beyond the cognitive domain of the system and left there forgotten (Bauman, this volume). More often that not, fear is ping-ponged between law and the city in a perpetual transfer of responsibility: logos and polis, force and violence, legitimation and public participation. The city receives the legal excreta only to stuff it back into the fissures of law, thinking that fear has been ostracised from the systemic boundaries.

But even after the most successful distanciation of fear from the walls of the system, there is always something left behind, an echo of absence: the fear *of fear* never really abandons the purified terrain, but remains within as a haunting *memento mori*. The fear of fear is equally insidious as fear, 'no nobler than any other fear' as the Chevalier reminds us in Poulenc/Bernanos's *Les Dialogues des Carmélites*. Fear of fear is the hidden end of the fear paradox: one end inside the system, the other outside the system, linked by an inoperability that paralyses, addressing the folds of ignorance within the system and always reminding it of the fear *extramuros*. However, since there is nothing for the system *extramuros*, the system is left with a gaping misdescription of a lost historicity, with a fear of fear. The system has no access to its environment, and *this* is the source of fear: as Bauman says, the source of fear resists mapping (Bauman 2005a, 17) – and its resistance is so successful because there is no map of the outside. The boundary between the system and its environment is what separates the system from nothing, the relative (but never in comparable terms) knowledge from the absolute ignorance – even the ignorance of ignorance. However, such ignorance does not bring bliss, but fear of fear, or, to put it differently, the *anxiety* of knowledge. Indeed, anxiety, as the state of heightened vigilance whose source is not traceable (Rachman 1998), is the way fear of fear manifests itself: 'precisely because anxiety is non-locatable it attains a terrible reality. It is fear of *fear*… This 'nothing' is the abyss above which the self, made conscious of its possibilities, balances, fearing to look down lest I should fall and be annihilated' (Davidson 2003, 60). Anxiety is often seen as a desperate but effective sign of strife for balance 'between signals of threat and signals of safety' (Rachman 1998, 125, talking specifically about agoraphobia). While the topography of fear is directed to specific objects or situations, that of anxiety is diffused and directionless. This is the kind of fear Bauman refers to when he talks about 'the decoupling of the fear-inspired actions from the existential tremors that generate the fear which inspired them' (Bauman, this volume).

Anxiety is the obvious result of the displacement of the boundary from around the system to within the system; or, as Bauman puts it, it is the moment that solidarity took over from belonging as the shield against fear (Bauman 2004, 98). Risk always comes from within: the law wonders about its role in a globalised context, not with respect to other systems and their colonising appetites (they have always been around), but because the questioning of the unutterable paradox of law's legitimation has already started ringing alarmingly within. Anxiety is to be found between law's edifices, comfortably nestled within the systemic operations, whispering the paradox that law itself wants to forget: is law lawful? Likewise, the city's risk comes from its very own body of emancipation, its inability to deal with its own consumption and production, its fear of becoming the only thing still operating as a cancerous formation on an apocalyptic planet. The city is facing an anxiety crisis: 'Anxiety was no longer kept outside the city, but outside its buildings' (de Muynck 2004, 12) populating the slits of distinction that the city has inflicted on its swelling body.

Anxiety is what is left after the expulsion of fear. The 'existential tremors' return and affect the system from within. The correspondence between internal and external ignorance leaves a scar on the skin of the system, and the draughty environment with all its threatening 'earthbound darkness' (Bulgakov 2004, 276) gusts in. The normality of the systemic 're-entry', namely the reproduction within the system of the difference between the system and its environment (Luhmann 1993), is compromised by an untraceable mis/correspondence between inside and outside. The issue, already quite taxing for the system, becomes even more so when one looks at a historical reciprocity, such as an instance of structural coupling. Does the outside resonate even more hollow inside? Is the ignorance of the specific alter (rather than the generic environment) a more nagging ignorance, precisely because it is wrapped in a coat of familiarity? And finally, to give the final blow to any impression of systemic self-control: is there any mechanism of dealing with an alien presence of identity formation that perpetually undermines the systemic priority of spatialisation? In other words, how does the system cope when put together with another system in a relation of perpetual *horizon*tal deprioritisation, in an ontological unit that is to remain invisible if it is to remain operable? The lawscape, as the paradoxical interweaving of postponed priority, puts to the system a much more trenchant demand than structural coupling: it demands that the system should nurture within its boundaries a growth of ignorance (the other system) with which it can never become familiarised, lest the system dissolve and become coextensive with its internal growth (because the paradox of the lawscape presupposes both continuum and difference). What is more, this very growth of ignorance is meant to be internalised by the system as prior to itself, always preceding any systemic construction of origin (because lawscape is the ever-receding horizon of priority).

It should now have become clear why the earnest systemic estoppel suggested in the previous section is not an adequate description of the way in which the system (either the law or the city) operates in the case of the lawscape. The 'and' of the lawscape never quite abandons the individual systems of law and city – they remain separate and continuous, always prior and consistently invisible (to themselves and to others) in their forced but always already occurring confluence. Even if the term 'lawscape' invisibilises it, the 'and' before it looms in front of it, as the signifier of both conflation and confinement, the enabler of continuum and difference, and the horizon of constant back-stepping, expressing thereby the epistemological and ontological tension between the law and the city, and elevating the observational relationship into an unresolvable paradox. The rigidity of the relation between observer and observed reveals itself majestically in the discovery of perhaps the most solid element of liquidity, as internalised, performed and invisibilised in the grottos of every system: the distinction between fear and its intentional attaché, namely fear of fear. Fear is the thing with which the system deals by not dealing with it, by ostracising it. But fear of fear, the anxiety of the boundary, the vertigo before the ever-receding limit of one's identity, is the thing with which the system cannot deal – at least not in the same way. Anxiety is the 'and' separating and bringing together the components of the lawscape, and invisibilising both each other and itself in a preternatural vanishing act. Anxiety appears in its blinding invisibility as the challenge of nothingness that has been outside and is now found inside, cancerously eating away the system's self-description. The system can only deal with what it can deal – namely, fear. Anxiety eludes the system, goes beyond its cognitive abilities, is nowhere to be located; yet, its 'absence' is felt by the system, its effect is constant and gnawing, its intentional link with fear bursts in and unsettles systemic operation.

This is where the text hits on its final paradox: anxiety operates on the system as its demon *and* its Margarita. Anxiety pushes and pulls the system's estoppel in such a way that without it, the system would not have been operational. Anxiety (in its intentional link with fear outside) reveals the unity of the lawscape by maintaining its inoperability, and mobilises each system to carry on operating within this inoperable unity. Noiselessly but fervently, anxiety urges the system towards an awareness of the boundary that separates it from the ever-receding horizon.

Nothing there

The unmappable environment lies at the end of the systemic boundary. The internal and external side of the boundary is a good way to conceptualise the totality of system and environment: not as separate enclosures (or apertures) but as the two sides of an interfolded totality. The system is what it is, as well as what it isn't. The environment is what the system isn't, the uncontainable nothing that elides observation. The two together are the totality of communicational meaning (what Luhmann calls 'society'). Positing a reflection of the system in its environment (in the guise of another system with which it is invited to coalesce) intensifies the conception of the boundary and pushes the system into further re-entries that constantly check on the validity of the boundary conception. The repetition is an anxious attempt to re-establish one's previous conceptions of boundary or adjust them to different information. It is not just identity of the self that palimpsestic repetition attempts to establish; it is, significantly, a reiteration of the expulsion of fear from within the systemic boundaries (a quest for security). Analogously, the further fear is shoved into the system's environment, the stronger the anxiety within. Two systems placed opposite each other and between two mirrors that reproduce infinite repetitions of reflections, one within the other, one melting into the other, jerking meaninglessly in order to distinguish which one is their reflection and which one is the other's. Anxiety is nested within each one of them, reaching out towards a thing that remains unadumbrated.

It is appropriate at this point to take the phenomenological turn and acknowledge what the text has been doing so far without naming it (arguably, for fear of naming it). In the usual formulation, fear in the lawscape is also fear of the lawscape, and in its intentional paralysis, it is time that fear conceded priority to a phenomenology of anxiety that escapes the strictly psychological or existential despite initial appearances. Indeed, Heideggerian anxiety is a mood, an affectedness, an existential attunement of *Dasein* which entails no thinking, just being in a state of throwness in the world. But this very anxiety reveals the nothing (*das Nichts*). The nothing for Heidegger is not *nihil absolutum* (Heidegger 1992) but a 'correlative' that conditions being by being the vehicle of its revelation. In his lecture *What is Metaphysics?* (1996) addressed to the scientific community, Heidegger presents the nothing as the precondition of knowledge, which, however, remains unacknowledged. Anxiety's revealing of the nothing augurs at the same time the impossibility of its acknowledgement, since revealing is essentially letting the totality of the meaningful world (including the one who finds oneself in a state of anxiety) 'slip away'. In other words, the nothing is precisely this slipping away, which is experienced at a state of anxiety as a loss of meaning. In that sense, the nothing is not revealed as a thing in itself, an entity ('The nothing reveals itself in anxiety, but not as being', Heidegger 1996, 102), but always as the negative correlative of being. The nothing is always of this world, always interfolded with the world and never taking one outside the world (an immanent, rather than Husserlian, transcendence). Nothing(ness) is not detached from being but belongs to it, swathing it with a bracketing negation that drains it from its meaning. But in so doing, the nothing reveals being. The disclosure of the nothing through anxiety is the enabler of the original openness of being; the passage through the unsettling slipping away of the nothing is the only way in which the boundary between *Dasein* and the nothing can be crossed. What is more, it is only in the nothing that *Dasein* can(not) be found: 'Da-sein means: being held out into the nothing' (Heidegger 1996, 103). And further: 'Without the original revelation of the nothing, no selfhood and no freedom' (Heidegger 1996, 103).

The ambiguity of the nothing is resonant of the ambiguity of anxiety. Anxiety can either make us take refuge in familiar things at hand, or can push us away from the familiar, detach us from ourselves and our thoughts, and throw us into the meaningless *Dasein*, which, in its turn, opens up the way to the unity of the world, by taking us back to being (Heidegger 1992, 141). The ambiguity of anxiety is reminiscent of another beautiful formation, this time by Kierkegaard: that of 'pleasing anxiety'. In *The Concept of Anxiety*, Kierkegaard deals with an ambivalent anxiety that is also connected with nothing in a circular way: nothing begets anxiety (Kierkegaard 2000a, 139), but nothing is also anxiety's object (Kierkegaard 2000a, 140; cf. Kierkegaard 2000b). Kierkegaard begins by positing that anxiety is a mood, 'a qualification of the dreaming spirit', during which 'the difference between myself and my other … is an intimated nothing' (Kierkegaard 2000a, 139). In anxiety, the confusion between guilt and innocence is at its most profound, crossing the boundary between the self and other in a frenzy of projected ignorance: 'innocence is precisely anxiety, because is ignorance about nothing. Here there is no knowledge of good and evil etc. but the whole actuality of knowledge projects itself in anxiety as the enormous nothing of ignorance' (Kierkegaard 2000a, 141). Anxiety is indeed about the ignorance of nothing – as opposed to fear, which refers to something definite (Heidegger makes a similar distinction) – and it is this ignorance that allows one to be innocent about one's knowledge. Anxiety pushes one to the other side of the binarism ignorance/knowledge by providing a vehicle for the possibility of possibility – in other words, the freedom of crossing: 'anxiety is freedom's actuality as the possibility of possibility' (Kierkegaard 2000a, 139). The nothing of anxiety opens up the other side of knowledge. Talking about the hereditary sin, Kierkegaard envisages the way Adam imagined the other side of the wall separating the garden from the outside:

> The prohibition induces in him anxiety, for the prohibition awakens in him freedom's possibility. What passed by innocence as the nothing of anxiety has now entered into Adam, and here again is a nothing – the anxious possibility of *being able* (Kierkegaard 2000a, 141, original emphasis).

It is not very difficult to run these thoughts parallel to the boundary that separates the system from its environment. Arguably, dealing with anxiety less as a psychological phenomenon and more in relation to the operations of a system may be an autopoietic faux-pas, but there are some grounds for forgiveness: anxiety is seen here as an opportunity for boundary readjustment in relation to ignorance – a variation on 'variation', the systemic accommodation of surprise (Luhmann 1995c). In that sense, it serves to explain cognitive operations of the system without altering fundamental positions with regard to the individual and society. Second, it reflects an epistemological projection on the level of a hesitant second-order observer, who cautiously proceeds into marrying law and the city. There is little doubt that as a utopian misconstruction and a transdisciplinary folly, the lawscape is likeable. There is less doubt that as an autopoietic experiment is fearsome. But trying to begin an ontological description while at the same time avoiding unilateral colonising advances is certainly ridden with anxiety, and this is projected in the text. Finally, systems theory tools are seen here as what they are: rather than a grand theory or at least the meticulous cogs of something grand, they are employed as a certain basis (amongst others) on which the problematic of the tension between two epistemological planes is described. As such, they are terrifically apposite because they enable the abstraction of a common operation (namely fear in the city and the law), without rendering the return to the mechanics of each system difficult. On the very boundary between the two systems (or the system and its environment), issues cropping up from either side are meaningfully projected and, at least in some sense, elevated to an appropriate level of abstraction, which can then be accordingly internalised by the systems.

To return, therefore, to the way anxiety enables the crossing of the boundary, it is important to draw some analogies. The nothing of the environment is not the *nihil absolutum*. It is correlative to the system. The system understands what it understands of itself through its misunderstanding of its environment, of the nothing that brackets it negatively and conditions its operations. Fear is invisibilised by and for the system, but anxiety remains painfully persistent within, not as an operation but as a 'mood', the ghost between operations, the friction of self-communication, the residue of mismatching re-entries. There is nothing in the system except for operations – but this 'nothing' is very much system-specific and the exact location of anxiety. The systemic nothing is at the same time begetter of and begotten by anxiety. Anxiety's destabilising apparition is dealt by the system with repeated re-entries and obsessive checks for locks and boundaries. In anxious repetition, the difference between the system and its environment becomes 'an intimated nothing', a dream of intentionality where the two ends of the thread are linked in a furtive unity.

Of course, there are always limits. The system is not able to apprehend the totality –'one thing the observer must avoid is wanting to see himself and the world' (Luhmann 1998, 111) – namely, the interfolded unity between itself and the nothing. The system still follows the golden thread of intentionality between its entrails and its vomit, its anxiety and the nothing outside, but it is forced to admit to its ignorance. Like the Kierkegaardian spirit, the system dreams of the nothing on which its ignorance is reflected, and believes such reflection to be the actuality of knowledge properly converted into systemic communication. But there can be no actual identification between these two sides of the same thing, despite the rupture of the self-description. Continuum and difference are maintained. System and system, floating about in a reciprocally frosty environment, are always already one thing, exchanging invitations backwards in time, to the time of totemic origins.

This ignorance retains its 'innocence': 'innocence is precisely anxiety, because it is ignorance about nothing' (Kierkegaard 2000a, 141). Ignorance stays wrapped in the unmappable inaccessibility of the environment, and as such it does not compromise systemic closure. The system is not exposed to the oxygen outside, and its precious immanence remains safely enclosed. However, something has changed, for now the environment arrives in the guise of rigidity, a resistance to the liquid non-connection, a glimpse of a historicity of coupling. This is exemplified in the rigid resistance of the lawscape which appears as a form that, in bringing together law and the city, allows the environment to 'flow in' the system (always in rigidity, always inoperable). The observational confluence of the lawscape is a resistance to the liquidity around, and a re-establishment of the systemic responsibility of fear. If, in view of the lawscape, fear can be described as habitually ostracised from each system and pushed into the confines of the other, as Kurosawa comments in *I Live in Fear*, then it is time the ostracised returned. Fear comes back from the environment and haunts the system in the form of an intentional link between itself and anxiety inside, in the fissures of law (for the city) and city (for law). This is the shadow of re-entry, as it were, that lurks in the system along the normal checking for consistency. The environment (law for city and city for law) is introduced into the system as the resistance formed between the observing and the observed systems in their intentional link between their mutually rejected fears and their echoing anxiety.

The observational rigidity becomes furtively employed by the system, only to be subsequently self-belied by the receding priority of invitation. This means, not only that any observational relation is contingent, but further, that the epistemological positioning of two observers in an observational merging that acknowledges both its historicity and its necessary invisibility, results in a coupling that can never be properly observed on account of its in-built recession. Thus, neither law nor the city can observe the lawscape; however, the lawscape has already 'entered' the systemic self-description. Not in its 'actual' shape of course (what is that anyway?), but as a ghost, an intentional link with its past expulsions, a memory of forgetting, a fleeting awareness of a blind spot, a reflective understanding of the collectivity of second-order observation, a computational mismatch of re-entries; in short, anything that the system experiences as a destabilising slit amidst its operations, a hole of ignorance on the wall of safety. Ignorance is circumscribed in an allure of knowledge, but this knowledge is self-referential: its object is precisely the ignorance that has been flown in from the outside. As a result, the system experiences the anxious slipping away of meaning, an indication that its boundaries are not land's end. For a fleetingly anguishing moment, the system describes itself as 'being held out into the nothing', where the nothing is already inside, enveloping the systemic self-description.

The link between fear and fear of fear is an adequate example of the reduced difference between description and self-description – or indeed, prescription and description. Fear and fear of fear constitute the Luhmannian 'form' which precedes any distinction: a form is an inoperative unity which needs to be ruptured and distinguished in order to be observable (Luhmann 1998). Fear, however, unlike habitual systemic distinctions, allows for no place (free from fear) from which it can be observed. Fear is on both sides of any distinction, precisely because it is interdigitated with the operation of distinction – any distinction – as its non-operative counterpart. The location of fear is intentionally formulaic, namely, a link in the manner of reconstituted form rather than a distinction (*contra* Luhmann 2002).[3] In that sense, fear transverses both system and environment as a paradoxical negativity that invisibilises one from the other, yet pulls them centrifugally together.

Thus, the nothing of the environment is never revealed to the system, either as a difference or a tautology. The environment, just like the Heideggerian nothing, negatively brackets the system while pulling it out of itself. Its vehicle, anxiety, pushes into liquidity as 'the possibility of possibility', 'the anxious possibility of being able' (Kierkegaard 2000a, 139, 141), and shakes the system into a state of loss: loss of meaning, of identity, of boundaries, of the environment. While meaning is slipping away, the system reassembles itself and plunges into a risky operation of self-exposure, self-discovery, self-annihilation – alas, always towards a reconstitution of the limits of its ignorance as knowledge. The system's rupture – the system's 'original openness' (Heidegger) – remains necessarily conditioned by the Edenic enclosure of ignorance, innocence, immanence. But even within the walls, there is a revelation. The 'and' of nothingness nags the lawscape from the inside, well internalised within the boundaries of the law and the city as the transcendence that could never describe itself as such. 'And' brings the fear of tautology, the tremor

3 In his analysis of Husserlian phenomenology, Luhmann (2002) looks at intentionality as a distinction. Here, intentionality is seen as the inoperable (in the sense of 'form') operation of the self – be this the system or consciousness – that links the latter with the horizon of possibilities.

of the form, the awe of the space before difference. 'And' reveals (because it hides) the immanent transcendence of the city and the law, their wet dream of justice, their utopia of self-extinction – for a just city is a utopia never to be found, and a just city is a city that has dispensed with the force of law. Fear never really leaves the city. If it had, the utopia of justice would have to be abandoned too:

> I advise my citizens to govern and to grace,
> and not to cast fear utterly from your city.
> What man who fears nothing at all is ever righteous?
> Such be your just terrors… (Aeschylus, *Oresteia*, 1953, 160).

Despite efforts to the contrary, fear is always within the city, brought in by the 'and' of nothingness, its intentional anxiety, the 'nothing' which is feared, and this fear fears itself more than it fears the outside. Fear and fear of fear is the lawscape's 'just terrors' – the internal limits that condition the confluence between law and city. Fear outside, its fear inside, linked by a hastily invisibilised 'and': where is fear in liquidity? The question can finally be answered and reformulated. Answer first: the demon of fear is everywhere, worthy of its title as the 'most sinister': a sin east of the garden of Eden (Bauman 2001, 9) that always returns into the enclosure, underlining every distinction, trammelling every difference, unsettling every boundary, and pushing further into liquidity by triggering rigid resistance. And now reformulation: if fear is everywhere, where can it be observed from? The paradoxical bilocality of fear spanning observer and observed, can only be observed from the privileged point of forced, fragile and contingent rigidity as encapsulated in the 'and' between observer and observed, the invisibilised boundary between continuum and difference, the islet of resistance in an ocean of flows – for how to snapshot liquidity if not through a sonorous *non-liquet*?

The Heideggerian paradox has a very strong affinity to the Kierkegaardian paradox, despite the fact that the first was addressing the scientific community and the second the theological community. Both requests are for the knowledge that pushes into ignorance that brings to knowledge without losing its ignorant halo – its 'immanence' or its 'innocence'. Knowledge is always 'held out into the nothing', the latter always remaining unmappable, unthinkable, undecipherable, unapprehendable, repulsive, and as such returning the quest back to the insular safety of the system. Safety, of course, is conditioned. Once dipped in the waters of the outside, the system never reassembles itself the way it was. The awareness of ignorance sets off the *perpetuum mobile* of anxiety, at once both 'pleasing' and 'despairing', which in its turn sets off the quest for the nothing outside, the terrain on which fear is negotiated and ignorance is projected as knowledge. Bauman has asked a question which underscores the inevitability of the paradox: 'Is it possible to vanquish fear while eliding tedium?' (Bauman 2005b, 166). The answer is of course the paradox itself: even when vanquished, fear remains as anxiety, decoupled from its original tremors and ready to venture out, where the fear has been ostracised. In such a frenzy of clandestine crossings, tedium is indeed elided and with it, an adventurous escape is reinstated in all its high ambivalence, 'whispering in one breath of blind fate and cunning, of craftiness and prudence, of aimlessness and determination' (Bauman 2004, 2).

References

Aeschylus (1953), *Oresteia*, trans. R. Lattimore (Chicago: University of Chicago Press).

Barber, B. (2003), *Fear's Empire: War, Terrorism and Democracy* (New York: W.W. Norton).

Bateson, G. (1972), *Steps to an Ecology of Mind* (New York: Ballantine).

Bauman, Z. (1998), *Globalization: The Human Consequences* (Cambridge: Polity).

Bauman, Z. (2001), *Community: Seeking Safety in an Insecure World* (Cambridge: Polity).

Bauman, Z. (2003), *Liquid Love* (Cambridge: Polity).

Bauman, Z. (2004), *Europe: An Unfinished Adventure* (Cambridge: Polity).

Bauman, Z. (2005a), 'The Demons of an Open Society', Public Lecture, LSE (London) <www.lse.ac.uk/collections/LSEPublicLecturesAndEvents/events/2005/20050919t0901z001.htm>, last accessed 10 November 2005.

Bauman, Z. (2005b), 'Seeking Shelter in Pandora's Box, or: Fear, Security and the City', *City* 9:2, 161–168.

Bauman, Z. (2005c), 'Living in Utopia', Public Lecture, LSE (London), 27 October, <www.lse.ac.uk/collections/LSEPublicLecturesAndEvents/pdf/20051027-Bauman2.pdf>, last accessed 10 November 2005.

Bauman, Z. (2005d), *Liquid Life* (Cambridge: Polity).

Bauman, Z. (2006), 'Uncertainty and Other Liquid-Modern Fears' in J. Přibáň (ed.) *Liquid Society and Its Law* (Aldershot: Ashgate).

Blomley, N., D. Delaney and R. Ford (eds.) (2001), *The Legal Geographies Reader* (Oxford: Blackwell).

Bourke, J. (2005), *Fear: A Cultural History* (London: Virago Press).

Bulgakov, M. (2004), *The Master and Margarita*, trans. M. Glenny (London: Vintage Classics).

Cooper, D. (1998), *Governing out of Order: Space, Law and the Politics of Belonging* (London: Rivers Oram Press).

Davidson, J. (2003), *Phobic Geographies* (Aldershot: Ashgate).

Davis, M. (1998), *Ecology of Fear: Los Angeles and the Imagination of Disaster* (New York: Metropolitan Books).

De Muynck, B. (2004), '"The Prosthetic Paradox" in Urban Affairs', in T. Hauben and M. Vermeulen (eds.), *Fear and Space* (Rotterdam: NAi).

Derrida, J. (1999) *Adieu*, trans. P. Brault and M. Naas (Stanford: Stanford University Press).

Ellin, N (ed.) (1997), *Architecture of Fear* (Princeton, NJ: Princeton University Press).

Hayward, K. (2004), *City Limits: Crime, Consumer Culture and the Urban Experience* (London: Glasshouse Press).

Heidegger, M. (1992), *Being and Time*, trans. J. McQuarrie and E. Robinson (Oxford: Basil Blackwell).

Heidegger, M. (1996), 'What is Metaphysics?' in D. Farrell Krell (ed. and trans.), *Basic Writings* (London: Routledge).

Holder J. and C. Harrison (eds.) (2003), *Law and Geography* (Oxford: Oxford University Press).

Husserl, E. (1973), *Cartesian Meditations*, tr. D. Cairns (The Hague: Martin Nijhoff).

Kafka, F. (1961), 'Before the Law' in *The Penal Colony: Stories and Short Pieces*, trans. W. & E. Muir (New York: Schocken).

Kierkegaard, S. [Vigilius Haufniensis] (2000a), 'The Concept of Anxiety: A Simple Psychological Orienting Deliberation on the Dogmatic Issue of Hereditary Sin' in H. Hong and E. Hong (eds.), *The Essential Kierkegaard* (Princeton, NJ: Princeton University Press).

Kierkegaard, S. [Anti-Climacus] (2000b), 'The Sickness unto Death: A Christian Psychological Exposition for Upbuilding and Awakening', in H. Hong and E. Hong (eds.), *The Essential Kierkegaard* (Princeton, NJ: Princeton University Press).

Levinas, E. (1981), *Otherwise than Being or Beyond Essence*, trans. A. Lingis (The Hague: Martinus Nijhoff).

Little, J. (1994), *Gender, Planning and the Policy Process* (Oxford: Pergamon).

Luhmann, N. (1990), *Essays on Self-Reference* (New York: Columbia University Press).

Luhmann, N. (1992), 'Some Problems with Reflexive Law' in G. Teubner and A. Febbrajo (eds.), *State, Law and Economy as Autopoietic Systems* (Milan: Guiffre).

Luhmann, N. (1992), 'Closure and Structural Coupling' in *Cardozo Law Review* 13, 1419–1442.

Luhmann, N. (1993), 'Observing Re-entries' in *Graduate Faculty Philosophy Journal* 16, 485–498.

Luhmann, N. (1995), *Social Systems*, trans. J. Bednarz, Jr. (Stanford: Stanford University Press).

Luhmann, N. (1995b), 'The Paradoxy of Observing' in *Cultural Critique* 31:1, 37–55.

Luhmann, (1995c), 'Legal Argumentation: An Analysis of its Form', trans. I. Fraser, ed. W. T. Murphy and G. Teubner in *Modern Law Review* 58:3, 285–298.

Luhmann, N. (1998), *Observations on Modernity*, trans. W. Whobney (Stanford, California: Stanford University Press).

Luhmann, N. (2002), 'The Modern Sciences and Phenomenology', trans. J. O'Neil and E. Schreiber in *Theories of Distinction: Redescribing the Descriptions of Modernity*, ed. and introduced by W. Rasch (Stanford: Stanford University Press).

Luhmann, N. (2004), *Law as a Social System*, trans. K. Ziegert, ed. F. Kastner, R. Nobles, D. Schiff and R. Zieger (Oxford: Oxford University Press).

Lyotard, J.F. and J. L. Thebaud (1985), *Just Gaming*, trans. W. Godzich (Minneapolis: University of Minnesota Press).

Moran, L., B. Skeggs, C. Tyrer and K. Corteen (2003), *Sexuality and the Politics of Violence* (London: Routledge).

Morrison, W. (1995), *Theoretical Criminology: From Modernity to Post Modernism* (London: Cavendish).

Philippopoulos-Mihalopoulos, A. (2004), 'Boundaries of Exclusions Past: the Memory of Waste', in R. Lippens (ed.), *Imaginary Boundaries of Justice* (Oxford: Hart).

Philippopoulos-Mihalopoulos, A. (2005), 'Dealing (with) Paradoxes: on Law, Justice and Cheating', in M. King and C. Thornhil (eds.), *Luhmann on Law and Politics: Critical Appraisals and Applications* (Oxford: Hart).

Philippopoulos-Mihalopoulos, A. (2006c), '*Before*: Gender, Identity, Human Rights', in *Feminist Legal Studies* 14:3.

Philippopoulos-Mihalopoulos, A. (2007a), *Absent Environments: Theorising Environmental Law and the City* (London: Routledge-Cavendish).

Philippopoulos-Mihalopoulos, A. (ed.) (2007b), *Law and the City* (London: Routledge-Cavendish).

Rachman, S. (1998), *Anxiety* (Hove: Psychology Press).

Rilke, R.M. (1995), *Ahead of All Parting: The Selected Poetry and Prose of Rainer Maria Rilke*, ed. and trans. S. Mitchell (New York: The Modern Library).

Robin, C. (2004), *Fear: The History of a Political Idea* (Oxford: Oxford University Press).

Rose, G. (1993), *Feminism and Geography* (Minneapolis: University of Minnesota Press).

Rose, G. (1996), *Mourning Becomes the Law: Philosophy and Representation* (Cambridge: Cambridge University Press).

Sarat, A. (1990), '"…The Law is All Over": Power, Resistance and the Legal Consciousness of the Welfare Poor', in *Yale Journal of Law and Humanities* 2:2, 343–380.

Schütz, A. (1994), 'Desiring Society: Autopoiesis beyond the Paradigm of Mastership' in *Law and Critique* 5:2, 149–164.

Schmitt, C. (1976), *The Concept of the Political*, trans. G Schwab (New Brunswick: Rudgers).

Seedo, N.M. (1964), *In the Beginning was Fear* (London: Narod Press).

Spencer Brown, G. (1979), *Laws of Form* (New York: Dutton).

Virilio, P. (2005), *City of Panic*, trans. J. Rose (Oxford: Berg Publishers).

Young, I.M. (1990), *Justice and the Politics of Difference* (Princeton NJ: Princeton University Press).

Zukin, S. (1995), *The Culture of Cities* (Oxford: Blackwell).

PART III
LIQUIDITY AND SOLIDITY IN POLITICS AND ETHICS

Chapter 5

The Politics of Liquid Modernity: Polanyi and Bauman on Commodification and Fluidity

Emilios Christodoulidis

The magnitude of the 'transformation': Bauman and Polanyi

In one of the occasional appearances that Karl Polanyi makes in Zygmunt Bauman's *Liquid Modernity* (2000), his *Great Transformation* (1944) is confronted with the logic of a further one, no less 'great' according to Bauman. Where Polanyi had 'proclaimed the treatment of labour as commodity to be a fiction' and unwrapped the consequences of the social arrangement based on that fiction, under the conditions of 'liquid society', Bauman insists that we are faced with 'a phenomenon *exactly opposite* to the condition which Polanyi took for granted' (Bauman 2000, 120). We are now faced with:

> the *disembodiment* of that type of human labour which serves as the principal source of nourishment of contemporary capital. . . . [C]apital got rid of the task which tied it to the ground and forced it into direct engagement with the agents exploited for the sake of its self-production . . . The disembodied labour of the software era no longer ties down capital: it allows capital to be exterritorial, volatile and fickle.
>
> While labour remains dependent on the presence of capital for its fulfilment, the reverse does not apply any more. *Capital can travel fast and can travel light* . . . counting on brief profitable adventures . . . and its lightness and motility have turned it into the paramount source of uncertainty . . . This has become the present-day basis for domination and the principal factor of social divisions. (Bauman 2000, 121).

And Bauman concludes:

> If the "managerial science" of heavy capitalism focused on keeping the "manpower" in and forcing and bribing it to stay put and to work on schedule, the art of management in the era of light capitalism is no longer burdened by such tasks. Brief encounters replace lasting engagements. One does not plant a citrus-tree grove to squeeze a lemon (Bauman 2000, 122).

Apt as the metaphor is, the question nonetheless arises of whether he may not be over-stating the break between the 'solidity' of Polanyi's account of capitalism and the 'fluidity' of his own. Note the assumptions he makes and the contrasts ('exactly opposite') that he draws. We are now faced with 'the disembodiment' of labour, he says; but then what else is commodification but disembodiment, an abstraction that crucially undercuts it as crucial expression of man's humanity? Capital was always 'volatile and fickle', it always 'travelled fast and light'; that is the point that Marx makes consistently when he talks of the 'promiscuity' of capital. Finally, in contrasting his own diagnosis with Polanyi's, is Bauman not, in fact, conflating what Polanyi identified as the logic of the process itself of the radical colonisation of society by the fictions of land, labour and money with the self-protective mechanisms that arose to counter the devastation?

Of course the point is not – and could not be – to 'catch out' Bauman, as it were, because that would be a meaningless exercise. It is instead to argue *with* Bauman *and* Polanyi for the conditions under which society might strive to counter the devastating consequences of a capitalism running amok. To explore this, what it demands, and what it entails, it is important to return to Polanyi's analysis of the revolutionary moment of the creation of a market in labour, land and money; the transformation of human economy into a self-adjusting system of markets; and his indictment of the commodification of the vital facets of human existence. It is to ask from within that context what, precisely, the transformation of capitalism into its 'liquid' phase entails, whether it is a radical break or merely a further unfolding of the logic Polanyi so brilliantly captures. And if we can trace a continuity with, rather than a break from, that first 'great transformation' that established what Polanyi identified as the *systemic* character of the market, it is to explore whether we can still draw resources from his careful analysis of the direction of flows under capitalist conditions, to further unpack them, and discern opportunities to stem them.

The reason for turning to Polanyi in this context is the power of his analysis of commodification as constitutive of – or at least as at the heart of – the liquidity that Bauman sees as the essential feature of late modern society. The significance of Polanyi's work is his insistence not just that the liquid 'flows' of modernity are flows that are strictly *regulated* and policed in market terms, but that they are first *made possible* through the commodity fictions of land, labour and money. In a market society the commodity fictions stand in and become indistinguishable from the elements that form the substance of society: human beings, their natural surroundings and their productive organisations. *The mode of substitution underlies and founds market society: commodification is the 'coinage' that sets free because it sets into circulation.* In this the rigidity of the constitution of entities and rules of circulation underlies and conditions the fluidity of late modern society. To look at Bauman's analysis through Polanyi's lens is to address the juncture between fluidity and rigidity and to rethink the question of the meaning of political action and self-determination beyond the banalities of so much of self-professed 'radical' democratic theory today.

Bauman's diagnosis

Bauman invites us to consider liquidity or fluidity as fitting metaphors, capturing something of the nature of the present – in many ways novel – phase in the history of modernity. Of course 'melting the solids', as Bauman rightly observes, was Marx's reference to the displacement of pre-modern forms of rigid social relations and the subsumption of the social bond to the logic of capital accumulation. The 'melting of the solids', as Bauman puts it, combining Marx and Weber, 'left the whole complex network of social relations unstuck – bare, unprotected, unarmed and exposed, impotent to resist the business-inspired rules of action and business-shaped criteria of rationality', laying the field open to 'the invasion and domination of (as Weber put it) instrumental rationality, or (as Karl Marx articulated it) the determining role of the economy.' Bauman's argument is that this initial melting phase is different from the condition we find ourselves in today because it re-emerged as a 'solid' order, in fact more 'solid' than the orders it replaced. And with 'most political or moral levers capable of shifting the new order broken . . . or rendered inadequate to the task, that order came to dominate the totality of human life' (Bauman 2000, 4).

What is very interesting at this point is how Bauman understands the dialectic between the simultaneous rigidity and liquidity of society. The term liquidity as Bauman understands it locates itself along the spectrum of the Marxian 'all that was solid melts into air'. For Marx, says Bauman, if the spirit was modern, it was modern in so far as it was determined that reality should be emancipated from the 'dead hand' of its own history. What is happening at presents is a re-distribution and reallocation of modernity's 'melting powers', so to speak:

> They affected first extant institutions the frames that circumscribed the realms of possible action-choices. Configurations, constellations, patterns of dependency and interaction were all thrown into the melting pot, to be subsequently recast and refashioned (Bauman 2000, 6).

This 'breaking of the mould' is of course, it should be added, a constitutive feature of Bauman's 'inherently transgressive, boundary-breaking, all-eroding modernity'. It seems that what distinguishes the current 'liquid' phase from its predecessor is that in *pre*-liquidity broken moulds were replaced, and that people let out from their 'old cages' were re-located in the 'niches of the new order: in the *classes*, frames which encapsulated the totality of life conditions and prospects' (Bauman 2000, 7). As I read him, it is the location in 'classes' that we are moving away from under conditions of liquidity.

> It is such patterns, codes and rules to which one could conform, which one could select as stable orientation points . . . We are presently moving from pre-allocated 'reference groups' into the epoch of 'universal comparison' . . . [where] patterns and configurations are no longer 'given', let alone 'self-evident'. . . The liquidizing powers have moved from the 'system' to 'society', from 'politics' to 'life-policies' – or have descended from the 'macro' to the 'micro' level of social cohabitation (Bauman 2000, 7).

Bauman follows Richard Sennett in speaking of *techniques* of 'speed, escape, passivity' that allow the system and its agents to remain radically disengaged. It is the inability to establish and act upon the continuity of the macro- and the micro-levels of society that undercut political action and radically hedge in the opportunity to challenge the sources of disempowerment. Politically the crucial question in this context becomes how to tap the frames that made possible action-choices of the transgressive, boundary-breaking kind, a question that Bauman identifies as increasingly difficult to address, let alone answer. This is a point to which we will return in the final section.

In the meantime, let us see how Bauman sums up his diagnosis of what is constitutive of the functioning of fluid capitalism. 'It is the patterns of dependency and interaction whose turn to be liquefied has now come' (Bauman, 2000, 8). 'The remoteness and unreachability of systemic structure, coupled with the unstructured, fluid state of the immediate setting of life politics . . . call for a re-thinking of old concepts that used to frame its narratives.' The old concepts Bauman identifies, and on which he structures the analysis of *Liquid Modernity*, are emancipation, individuality, time/space, work and community:

> Social disintegration is as much a condition as it is the outcome of the new technique of power, using disengagement and the art of escape as its major tools. For power to be free to flow, the world must be free of fences, barriers, fortified borders and checkpoints. Any dense and tight network of social bonds . . . is an obstacle to be cleared out of the way. Global powers are bent on dismantling such networks for the sake of their continuous and growing fluidity, the principal source of their strength and the warrant of their invincibility. And it is the falling apart, the friability of human bonds and networks that allow these powers to do their work in the first place (Bauman 2000, 14).

But at this point a first suspicion is raised. Could it be that Bauman is actually overstating the break and that the problem remains that certain nodal points and negotiating posts remain firmly in place as facilitating the flows of liquid society? The argument that this chapter makes is that it is still the markers of the 'old' solidity, its mainstays and organising concepts, its gathering orders and logic of commodification, its 'fences, barriers' and anchorage points, that allow the vastly increased flexibility that capitalism possesses in what Bauman characterises as its fluid, liquid or 'light' phase. To look at this let us in the next section look at what Bauman says about work – which Bauman also identifies alongside emancipation, time/space, individuality and community as constitutive dimensions of liquid society – and compare it to Polanyi's analysis of the commodification of labour. This will allow us to assess whether the situation has changed to the point where the 'old' critique of the commodification of labour remains crucially inadequate for the task, as Bauman implies. We will then generalise the insight to the level of production in general; and in the last section look at how the possibilities of resisting the ravages of the world market are envisaged by Polanyi and Bauman, severally and jointly.

The commodification of labour

For Bauman 'the passage from heavy to light capitalism and from solid to fluid or liquefied modernity constitutes the framework in which the history of the labour movement has been inscribed' (Bauman 2000, 167). The passage also signals the end of the era of mutual engagement between the supervisors and the supervised, capital and labour. The relations of production under capitalism were antagonistic yet this antagonism says Bauman, borrowing from Lewis Coser's famous analysis of conflict, was a case of 'functional' conflict. The contract of employment created a context of mutuality and dependency such that 'strengthened the unity of the conflicting parties precisely because none of them could go it alone and both sides knew that their continuous survival depended on finding solutions that they would consider acceptable' (Bauman 2000, 146–7). There is some equivocation over the meaning of 'unity' in the above statement but Bauman's message is nonetheless clear. The context of mutual dependency made political action and workplace demands meaningful. 'If the employees fought for their rights, it is because they had confidence in the holding power of the frame in which, as they hoped and wished, their rights would be inscribed' (Bauman, 2000, 166).

But now precariousness is everywhere: insecurity has become constitutive of the experience of social life. 'Downsizing', 'streamlining' or 'rationalising' against erratic shifts of market demand and the irresistible pressure of 'competitiveness' and 'flexibility', and an unemployment that has become 'structural', have made the workplace the exemplary locus of insecurity and the lives of those already unemployed 'brittle and uncertain' (Bauman 2000, 161). Pierre Bourdieu has written extensively on this. He says: 'In the face of the new forms of exploitation, favoured notably by the deregulation of work and development of temporary employment, the traditional forms of unionist action are felt inadequate' (Bourdieu 1993, 628). Recent departures, he adds, 'have broken the foundations of past solidarities.' Bauman summarises it thus: 'The present day liquefied, flowing, dispersed, scattered and deregulated version of modernity . . . augurs the advent of light, free-floating capitalism, marked by the disengagement and loosening of ties linking capital and labour' (Bauman 2000, 149).

There is much truth in this, though I would be reluctant to see the problem in the 'disengagement of capital from labour' but, rather, in modalities of its selective engagement with it. The problem for workers, in the first or third worlds, unionised or not, legal or illegal, has been capitalism's successful circumvention of the 'hindrances' of unions organised *nationally* against the forces of capital organised *globally*. It is the circumvention that is the problem and 'liquefication' does not quite capture the nature of the strategy. But if circumvention is what is at stake then the problem is the renewal of an older one, and it calls for strategic action to confront it. This can vary from a strategy to contain or even 'lock in' capital to an attempt to unionise in broader constituencies, in the context, for example, of a 'social Europe', and there are of course many other strategies of societal self-protection. None of this is easy, obviously. But I am not sure how helpful it is to identify the problem in terms of a 'melting' of the solids, if what is meant by that is capitalism's successful adventure outside the confines of national economies and the vast extent to which that circumvention has allowed an unprecedented exploitation of labour across the globe.

To see whether we have here a shift of a *paradigmatic* dimension, best captured in terms of liquidity, or whether we can make sense of current conditions of disempowerment in terms of the 'older' paradigm of the development of a market system in labour, let us return to the most acute of analyses, Polanyi's *Great Transformation*. One of the most important lessons to be learnt from this important work in economic history is that liberal economy – 'this primary reaction of man to the machine', as Polanyi characterised it – was a violent break with the conditions that preceded it. The isolated markets that predated the age of industry were transmuted into a self-regulating *system* of markets. The autonomy of the market system was emphatically not an expression of a natural primary economic motive in humanity, a release of some kind of a natural propensity 'to exchange and to barter' as Adam Smith would have it. 'Single out whatever motive you please' counter-suggests Polanyi in a later paper,

> and organise production in such a manner as to make that motive the individual's incentive to produce, and you will have induced a picture of man as altogether absorbed by that particular motive. Let that motive be religious, political or aesthetic; let it be pride, prejudice, love or envy; and man will appear as essentially religious, political, aesthetic, proud, prejudiced, engrossed in love or envy. . . . As a matter of fact, human beings will labor for a variety of reasons as long as things are arranged accordingly (Polanyi 1947, 113).

The thought experiment underlines the argument that conditions are not given but created; among them, crucially, the transformation of the motive of action: 'for the motive of subsistence that of gain [had to] be substituted' (Polanyi 1944, 41). The medium of exchange had to be introduced into every articulation of industrial life. Neither was the emergence of the market system the spontaneous emancipation of the economic sphere. Instead the system of the self-regulating market (as distinguished from the existence of markets in pre-capitalist societies) 'has been the outcome of a conscious and often violent intervention on the part of government which imposed the market organisation on society' (Polanyi 1944, 250).

> Economic liberalism created a novel mechanism out of more or less developed markets, and co-ordinated their functions in a single whole. . . . Yet institutional change, such is its nature, started to operate abruptly. The critical stage was reached with the establishment of a labor market in England, in which workers were put under the threat of starvation if they failed to comply with the rules of wage labor. As soon as this drastic step was taken, the mechanism of the self-regulating market sprang into gear (Polanyi 1944, 216).

Here is Polanyi on 'the birth of the liberal creed':

> There was nothing natural about laissez-faire; free markets could never have come into being merely by allowing things to take their course . . . Laissez-faire itself was enforced by the State. The thirties and forties saw not only an outburst of legislation repealing restrictive regulations, but also an enormous increase in the administrative functions of the state which was now being endowed with the central bureaucracy able to fulfill the tasks set by the adherents of liberalism. . . . It was the task of the executive to collect statistics and information, to foster science and experiment, as well as to supply the innumerable instruments of final realization in the field of government (Polanyi 1944, 139).

Adam Smith's 'simple and natural liberty' involved an enormous effort to bring it about. Free markets, explains Polanyi in his careful historical analysis of the period, did not do away with the need for control, regulation and intervention but, rather, increased that need enormously. Of course the peculiarity of the market system is that once established it must be allowed to function without interference: 'a self-regulating *system* of markets is what we mean by a market economy' (Polanyi 1944, 41). And yet 'the road to the free market,' he insists, 'was opened and kept open by an enormous increase in continuous, centrally organised and controlled interventionism' (Polanyi 1944, 140). The road was policed through violence and it is significant that at various times it was economic liberals themselves that ran to the defence of violent restrictions to laissez-faire when it came to the free association of labour, the right of workers to combine. In all:

> economic history reveals that the emergence of national markets was in no way the result of the gradual and spontaneous emancipation of the economic sphere from governmental control. On the contrary, the market has been the outcome of a conscious and often violent intervention (Polanyi 1944, 250).

Throughout all this Polanyi provides an unparalleled (outside the Marxist canon) defence of the importance of labour. 'Labour is only another name of a human activity that goes with life itself.'

To allow the market mechanism to be the sole director of the fate of human beings and their natural environment:

> involves no less a transformation than that of the natural and human substance of society into commodities. . . . It is not for the commodity to decide whether it will be put up for sale, to what purpose it should be used, at what price it should be allowed to change hands, and in what manner it should be consumed or destroyed (Polanyi 1944, 176).

'The commodity fiction handed over the fate of man and nature to the play of an automaton running in its own grooves and governed by its own laws' (Polanyi 1947, 110). This:

> would result in the demolition of society. For the alleged commodity 'labour power' cannot be shoved about, used indiscriminately, or even left unused without affecting the human individuals who happen to be the bearers of this particular commodity. . . . In disposing of man's labour power the system would, incidentally, dispose of the physical, psychological and moral entity 'man' attached to that tag. Robbed of the protective cover of cultural institutions, human beings would perish from the effects of social exposure.

The conclusion, though weird, is inevitable: 'the dislocation caused by such devices must disjoint man's relationships and threaten his natural habitat with annihilation.' (Polanyi, 1944, 42). According to Polanyi:

> To separate labor from other activities of life and to subject it to the laws of the market was to annihilate all organic forms of existence and to replace them by a different form of organization, an atomistic and individualistic one. Such a scheme of destruction was best served by the application of the principle of freedom of contract. (Ibid.)

Using a language strikingly similar to Bauman here, Polanyi adds that in practice 'this meant that the non-contractual organizations of kinship, neighbourhood, profession and creed were to be liquidated since they claimed the allegiance of the individual and thus restrained freedom.' But he is quick to point out that – and this may indeed be key to countering Bauman's image of liquidity:

> To represent this principle as one of non-interference, as economic liberals were wont to do, was merely the expression of an ingrained prejudice in favour of a definite kind of interference, namely such as would destroy non-contractual relations between individuals and prevent their spontaneous re-formation (Polanyi 1944, 163).

The systemic continuity

In an article written over a decade ago, Maurice Glasman offered a brilliant theoretical rebuttal to the mainstream liberal defence of the West's efforts to deliver the promises of the market economy – the 'terror of planned spontaneity', Glasman calls it – to an Eastern Europe recently liberated from the communist yoke. His focus is Poland, Bauman's homeland, and he uses Polanyi's work to argue the case against 'market utopia'. His question was why it was that 'market utopia' was exported as a model for the reconstruction of Eastern Europe instead of the West German post-war settlement – 'the most successful model of economic and social reconstruction in world history' (Glasman 1994, 59) – with its straddling of markets, liberal institutions, a constitutive dual commitment to welfare policy and, in 'co-determination' in industry, to industrial or economic democracy. His question was all the more pressing given that it is was asked against the backdrop of the Polish '*autogestionnaire*' tradition of syndicalism that found an exalted expression in the discourse and constitution of the 'Solidarity' movement, and which would have provided the natural habitus for a *different* kind of transition than the one forced through by the IMF, the World Bank and the West's other market commissars. What is most important in this context is precisely that the framework of professed spontaneity into which the societies were 'released' was in fact one that it took an immense effort to force through and police. A reform strategy was imposed 'the likes of which no Western nation had ever considered imposing on itself for fear of the effects it would have on people's lives and livelihoods' (Glasman 1994, 81), justified on the grounds that all economic reforms have a social cost of one kind or another. The conditions of privatisation and usurpation of Poland's resources by, predominantly, criminal organisations (a pattern to be repeated depressingly frequently since) on the one hand, and of the undermining of any institution 'that might have served as a buffer in the market storm that denuded Polish culture' on the other, are the twin achievements of the Sachs/Balcerowicz/IMF/World Bank stabilisation plan. 'Solidarity' was to 'dissolve itself as an economic agent while acting as a social pacifier and government apologist' (Glasman 1994, 82). They were not led to the position through betrayal, corruption or weakness. They were the losing side in a political struggle waged successfully by the forces of the market imposing, at immense social cost, 'the prevailing orthodox paradigm of economic, political and societal progress institutionalised in the dominant international organizations of political and economic regulation' (Glasman 1994, 83). Now 'libertarian atomism' ensured that each citizen faced the world without any institutional solidarity or protection:

> The deregulation of rents and heating has led to homelessness and hypothermia; the rise in the price of food has led to hunger. The educational and health-care systems are crumbling, leading to the development of private systems for the old and new rich and the virtual abolition of welfare for the rest of society (Glasman 1994, 85).

There is no 'evasion or slippage' here; no 'speed, escape and passivity.' What there is, is a rigid dismantling of a system, an active disarticulation of alternatives and the institution of a framework of guarantees for capital. As ever, the liquid flows of capital require entrenchment and rigidity. The experience is of course not limited to the fast-tracking of Eastern Europe. The IMF's tight fiscal monetary policies shrink economies, austerity policies leading to expenditure-cuts that suffocate ailing national economies. When, after the collapse of the Thai currency in 1997, concerns were raised even from within the global instruments of market integration (notably the World Bank's chief economist Joseph Stiglitz), the IMF's response was that 'East Asia simply had to grit it out.'[1] As unemployment increased tenfold and wages plummeted, the IMF demanded that the Thai Government cut food subsidies. In 1997, the ANC in South Africa embraced GEAR, ironic misnomer for 'Growth, Employment and Redistribution programme', which is as thoroughgoing a privatisation/deregulation programme as has yet been devised, involving savage public sector cutbacks and a regressive sales-tax policy, with the help of which South Africa surpassed Brazil in claiming the most polarised income levels in the world. The construction of Africa's largest dam has made potable water unaffordable for a record number of residents of Johannesburg, while the ANC leadership continue to court foreign investment by promising capital-protection measures and guaranteeing the repatriation of profits.

I do not need to provide further examples to make the point. And Bauman will almost certainly say that this was his point all along. In the example of Thailand, the country benefited from a flood of short-term capital which created an unsustainable boom; when the 'hot money' was withdrawn the bubble burst. Here we have a prime example of liquid flows of fickle capital he might say. But there is something that the 'liquidity' argument misses here. What it misses is that the conditions for the flow of capital are set down and entrenched (the IMF in Stiglitz's words, 'delivering the same medicine to each ailing nation that showed up on its doorstep' (Stiglitz 2000, quoted in Wade 2001) in measures that release resources into its flow, securing guarantees for financial returns to the detriment of society. 'For power to be free to flow,' Bauman had insisted in his definition of 'liquidity', 'the world must be free of fences, barriers, fortified borders and checkpoints.' But *barriers, fortified borders* and *checkpoints* are exactly what, in these examples, *have allowed the flow*. They are installed by international economic organisations and policed vigilantly. And this is not just at a local or EU level, but at the global level. The 'constitution of global capital', as Stephen Gill calls it, is constitutively connected to institutional mechanisms which discipline markets and states. These force states, for example, to restructure internally, often through a legal re-structuring of market and regulatory institutions. This is done, says Gill, to accord with the 'three Cs': confidence of

1 IMF Managing director Michel Camdessus, quoted in Wade (2001, 124).

investors, consistency of policies, and credibility of governments' (Gill 2000). It is in this sense that Scott Veitch, in contrast to Bauman's picture of a withdrawal of law, speaks instead of our witnessing a '*fifth* juridification thrust', where:

> national, but also EU institutions and policies, have to adapt to transnational networks and de-regulated markets, such as agreements on competition in services and intellectual property in formerly locally protected markets. Significantly, these forces are locked in through more or less formal legal agreements and conventions, and are implemented by a range of legal institutions – EU, WTO, IMF, central banks – operating at different levels of locality. For these reasons it is appropriate to talk about a 'constitution' of global capitalism (Veitch 2004, 92).

From the privatisation of public resources, the granting of patents to public knowledges, the commodification of life and labour down to the minutiae of investment rules, withdrawal clauses for corporate investment, the IMF's promulgation of unrestricted short-term capital flow, we witness a massive strategic intervention in the social field to create and sustain a world market. The most important part of this involves the institutional separation of the political from the economic sphere as constitutive of market society which, as Polanyi had insisted, was at the root of the 'great transfomation'. The point is that it is the same, continuing story of establishing the conditions for the operation of capital. Already, under the auspices of 'the international gold standard', Polanyi reminds us:

> the most ambitious market scheme of all was put into effect, implying absolute independence of markets from national authorities. World trade now meant organisation of life on the planet under a self-regulating market, comprising labor, land, and money, with the gold standard as the guardian of this gargantuan automaton. Nations and peoples were mere puppets in a show utterly beyond their control.

And as he has shown, economic imperialism has always been a struggle of the Powers for the privilege of extending their trade into politically unprotected markets.

In the words of one commentator, '[e]conomic self-regulation breaks the power of intermediate institutions and solidarities while severing politics from economics through the elevation of private property claims to the level of human right' (Glasman, 1994). The fact that the 'land question' has been placed outwith the constitutional agenda and beyond constitutional scrutiny in South Africa is a case in point. But in this, the South Africans are following the celebrated precedent of the American Constitution which famously isolated the economic sphere entirely from the jurisdiction of the Constitution and, despite universal suffrage, left voters powerless against owners.[2] Under the unrelenting strain of commodification, Glasman contends, society invariably disintegrates. The lack of intermediate institutions then leads to the construction of an abstract community enforced by the state apparatus in order to restore 'order' and the values of community. While the creation of an

2 'The American Constitution, shaped in a farmer craftsman's environment by a leadership forewarned by the English industrial scene, isolated the economic sphere entirely from the jurisdiction of the Constitution [and thereby] put private property under the highest conceivable protection' (Polanyi 1944, 225–6).

abstract community has merely shifted from the state communities to the even more abstract banalities of cosmopolitan or world communities, the 'order' of the police is now enforced not by state but by international apparatuses, from strategies of humanitarian intervention to international active enforcement of guarantees and sanctions for investments across state borders.

The results are devastating and Bauman, amongst many here, develops it powerfully in his work. A functionally integrated global society repeats the logic of the self-regulating market, its promise of freedom as uncoerced exchange of property holdings, facilitated through enforced flexibilisation of labour, privatisation of common resources and liberalisation, the performance of partners policed by an ever more complex system of sanctions and guarantees, the rigidity of which makes a mockery of state power and the severity of which destroys populations. Any possibility of democratic involvement in the workplace as well as welfare provision are cut at the root. Spontaneous reactions to market dispossession are condemned as going against reason and history.

Resistance and self-determination

One of the most intriguing aspects of Polanyi's analysis is his optimism that 'however stultified by a legacy of a market-economy . . . civilization must [and will] find a new thought pattern.' (1947) In the *Great Transformation* we find the same logic repeated. When the mechanism of the self-regulating market springs into gear, its impact on society is so violent that, almost instantly, and without any prior change in opinion, powerful protective reactions set in (see, indicatively, Polanyi 1944,216). In each case strains induced from the market were picked up politically and translated into political events which are the core of history. He contends that 'since the market was permitted to grind the human fabric into the featureless uniformity of selenic erosion, man's institutional creativeness has been in abeyance.' (Polanyi 1947, 117) But as Roberto Unger might put it, it is always 'false necessities' perpetuated by market forces that lead to a sense of disempowerment in politics and the entrenchment of what is contingent as a-historical necessity. And where lies contingency, institutional imagination can always be re-awakened. (Unger 1996)

Not so for Bauman, however, and it might be at this point that we should remain particularly attentive to the reasons why (not). Bauman identifies as the 'main contradiction' of 'fluid modernity' the distance between the right to self-assertion and the control of the social settings which would make it feasible. The complexity of modern society spells paralysis to the extent that any attempt to act politically to challenge the 'order' of the market is virtually precluded as inadequate, futile or dangerous, because of the undermining differentiation and the integrity of systems. Bauman argues that this means that:

> however free the subsystems of that order may be singly or severally, the way in which they are intertwined is rigid, fatal and sealed off from any freedom of choice. The overall order of things is not open to options. It is far from clear what such options could be, and even less clear how an ostensibly viable option can be made real in the unlikely case of social life being able to conceive it and gestate. Between the overall order and every

> one of its agencies, vehicles and stratagems of purposeful action there is a cleavage – a perpetually widening gap with no bridge in sight (Bauman 2000, 4–5).

He adds this: 'The liquidizing powers have moved from the 'system' to 'society', from 'politics' to 'life-policies' – or have descended from the 'macro' to the 'micro' level of social cohabitation.' The system and its agents remain radically disengaged. It is the inability to establish and act upon the continuity of the macro- and the micro-levels of society that undercut political action and radically hedge in the opportunity to challenge the sources of disempowerment. The crucial question in this context becomes how to tap the frames that made possible action-choices of the transgressive, boundary-breaking kind.

In this chapter I have attempted to draw a continuity between Polanyi's account of the rise of the market order through intervention and violence and the conditions that allow the flows of capital in 'liquid' modernity and release lives and knowledges into the flow of capital. Deregulation, liberalisation, flexibilisation, casualisation are all sustained through planning, direct and constant interventionism, and frequent recourse to violence to ensure the suppression of alternatives. Like Polanyi's picture, Bauman's too is a picture of commodification writ-large, the commodity logic, as we said, the coinage that sets free because it sets into circulation. As ever, the institutional imagination is called to counter the effects of ideology and in Bauman's analysis, perhaps attempt to reconnect policy choices with politics proper, of that 'transgressive, boundary-breaking kind.' I cannot pursue this further here except to say that the disarticulation of the two, between the right to self-assertion and the control of the social settings which would make it feasible, *may* be understood as contingent and thus redressable.

When Bauman called Socialism an 'active utopia' he spoke of utopian thinking as involving the 'ability to break habitual associations, to emancipate oneself from the apparently overwhelming mental and physical dominance of the routine, the ordinary, the normal' (Bauman 1976, 11). The function of utopias is to 'relativise the present' . . . 'the boldness of the utopian insight is its ability to cut loose and be impractical' (Bauman 1976, 13) . . . 'Utopia is an integral element of the critical attitude' (Bauman 1976, 15) . . . 'obstinate reminders of the never-plugged gap between the promise and the reality' (Bauman 1976, 16). And on the point about ideology: 'If the reality-protecting ideology attempts to disguise history as nature, the activating presence of utopia in human action, on the contrary, unmasks the historical status of alleged nature' (Bauman 1976, 15–6). One way to put the claim of this chapter to Bauman is to urge him to retrieve *that activating presence* of utopia rather than the more mainstream understanding of that which has no locus, into which his thoughts are taking him. And as he put it all those years ago, there is no more active and activating utopia than Socialism, with its promise, in the words of Polanyi, 'to transcend the self-regulating market by consciously subordinating it to the democratic society' (Polanyi 1944, 234).

References

Bauman, Z. (1976), *Socialism: The Active Utopia* (New York: Holmes and Meier).

Bauman, Z. (2000), *Liquid Modernity* (Cambridge: Polity).

Bourdieu, P. (1993), *La Misère du Monde* (Paris: Seuil).

Gill, S. (2000), 'The Constitution of Global Capitalism', at www.globalsite.ac.uk

Glasman, M. (1994), 'The Great Deformation: Polanyi, Poland and the Terrors of Planned Spontaneity' in *New Left Review*, 205, 59.

Polanyi, K. (1944), *The Great Transformation* (Boston: Beacon Press).

Polanyi, K. (1947), 'Our Obsolete Market Mentality: Civilization Must Find a New Thought Pattern', in *Commentary*, 3, 109–117.

Stiglitz, J. (2000), 'What I Learned at the World Economic Crisis' in *New Republic*, 17 April.

Unger, R. (1996), 'Legal Analysis as Institutional Imagination' in *Modern Law Review* 59, 1.

Veitch, S. (2004), 'Legal Right and Political Amnesia', in K Nuotio (ed.), *Europe in Search of 'Meaning and Purpose'* (Helsinki: Forum Iuris).

Wade, R. (2001), 'Showdown at the World Bank' in *New Left Review*, 124.

Chapter 6

Facing Past Human Rights Abuse: A Way from a Liquid to a Solid Society

Grażyna Skąpska

> The singular, explosive, incalculable political power of living within the truth resides in the fact that living openly within the truth has an ally, invisible to be sure, but omnipresent: this hidden sphere of authentic existence. It is from this sphere that life lived openly in the truth grows; it is to this sphere that it speaks and in it that it finds understanding. This is where the potential for communication exists. … Living within the truth is humanity's revolt against an enforced position, is … an attempt to regain control over one's own sense of responsibility.
>
> Václav Havel, *The Power of the Powerless*

The life of contemporary society, as concisely depicted in the title of Milan Kundera's book, represents an unbearable lightness of being. A 'lightness of being' is expressed in the concept of life as liquid (Bauman, 2005), and society as fluid (Giddens, 1984, 23). It is a succession of episodes '... free from the worry about consequences' (Bauman, 2005, 5). It is the life of a consumer society of fluid identities and it consists of liquid moderns – vagabonds and tourists – who not only have lost their faith in the future, but who cannot commit to relationships (Bunting 2005, 2).

In such a society, the past, even the most horrible one, takes – in the best case – a frozen, clean and sterilized form of referential *simulacra* transplanted from the real order to an order of history, science, museums (Baudrillard, 1994). In the worst case, as recent examples indicate, the horrific past of Auschwitz and the gulags is used to enhance a decadent consumption, to stir unhealthy emotions. It takes the form of masquerade, of a Waffen SS uniform thought suitable for a discotheque in a catastrophic annihilation of meaning, as shown by the example of a member of the British Royal family; the possibility of experiencing fake horrors, as in the cases of gulags turned into tourist attractions, where a tourist can spend a few days in the original barracks eating the prisoners' food; or of a techno event organized in the Netherlands on 4 May – Victims Commemoration Day – advertised on the Web.[1]

1 I am referring to the event that stirred public opinion and caused public outrage: the invitation to a huge techno dance organized in the Netherlands on 4 May 2005, under the title 'Housewitz'. Two DJ's clad in Wehrmacht uniforms invited '7 million dancers' – against the shouts of 'Sieg Heil', and the slogan 'Tanzen macht frei' on the photo of the real gate to Auschwitz in the background, accompanied by such information as 'obligatory costume: starving Jew' (a photo of real Auschwitz prisoners, naked, in the background), 'free

The latter examples present a grotesque type of contemporary liquidity, where the boundary between consumers' fantasies and the most horrible reality is perceived as a mere optical illusion.

A fluid society is ruled by liquid laws: purely technical legal fictions, devoid of any ties to morality or ethics. When confronted with the task of redressing the horrors of the past, this law – the purely formal rule of law – brings about an alienating justice or rather, an alienating injustice (Skąpska, 2005, 227–31; with reference to Teubner 2001, 21–44; Luhmann 2000, 3–21).

However, even the fluid and liquid society can acquire some solid features thanks to moral drives or impulses, to feelings such as guilt, shame or pride stirred by the unusual, extraordinary circumstances: it can have its moral moments (Bauman, 1989, 19). Such impulses may also be decisive in the critical debate about its institutions, laws and above all, the constitution, as the source of a new social and political order. In this chapter I will argue that such moral moments act as catalysts that may lead to the acquisition of some solidity by a liquid society, when confronted and forced to reckon with its own past of human rights abuse, its own involvement in horrors. Facing the shameful past and instituting a search for the truth about it has an enlightening potential: it may arouse public consciousness and make people think in terms of good and evil. Therefore, paradoxically, the enlightening truth delivered through social communication about past human rights violation may help a liquid society acquire some solid features, to enlighten, to mature, in accord with Immanuel Kant's definition of Enlightenment as the exit of the human-being from self-incurred immaturity.

Such enlightening and healing experiences are conditional, though. The 'exit from immaturity' through communication and learning the truth about the crimes committed in the past, although possible, proves to be very difficult. It depends not only on installing democracy and opening the public sphere to critical debate, but also on the mundane experiences of ordinary citizens, on the social memories of the past, and on the deeply rooted, residual structures of thinking about justice, crime, guilt and punishment, not to mention power relations and the vested interests of those who would like to hide and silence past atrocities, or use the past in the political struggle. Because truth about the past is so wrapped up with the quotidian definitions of the situation, in the memories, and the experiences of ordinary people – for instance, the long-term and close coexistence of victims and perpetrators – it is at the same time a truth about everyday opportunism, cowardice, toleration of human rights abuses, or, on the contrary, about the civil courage of ordinary people, those unsung heroes of world history. The public debate about past human rights abuse that may become possible, and the ways in which people 'come to terms' with it, reflects the various experiences of victims, of their families, of perpetrators, of

---

showers' (a photo of gas chamber in the background), 'free taxi ride home' (a photo of a car loaded with naked bodies in the background). At the end Hitler's head appears and a voice says 'make your body free' (www.geenstijl/nl and www.stopklatka.pl). This category also included a discotheque established in the close vicinity of the Auschwitz camp, in the former 'Lederfabrik' where prisoners worked, or a discotheque in the former Gestapo place of torture in Krakow.

collaborators and instigators, of simple cowardice, of everyday courage, as well as different techniques of remembrance, justification and legitimization of the wrongs of the past.

In order to ponder upon the question of a society's ability to face difficult truths, to consider them, to demythologize public memories, and consequently to acquire solidity – both cognitive and institutional – I will briefly discuss the experiences of Eastern European societies which lived under the peculiar form of totalitarianism called Stalinism, and which originally inspired Milan Kundera to call his famous book, *The Unbearable Lightness of Being*. Here the concept of Stalinism, and of late Stalinism, is used to identify the system, initially based on terror, with modifications of its scale and range, which was installed after the Bolshevik Revolution in Russia, and later on in Eastern Europe, and which, in the form of late Stalinism, deeply penetrated those societies, and transformed terror into spying, collaboration, denunciation of fellow citizens, and finally into liquid cynicism and moral devastation.

In this chapter I will discuss Stalinism as a way of life, and Stalinist and late-Stalinist regimes as such, in which the subjects of human rights abuse were not some external 'Others' but predominantly 'the enemies within', the ones among us. Then I will briefly discuss the issue of critical public debate and its potential to combat Stalinism so understood, to demythologize memories and consciousness, to impart some solidity to the liquid post-Stalinist societies. Finally, I will consider the question of the institutions responsible for bringing some solidity to liquid and morally devastated societies.

Stalinism and Late Stalinism as a way of life

In his essay on the power of the powerless from which the initial quotation in this chapter is taken, Václav Havel describes the behaviour of a greengrocer, who endlessly repeats seemingly meaningless rituals connected with communist First of May celebrations. The case of this greengrocer represents a good frame for the debate on the peculiar societal aspects of Stalinism and late Stalinism (wrongly labelled post-totalitarianism by Havel) with respect to the social relations between victims and perpetrators, the definition of enemy, of crime, and last but not least, the involvement of society in the functioning of the system, as well as in the opposition to it.

It was argued that such a system – because of its constitutive features – could be installed at any time or in any country. These constitutive features of Stalinism consist of the maximization of domination and control by the minimization of costs (Kurczewski 1991, 2). As Jacek Kurczewski observes, those who install Stalinism in their country do not have to be called Stalin (Kurczewski 1991, introduction). It could, for instance, be the Argentinian junta. According to Michel Foucault, for example, this could be achieved through the education system and, above all, by installing an omnipresent spying Panopticon. That, in turn, broadens societal power relations because those who spy exercise a considerable, often limitless, power and control over their subject, be they colleagues, neighbours, friends, or family members. This definition of Stalinism differs considerably from other definitions, which stress modernization concentrated on the development of heavy industry, the collectivization of agriculture, and the centrally planned economy, and also on the destruction of law, and the omnipresence of ideology. A Polish philosopher – who herself spend many years in a gulag in Siberia – describes Stalinism, among other things, as a paradise for mediocre people, and the functioning of Stalinist system as based on the circulation of power between the highest and the lowest echelons of society (Skarga, 1991, 5). Hence, she points directly to the societal features of Stalinism, noting, most importantly, the already mentioned Foucauldian circulation of power as its main characteristics. There are also other important features of Stalinism as a social phenomenon, and as a social way of life.

In analyses of totalitarianism, especially of Nazi totalitarianism and Nazi genocide, 'otherness' and distance is stressed. If the enemy was defined as the Other, then the processes of distancing and exclusion became possible. In the widespread discussions on the Holocaust, it is stressed that it was preceded by a complex habitual and mental process imposed and directed by the government in Nazi Germany. It consisted of the deindividualization and dehumanization of Jews, because of their collective characterization as 'others'. In its extreme form, it consisted of the German descriptions of Jews as anti-human: as *Gegen-Menschen, Anti-Menschen*, and *Anti-Rasse*. To this was added spatial and social distancing, the ghettoization of 'others' who would disappear from their neighbourhoods, offices, firms, associations, theatres, streetcars, and parks. That represented an important step toward their transportation to extermination camps in faraway places, where nobody even knew any of them, and also did not speak their language (Another telling example of distancing as a step toward human rights violations was apartheid in South Africa.).

In contrast, the first characteristic feature of Stalinism was the peculiar closeness of victims and perpetrators, their proximity and mutual involvement in complex relationships. Thus, the functioning of Stalinism is characterized by the deep penetration of the system's structures into the private lives of people, by the close-knit relationships between system functionaries from the lower echelons of the hierarchy and the rest of society, because they were often living in close proximity (or even in the same apartments – so-called communal apartments in which many families shared the same kitchen and bathroom) to their victims who were their classmates at the universities, colleagues in the work-place, and even members of their own families. In words of another witness, Stalinism grooved (channelled) ruts in which life ran. Such ruts went deep into the society; they penetrated the walls of private houses and spontaneous, informal social circles. It was not a world that consisted only of police terror situated outside society. It was formed from within too, thanks to mechanisms of social accommodation and control (Świda-Ziemba 1991, 18, 23, 26–43).

In the Stalinist system – after the first years of the 'dictatorship of the proletariat' aimed at the annihilation of the bourgeoisie – the enemy was not predominantly perceived as an 'other'. Any friend, close relative or close family member could turn out to be an enemy, known as 'the enemy within', inconspicuously living among us, if his or her behaviour merely questioned in the slightest the official and actual interpretation of ideology, threatened the functioning of the system in any way, or in any way failed to conform to its rules. Thus, severely punished crimes committed by such enemies also included telling jokes, spreading information about the functioning of the system (which was called 'whisper propaganda' in the penal codes), selling anything on the black market, and even dressing in Western fashions or sporting Western hair styles. The penalties for such petty crimes included imprisonment, and sentencing to hard labour, often in militarized labour camps. Characteristically, many such 'crimes', defined in the first decrees issued during the years of terror, were later incorporated in the regular penal codes valid until the early 1990s (Ziemba, 1991, 159ff.).[2]

Apart from the penal law, the Stalinist government had at its disposal a plethora of possible punishments, from depriving people of passports to banning university education, to installing political police families in one's own apartment. Thus, one of the important reasons why the greengrocer – the main hero of Václav Havel's essay on the power of the powerless – displayed the symbols of his loyalty to the system and its rituals in his shop window was his conviction that he himself could be accused of being the enemy within, reported to authorities and somehow punished should he not conform to rituals. People who thought in a similar way participated in fake elections, faked enthusiasm during demonstrations, became members (sometimes unknowingly) of mass organizations of women, pioneers or associations of friends of the Soviet Union. These were ordinary people, neither great victims, nor great perpetrators. Others denounced their friends and relatives and spied on them in order to maintain their close relationships with the authorities, to win some reward, and maybe also to enjoy exercising power over those close to them. Still others decided to make a career at all costs. The authorities, on the other hand, took great pains to involve the greatest possible numbers in collaboration with the Stalinist system, making people sign declarations of loyalty, enrol in the above-mentioned mass organizations of pioneers, socialist women, friends of the Soviet Union, and so on, and also to spy. They used blackmail or open threats; they broke people through torture. They also used all kinds of rewards, on the other hand, because everything – apartments, good jobs, better food or clothing, the possibility of a career, particularly a scientific one – was in their hands. Hence the great numbers of collaborators, but also of victims involved in the mutual complex networks and relationships.[3]

One important feature of the Stalinist system is its stress on collectivity and the collective bonds of party members, neighbours, and company employees. Collectivity, belonging and comradeship represented a way of accommodating victims and perpetrators alike to the system. This suggests another possible reason for the greengrocer's reluctance to challenge the system's rituals and its lies: it would mean exposing the hypocrisy and cowardice of his neighbours and possibly that

2 See Ziemba on penalized behaviour during first 12 years of Stalinism in Poland. In his opinion, after Stalin's death and the 1956 'thaw' in Poland, the most significant features of the Stalinist legal system were not changed. Many of them were incorporated into the new penal code, and the regulations concerning political crimes, still binding in 1989, were no less severe than they were before 1956.

3 According to very rough data, the numbers of communist political police secret collaborators in Central and East European countries was somewhere between half a million and one million. *Rzeczpospolita*, 1 January 2004.

of friends and family members too, and therefore putting himself outside, or even above, society by challenging important social bonds.

All such cases demonstrate the different types of social solidarity on which Stalinism, as a way of life, was founded: from a hypocritical and unspoken rule not to question the lies of the system, through a shabby joint complicity in the crimes of the system, to solidarity based on an unquestioned subordination of the individual to the collectivity.

Finally, there is the place – mental and also purely geographical – of gulags: detention camps, defined as correction or labour camps. The Stalinist system took its terrible toll: the deaths in those camps numbered tens of millions, mostly of fellow citizens, even if gulags were not defined as extermination camps. The deaths resulted from the devastation of people by hunger and forced, slave labour – used as a cheap means of modernization and, by the same token, to reform fellow citizens – not only through executions (Applebaum, 2003). Thus, the aim of such labour camps was to help the 'enemies within' transform themselves into useful people, unless they died first. Some camps were located in faraway places, easily possible in such a country as the Soviet Union but others were on the outskirts of cities, in close proximity to firms, schools, hospitals, universities. Their inmates mingled with people outside the camps in everyday encounters.[4]

On the other hand, late Stalinism was characterized also by growing consumerism – an important contribution to the liquidity of late-Stalinist societies – even if it was rather meagre and consisted of new opportunities to buy the most trivial things, like better food, or cheap furniture or to go on holidays to Bulgaria. Consumerism represented an important intervening variable between the system and the people involved in the machinery of its functioning. This meagre consumerism had different names: it was called 'goulash communism' in Hungary, 'small stabilization' in Poland, and 'normalization' in the then Czechoslovakia.

To challenge such a system, to expose its lies, to denounce its atrocities demanded morally and cognitively mature people – a proper civil society characterized by civil courage – people who had chosen this seemingly hopeless exit from it. They opted out from hypocrisy, from the late-Stalinist lightness of being, from the benefits of 'goulash communism' or 'normalization'. Therefore, Stalinism was characterized not only by collaboration and spying or mere opportunism but also by reckless acts of civil courage in everyday-life situations undertaken not only by famous dissidents but by ordinary people, by those who had not subscribed to mass organizations, were not blind to state crimes, who tried to help the victims, and to perform honestly in their professions as teachers, judges, lawyers: in short, those who practiced an 'anti-politics' in everyday-life situations (Konrad 1988).

4 In Poland, in the big cities, political prisoners often worked in regular enterprises, big construction companies, coal mines, side by side with 'regular' employees, but under different working conditions and regulations.

Democracy and public debate

There are several questions about the way out of liquidity when society is confronted with its own past, with the deep-rooted entanglements of victims and perpetrators, on the one hand, but not characterized by a lack of civil courage, on the other. The most important question is the role of public critical debate for the process of enlightenment, maturity and emancipation from Stalinism brought about by democratization. Then democracy – if not understood as pure arithmetic – brings not only self-governance but also opens new areas of discourse and deliberation on topics that were excluded from the public arena by the oppressive regimes. Therefore, democratization supports, at least in principle, a reckoning for past atrocities. Such initially suppressed issues which could be debated after democratization included – in Poland – the killing of Jews by their neighbours during the Second World War. They also included the mass-resettlements of ethnic minorities and confiscation of their property, often by looting and plunder, after the Second World War. In other parts of the world, democratization brought about the disclosures of atrocities committed by military regimes in Argentina, Uruguay, Chile, El Salvador, Honduras, and of the operation and organization of apartheid in South Africa. In all those countries, societies were faced with horrors committed by oppressive regimes that stirred public emotions and started public debate on mass human right violations as part and parcel of the democratization process. However, the relationship between democracy and critical public debate is not an easy or a simple one. As the empirical examples show, critical debate on Nazi crimes is still problematic in Germany (Schwan, 1997). In Poland, the first years of Stalinist terror and the involvement of people in its functioning are very seldom publicly discussed even now, let alone the function of late Stalinism: its hypocrisy, its small stabilization and also its crimes, particularly the 'darker side of the system change', that is, '...the unencumbered opportunities for advancement of the old regime's power-networks interests' (Łoś and Zybertowicz 2000, 262). In Poland too, the policy initially adopted was that of drawing a 'thick line', that is, a policy based on the consolidation of social efforts aimed at the future reforms, and not on the consideration of past wrongs. This policy seriously limited the scope and range of public debate and excluded many of its potential participants, namely, the victims and their families. All such examples demonstrate that democracy has only a limited and conditional enlightening potential.

Political vested interests are not the only ones involved. In order to debate a way forward from the liquidity of a post-Stalinist society, one has to reconsider the truths that emerge from the public debate and the character of the evidence on which these truths are based. One has also to bear in mind the peculiar character of Stalinism and the complex entanglements of victims and perpetrators within Stalinist society. One has also to reflect on factors such as self-esteem, as well as guilt and shame, that stir the public consciousness, stir the moral emotions, and provoke a reconsideration of history – and also of one's own history in the broader context of good and evil.

The variety of social truths is illustrated in a series of notably conflicting statements concerning some indisputable facts documented in an analysis of Polish parliamentary debates on lustration (screening of the past) and decommunization (banning former communist from some official functions). That analysis revealed many conflicting and partial truths about the political past within the same society because these truths and the interpretations of facts reflected various definitions of the situation and of particular experiences as well as the various values and ideas of people living in a Stalinist or late-Stalinist society, not to mention the vested interests of persons who were profiting by it (Loś 1995, 192).

My own experience in the Polish court was with the victims of Stalinism – two elderly ladies and an elderly man, all three former members of the Polish underground fighting the Nazis during the Second World War, denounced as the West's spies by the communist authorities, put in prison and severely tortured. Their torturer, Adam Humer, also an old man at the time of trial, treated the victims, who were witnesses in his trial, with the utmost scorn and contempt. He did not question the facts and well remembered his own power over his victims and their weakness. Maybe he also remembered other cases in which his victims, who could not withstand torture, broke down and promised collaboration with the communist secret police. He felt entirely justified by the ideology of class struggle: for him all three present at that trial and his other victims were representatives of the enemy – Western capitalism or 'imperialism' – as he constantly repeated. He, on the other hand, defended 'social justice'. Perpetrators of this type see themselves as servants of the state, most often of national states surrounded by aggressors. They are just functionaries, such as Eichmann in his office. They see themselves as soldiers in an inevitable and just war. However, although their trials do not change their self-assessment, they at least lead to public debate on the revealed facts, and more importantly, they contribute to the new interpretation of these facts.

Partial truths are linked with the memories of past events. It is obvious that none of us could survive the memory of all that we might have remembered. It would mean an overload. So, even if we do register something, we remember only a fragment. It is also obvious that we are highly selective in what we see, in what we store, in what we recall, and how we recall it, especially if these recollections are shameful, if they reveal a shameful past. In a similar vein, what was an heroic act to a member of the underground opposition could be a disturbance, a nuisance to those who would prefer a quiet life. As Niels Christie writes, we perceive selectively, we remember selectively, we recall selectively. We construct, but above all we interpret. In respect of the truths based on memory, this recollection by the prominent Norwegian criminologist illustrates the above:

> I was a child in an occupied country during World War Two. I did the usual things. (...) Nevertheless, I cannot remember anything about the time that the Jews were deported; I cannot remember one single comment about it in my generally patriotic circles. The Jews were apprehended by the ordinary Norwegian police. Since they were so many and yet so few, one hundred ordinary taxis were used to transport them to the ship that brought them to Germany. I suppose the drivers soon forgot this episode in their lives. When the few survivors came home from the camps, they came to a country that to some extent had forgotten that they had ever been there. And their property was mostly gone. It was not until 1996 that they – or mostly their children and grandchildren – got decent compensation (Christie, 2003, 338).

One can quote similar acknowledgments, by ordinary Poles but also by Polish intellectuals, not only about the Holocaust, but also about events that happened after the Second World War, until the very end of Stalinism as a political system. One can hear the accusations that the displaced people were the enemies of the Polish nation, on the lines of the official communist propaganda (Skąpska, 2005, 219), denials of state crimes, appraisals of small stabilization or goulash communism, and of martial law declared in Poland in 1981 as a 'lesser evil' or even a necessity.

Such examples clearly illustrate that social truths, especially if they concern the past and are based on memories, are highly complex and unclear phenomena: they are founded on fragmentary information about some indisputable facts and consist mostly of interpretations of those facts. These complex and unclear interpretations of facts mirror the complexities and entanglements of Stalinist societies; they are linked with particular perspectives and definitions of situations, with the experiences of ordinary people, and with social memories that are incomplete and selective. Moreover, social truths, if they refer to atrocities or to human rights violations, are entangled with strong emotions and traumas. They are not value-neutral.

The input side of these truths is based on beliefs and convictions, however incomplete and unclear, stereotypic, or ideological. Their output is linked with desired consequences. Moreover, according to the psychological concepts of social truths, because of the emotions they provoke they are 'rich' and in a way 'hot' (Taylor 1985, 35). They are expressed in ordinary colloquial language and refer to such emotions as guilt, crime, punishment, genocide, and reconciliation. They appeal to cultural and even religious stereotypes and archetypes (Skąpska 2002, 208). Therefore, social truths mirror the characteristics of Stalinist society: the everyday-life closeness of victims and perpetrators, the complex power-relations, and the moral costs of benefits.

The challenge to such social truths, for instance in the form of information about atrocities, is a challenge to popular definitions of situations but also to the emotions on which self-assessment is based. Such a challenge could support pride but it could also result in shame and guilt. Hence the transformative potential of a debate on past human rights violations: it makes one reconsider the beliefs on which self-esteem is based, it can provoke shame and maybe also feelings of guilt and thus lead to the redefinition of situations. It results in a change of perspective and new self-conceptions in the process of a double hermeneutics of a sort. Therefore, the truth about an atrocious past made public, debated, and eventually put on trial functions as a catalyst and as an important moral impulse to a society to rethink the beliefs on which its self-assessment is based.

> There are other important extra-cognitive aspects of democratic free communication about past atrocities: the afore-mentioned sense of responsibility for the future, the will to avoid gulags and Auschwitz, not to mention a democratic resolution to protect the dignity of victims and to involve them in public communication.

Thus, although social truths are complex and at the same time fragmentary, entangled with various, even conflicting experiences, the debate about them often reveals unknown facts and even unthinkable interpretations. It potentially provokes deep emotions and changes in self-assessment which eventually may lead to emancipation and contribute to societal maturity. Such a debate may then show a way towards societal solidity.

The concept of maturity is applied also to the characteristics of social conditions that promote or impede individual cognitive and ethical development. In this regard, a debate about past human rights violations, and the eventual semiosis of the most recent history emerging from such a debate, has a transformative and even emancipatory potential for individuals and collectivities: it can shatter taboos and uncover stereotypical thinking and collective hypocrisies. For society at large, it represents an opportunity for many to learn about its authentic identity; it is linked with people's ability to adopt a critical stance vis-à-vis themselves and their institutions. Since critical self-evaluation can be a humbling and humiliating experience that results in feelings of guilt and shame, a great deal of civil courage is demanded of societies undergoing this painful process – a process that is likewise essential to the development of those social sciences that have been twisted by oppressive ideologies and conditions of life under Stalinism.

With regard to maturity and emancipation, social scientists are interested in the relations between victims, perpetrators and instigators, in techniques of silencing the truth, that is, distorting social communication, and in the effects – social and political – of unimpeded communication about past atrocities. In their view, if societies cherish their self-image at the expense of truth, critical voices are silenced, authors ridiculed or, at best, marginalized, and the social order is legitimized by myths that support a social structure in which there is no place for victims. As Christie observes:

> Silence is one of the answer to atrocities. Silence, because there is nobody around to listen. Therefore isolation of the victims is one of the major features in social systems when illegitimate violence is applied. There is nobody to tell, and there is no end to attempts by oppressors to silence their victims. Nor is there an end to the continuous struggle to break the silence (Christie, 2003, 339).

There are several ways of silencing. It could happen that the victim's intellectual need for an explanation is eventually directed toward his/her own deficiencies, and silences the protests. In her review essay on Gulag literature, Anne Applebaum refers to the extraordinary silence of the victims of the Soviet terror, and to the phenomenon of the shunning of persons returning home from the Soviet camps, by their professional colleagues, friends, and even families (Applebaum, 2002). Because the Soviet élite had never quite admitted the wrongdoing, victims were not, until the glasnost reform of the 1980s, allowed even to discuss what had happened to them in public. In her words '... silence was mandatory and repressions [*of these persons*] obligatory' (Applebaum 2002, 18). To change this, it is essential that the victim emerges from isolation and gains access to an audience that will not reinforce the victimization: the definition of the situation imposed by the oppressors. Hence, silencing people, concealing the truth about past atrocities is not only an important psychological strategy, but also a social and political one – and not only in dictatorships but also in democratic societies. The truth about the past could devastate not only individuals but also social and national self-conceptions, national ideologies and myths. Thus, one can at least try to understand this strange reluctance of Gulag victims to talk about their experiences. They felt that they somehow challenged national solidarity, and that to denounce the things done to them would mean to compromise the way in which the nation functioned, even if they had been wrongly accused. There emerges also the uneasy truth that they were denounced by their friends, even family members, that their nearest turned to be their oppressors.

The silencing of past atrocities could thus be an object of vested political interests and the process of dealing with the past follows the rules of power and selectiveness (Reinprecht, 2002, 103). Élite-governed policies pertaining to the past attempt to legitimize the new state of affairs; a public discourse and a novel topography of collective memory is generated by new policies of symbolism which, on the one hand, help to construct, or to reconstruct a collective identity, and, on the other, legitimize the newly constructed political and legal institutions. Considering the character of intangible social truths and social memories and the closeness of victims and perpetrators and, indeed, the very number of doubtful, unclear and highly disputable cases, it is then even more important to debate factors that influence the critical public debate and, therefore, decide how democracy will function after the collapse of an oppressive regime.

Post-communist 'Lightness of Being': Impediments on the way from liquidity to solidity

Sociologists indicate several phenomena characterizing post-Stalinist society lifeworlds, that have a striking 'elective affinity' with Habermas's 'new untransparency' proposition (Habermas, 1985). There are features of these lifeworlds which impede any public debate on past atrocities that help to avoid difficult topics, to avoid responsibility, not to mention feelings of guilt or shame. They include consumerism, a specific form of political correctness that promotes conformity in mainstream popular opinions, and the peculiar ideology of progressivism that imposes oblivion combined with purely utilitarian attitudes to politics based on conflict-avoidance and on the cost-benefit *calculus*. They also include the purely utilitarian and technical concept of law.

As we have observed, the culture of consumerism consists of the elevation of private well-being and legitimizes the conscious concealment and silencing of a difficult past because of present prosperity as exemplified by the slogan 'living well [*economically, that is*] is the best revenge' (Halmai and Scheppele, 1997, 155). It is based on the clear preference given to economic stability, to a life without moral responsibility, and the avoidance of the difficult topic of human rights violations in exchange for the present abundance of consumer goods.

Critical public debate is badly served by forms of political correctness based on the principle of not tackling uncomfortable subjects, not calling things by their real names, not questioning the status quo that is, not challenging the social cohesion based on the similarity of opinions. That leads to the silencing of awkward voices, of all difficult truths that do not fit mainstream opinion and, in effect, to the exclusion of troublemakers and their increasing suppression. Moreover, because of concerns about social cohesion and an unwillingness to underline points of disagreement this new political correctness results in the denial of the deep divide between supporters and opponents of authoritarian and totalitarian regimes in the past based on the highly unfair – even accepting Stalinism as a way of life – supposition that 'all of us were smeared' and profited from the former regime.

Finally, there is an imposed progressivism, the 'forgetting about the difficult past for the sake of the future' ideologies, the ideologies of the 'thick line' dividing the past from the present. If such ideologies are combined with utilitarian reasoning on costs and benefits, they further eliminate important social experiences and their bearers and exclude from the public realm those who have justified grievances, such as prisoners of gulags and detention camps, and the experiences and arguments of the families of disappeared persons as if they have less weight than projects for future well-being. That form of progressivist liquidity has two important consequences for the transformation of post-totalitarian or post-dictatorial societies. First, it has political consequences that contribute to the above-mentioned artificial blurring of differences between the regime's supporters and its opponents, and between perpetrators and their victims. Secondly, it results in a peculiar form of democracy that excludes the voices and complaints of the victims of the former regime.

Thus, in order to discuss the enlightening and emancipatory potential of a public critical debate on past human rights violation in societies which have experienced Stalinism, one has to make an important supplementary point. This is based on Foucault's famous criticism of the Kantian concept of Enlightenment and his conceptualization of the 'power-chain' that exists in the most simple communicative relationship because of inequalities in knowledge and rhetorical skills. Foucault's interpretation of Kant places an emphasis on the word 'exit', 'opting out', leaving the status quo through constantly developing one's authenticity (Foucault, 1986). There is no place in this chapter for a critical discussion of this conceptualization of exit, with authenticity as its outcome, but certainly one should add that considering past atrocities gives a direction to such an 'exit' from the existing truths. At least we know what to avoid: we can repeat the slogan 'never again' knowing exactly what must not be repeated, knowing how to avoid the 'gulag'.

Institutions imparting solidity to post-Stalinist society: brief concluding remarks

Finally, an important impediment on the way out from liquidity is the institutional and, especially, the legal infrastructure applied in a self-referential way, that is, with reference to the existing legal system only. Such a self-referential concept of law, devoid of any links to morality and ethics, proves to be entirely insufficient in dealing with past atrocities. It even leads to a situation of equivalence between victims and perpetrators in which perpetrators could defend themselves as officials of the state who were acting in defense of it. On the other hand, considering the close proximity and intertwined lives of victims and oppressors, perpetrators and instigators, the large grey area of doubtful facts, of blackmail and the corruption of people, it is very doubtful whether the rule of law could help and whether it could function as a means of solidifying post-Stalinist society as it emerged from moral devastation. Thus, in these concluding remarks, it seems feasible to consider how such institutional frameworks, which solidify exit and opting out, contribute to the efforts of society not to repeat the Gulag and to protect the dignity of victims.

As argued above, how and why the gross human rights violations happened, who caused the victimization, and how many became victim has seldom been exposed by national governments or international bodies. Enshrining the rule of law into new constitutions was not entirely helpful and efforts to confront past human rights violations, to take account of them, to compensate victims and to punish perpetrators and instigators have been strongly criticized (Skąpska, 2002). The task of reckoning and accounting and, above all, of bringing these issues to public notice has been mainly undertaken by NGOs with all their understandable limitations: movements such as such as the 'Memorial' organization in Russia or the organizations of the mothers and families of the disappeared in Latin America, dedicated journalists and committed researchers to whom so much is owed for fulfilling this much needed task (Bassiouni, 1996, 11). The role of civil society must be stressed as an important factor on the way from liquidity to solidity, as a salient component of large-scale social enlightenment.

On the other hand, debates and analyses of social approaches to the past demonstrate that social values and emotions play an important part in this mostly cognitive process. In fact, a purely cognitive enlightenment would be neither possible, nor sufficient to fully confront the most difficult facts. The very decision to review the past is linked with some fundamental values and also with strong popular emotions like shame, guilt, pride and civil courage. These two factors – the engagement of civil society and the moral moments stirred by emotions that result from deeply rooted values – make one think of the importance of institutions such as truth commissions and truth and reconciliation commissions for public critical debate, discussions about complex truths and complex experiences, honoring the victims and exposing the perpetrators and instigators as possible exits from liquidity.

References

Applebaum, A. (2003), *Gulag – A History* (New York: Doubleday).

Applebaum, A. (2002), 'After the Gulag', *The New York Review of Books*, 24 October, 40–41.

Bassiouni. M.C. (1996), 'Searching for Law and Achieving Justice: The Need for Accountability', *Law and Contemporary Problems* 59/4.

Baudrillard, J. (1994), *Simulacra and Simulation* (Ann Arbor: University of Michigan Press).

Bauman, Z. (1989), *Modernity and the Holocaust* (Oxford: Blackwell).

Bauman, Z. (2005), *Liquid Life* (Cambridge: Polity).

Bunting, M. (2005), 'Passion and pessimism', interview with Zygmunt Bauman, Guardian Unlimited Books, http://books.guardian.co.uk/review/story 27 November.

Christie, N. (2003), 'Answers to Atrocities', in G. Skąpska, A. Orla-Bukowska, K. Kowalski (eds.), *The Moral Fabric in Contemporary Societies* (Leiden-Boston: Brill).

Foucault, M. (1986), *What is Enlightenment?*, Polish tr. 'Aufklaerung i rewolucja', *Colloquia Communia* 4/5.

Habermas, J. (1985), *Die neue Unübersichtlichkeit* (Frankfurt: Suhrkamp).

Halmai, G. and Scheppele, K.L. (1997), 'Living Well Is the Best Revenge: The Hungarian Approach to Judging the Past', in A.J. McAdams (ed.), *Transitional Justice and the Rule of Law in the New Democracies* (Notre Dame: University of Notre Dame Press).

Kurczewski, J. (1991), 'Słowo wstępne' [Introductory remark], in J. Kurczewski (ed.) *Stalinizm* (Warsaw: Uniwersytet warszawski, Instytut Profilaktyki Społecznej i Resocjalizacji).

Luhmann, N. (2000), 'Die Rückgabe des zwölften Kamels: Zum Sinn einer soziologischen Analyse des Rechts', *Zeitschrift für Rechtssoziologie* 21, 3–21.

Loś, M. (1995), 'Lustration and Truth Claims: Unfinished Revolutions in Central Europe', *Law and Social Inquiry* 20, 117–61.

Loś, M. and Zybertowicz, A. (2000), *Privatizing the Police-State. The Case of Poland* (London: Palgrave/Macmillan).

Reinprecht, C. (2001), 'The Role of Collective Memory in the Process of Democratization: The Austrian Experience', in H. Pascher and G. Skąpska (eds.), *A Work in Progress. Social and Political Change in Contemporary Poland and Austria* (Krakow: Universitas), 101–117.

Schwan, G. (1997), *Politik und Schuld. Die zerstörerische Macht des Schweigens* (Frankfurt: Fischer).

Skarga, B. (1991), 'Stalinizm' [Stalinism], in J. Kurczewski (ed.) *Stalinizm* (Warsaw: Uniwersytet warszawski, Instytut Profilaktyki Społecznej i Resocjalizacji), 3–6.

Skąpska, G. (2002), 'Moral Definitions of Constitutionalism in Eastern Europe', *International Sociology* 18/1, 199–218.

Skąpska, G. (2005), 'Restitutive Justice, Rule of Law and Constitutional Dilemmas', in A. Czarnota et al. (eds.), *Rethinking the Rule of Law in Post-Communist Europe: Past legacies, Institutional Innovations and Constitutional Discources* (Budapest: CEU Press).

Świda-Ziemba, H. (1991), 'Stalinizm i społeczeństwo polskie', [Stalinism and Polish Society], in J. Kurczewski (ed.) *Stalinizm* (Warsaw: Uniwersytet warszawski, Instytut Profilaktyki Społecznej i Resocjalizacji), 15–98.

Taylor, G. (1985), *Pride, Shame and Guilt. Emotions of Self-Assessment* (Oxford: Clarendon Press).

Teubner, G. 2001, 'Alienating Justice: On the Surplus Value of the Twelfth Camel', in J. Přibáň and D. Nelken (eds.), *Law's New Boundaries* (Aldershot: Ashgate), 21–44.

Ziemba, Z.A. (1991), 'Prawo karne Polski Ludowej w latach 1945–1956', [Penal law in People's Poland in the years 1945–1956], in J. Kurczewski (ed.) *Stalinizm* (Warsaw: Uniwersytet warszawski, Instytut Profilaktyki Społecznej i Resocjalizacji), 97–164.

PART IV
EUROPEAN ADVENTURES AND IDENTITIES

Chapter 7

European Legality and its Critique: On Bauman's Concept of an Adventurous Europe

Jiří Přibáň

There are many political and cultural reflections on European identity. These reflections contribute to the self-identification of the inhabitants of the European continent as Europeans and even cause conflicts over which political processes and visions are more European. In his 'adventurous' search for Europe, Zygmunt Bauman described modern European culture as a 'thorn in society's flesh' (Bauman 2004, 13) that destabilises norms and conventions and makes change and protest its constitutive virtues. According to him, European culture is not a culture of unity that could provide solid normative foundations for society. Europe is 'a mission' and 'a labour that never ends, a challenge always still to be met in full, a prospect forever outstanding' (Bauman 2004, 2). It is determined by its search for the infinite, typified by intrinsic paradoxes and antinomies, and thus powerfully balances its morality and immorality.

Bauman's search for Europe as an adventure is part of strong European intellectual tradition. For instance, Friedrich Nietzsche claimed more than a century ago that Europeans need to embrace 'the art of disguises' necessary for living in the 'labyrinths' of a culture of ambivalence and multiplicities (Nietzsche 2000, 335). European culture is a culture of contradictions and aporias which cannot define solid moral foundations for European societies. Similarly, Bauman recognises the contradictory, ambivalent and liquid character of modern European culture. Nevertheless, he also seeks to reconcile the creative and destructive power of Europe and make them part of a profoundly ethical enterprise and global legacy.

Cosmopolitan Europe and its transgression

Unlike Nietzsche, Bauman resorts to a more conventional call for a cosmopolitan ethos which is deeply entrenched in modern European humanism and does not pursue the radical adventure of an ultimate re-evaluation of all modern values. He critically reflects on the crisis of European culture and humanity and pursues the goal of saving it through its very spirit of universal humanity and ethics.

Like Edmund Husserl and many other humanists, Bauman believes that European crises can only be successfully resolved by the further 'Europeanisation of Europe' and by injecting cultural universals into the specific and technical problems of modern European societies (see, for instance, Husserl 1970, 275). In many respects, Bauman's unfinished and unfinishable European adventure resembles the phenomenological pursuit of an 'ideal image whose dimension is the infinite' (Husserl 1965, 159). It is an effort to save a particular European spirit and cultural tradition from oblivion. It is a struggle against moral and cultural crises threatening to obliterate the origins and very meaning of the existence of modern Europe.

In his outline of European political, moral and cultural prospects, Bauman eventually follows two distinct streams in modern European thought – the Kantian universalistic discourse of humanity, and the traditional respect for tolerance and diversity formulated in the moral theories and philosophies of Emmanuel Lévinas and Hans-Georg Gadamer. He reflects on the fact that Europe has never had fixed borders and has successfully transgressed all attempts to anchor its identity to a particular space and time. European civilisation has spread to the furthest parts of the planet making it a truly global and interconnected space. It has unbound the contradictory forces of globalisation and made its social and political institutions planetary. These institutions have been responsible for some of Europe's worst 'civilisational' atrocities but they are still the only available framework for the contemporary globalised world of humankind. Globalisation is a consequence of European expansion and the export of its universalistic culture. It implies the destructive global spread of industrial waste and political domination. However, it also advocates a peaceful and hospitable world of universal humanity and respect for difference and otherness.

In this depiction of Europe's ambivalent modernity, there is another strong intellectual inspiration that turns out to have had a significant impact on Bauman's approach – Marx and Engels's radical dialectic philosophy. According to this philosophical tradition, the dawn of modernity is marked by the bourgeoisie's advancement of the instruments of production and means of communication that 'draws all, even the most barbarian, nations into civilisation' (Marx and Engels 2002, 224). This European civilisation compels all nations to adopt new economic and political patterns of social life and thus creates new contradictions, forms of exploitation, collective violence, danger and ultimate disorder. According to Marx and Engels, there is 'too much civilisation' (Marx and Engels 2002, 226) spreading globally which eventually demands a global proletarian revolution bringing social peace and the ultimate harmony of humankind.

Leaving aside the modernist utopia of the proletarian revolution, Bauman also believes that European civilisation can internalise contradictions and deal with its ambivalent forces and is therefore both 'a transgressive civilization' and 'a civilisation of transgression' (Pomian 1992; quoted in Bauman 2004, 7). Bauman and other adherents of the Kantian cosmopolitan Europe claim that normative universalism needs to be reconciled with specific social and political heterogeneities if it is to inspire the European feeling of belonging and identity. In this manner, Jürgen Habermas, for instance, seeks to construct European collective identity as the creative interplay of sameness and otherness when he depicts it as an identity which would guarantee that '[C]itizens who share a common political life also are others to one another, and each is entitled to *remain* an Other' (Habermas 2001,

19). European identity can be imagined as the culture of unity and difference, externalisation and internalisation. As Bauman says, paraphrasing a comment made by Hans-Georg Gadamer: '[T]he European way of life is a continuous negotiation that goes on despite the otherness and the difference dividing those engaged in, and by, negotiation' (Gadamer 1989; quoted in Bauman 2004, 7). Europe's identity may have the Other as its necessary component (Bauman 2004, 41), but this 'otherness' can eventually exist only because of the legacy of Kant's *allgemeine Vereinigung der Menschheit* and the Enlightenment notions of equality, rule of law, human reason, and solidarity (Bauman 2004, 16).

The Kantian notions of cosmopolitan identity and citizenship have been popular as a response to our contemporary, globalised social and political condition (see, for instance, Bohman and Lutz-Bachman 1997). They also have often been used as a response to problems of European integration, globalisation and international conflicts. The fantasy of the international community, which emerges as a constitutionalised world society, organises sovereign collectivity and specifies the decision-making hierarchies of this cosmopolitan equivalent of the nation-state, has been an intrinsic part of contemporary legal and political theory (see, for instance, Fasbender 1998, 529–619; for a critique of these fantasies, see, especially, Schutz 1997).

However, philosophers and politicians tend to ignore Kant's deep irony present in the concept of 'perpetual peace'. As Wolf Lepenies remarks, it was taken from the 'satirical inscription on a Dutch innkeeper's sign upon which a burial ground was painted' and one, therefore, should conclude that '[P]erpetual peace was for the dead, not for the living. It was a regulative idea, not an idealist misconception of harsh reality' (Lepenies 2006, 196). Furthermore, Kant used the notion of cosmopolitan identity and citizenship as an ethical category and not as a prerequisite of world political organization. For Kant, there is a difference between cosmopolitan politics and ethics, and citizens of a cosmopolitan federation of states still need their individual republics in order to be citizens at all (Benhabib 2002, 183). While ethics should be universal, political communities keep their particular nature. Civil ethics can be cosmopolitan but political citizenship may be exercised only within the boundaries of particular political societies.

According to Kant, states must finally enter into a cosmopolitan constitution due to the constant wars and 'form a state which is not a cosmopolitan commonwealth under a single ruler, but a lawful *federation* under a commonly accepted *international right*' (Kant 1971a, 90). This federation guarantees 'perpetual peace' in the international state where it is impossible for the nations to constitute a utopian '*world republic*' (Kant 1971b, 105). In this state, cosmopolitan ethics is restricted to the conditions of universal hospitality and legally specified by the cosmopolitan *right* 'of a stranger not to be treated with hostility when he arrives on someone else's territory' (Kant 1971b, 105; for further comments, see, for instance, McCarthy 2002, 249).

Despite Kant's distinction of ethics, national politics and international law, Europe has been frequently depicted as a principally cosmopolitan project that can morally mould and politically lead global society. According to these views, Europe has transgressed the nationalistic culture of war and replaced it with international diplomacy, coming ever closer to the cosmopolitan philosophers' dream of eternal global peace for which Europe may be an exemplar and starting point.

Contemporary social and political scholars of both the political right and left often describe Europe as 'Kantian' and contrast it with the 'Hobbesian' United States of America. These descriptions may be both complimentary and critical. Contradicting Robert Kagan's defence of Hobbesian US foreign policy and critique of Europe's political incapacity legitimised by Kantian ethical utopianism, Bauman thus says that 'Europe is well prepared if not to *lead*, then most certainly to *show* the way from the Hobbesian planet to the Kantian "universal unification of the human species"' (Bauman 2004, 40). While Kagan perceives Kantianism as evidence of Europe's decline (Kagan, 2004), Bauman perceives it as Europe's universal legacy and, setting aside current US foreign policy, contrasts it with the dark 'Herderian' tradition of modern ethnic nationalism. In this context, he comes surprisingly close to Habermas who considers Kant's idea of republican autonomy and self-legislation a triumphant tradition which lies behind the modern welfare-state democracies and needs to be developed beyond nation-state limits (Habermas 2001, 60–1). It should become a formative trend in globalisation leading to a 'post-national constellation'.

Neo-tribalism and the deserted *agora:* on the European politics of identity

The infinite search for European identity is a synthesising ethical effort stretching beyond the temporal horizon of European culture and its pluralistic manifestations in different nations of Europe. It searches for transcendental unity and meaning in human artefacts, traditions and patterns. It, therefore, is important to establish which political traditions and cultural patterns and symbols have been formative for European politics in recent history. As Bauman comments, tradition operates paradoxically because 'it prompts us to believe that the past *binds* our present; it augurs, however (and triggers), our present and future efforts to *construe* a "past" by which we need or wish to be bound' (Bauman 1999, 132; emphasis in original).

Shaping a European, cosmopolitan, ethics-based political identity thus emerges as a complex reflexive interplay of the establishment of new political and legal rules and practices challenged by the typically modern European difference between civic and ethnic traditions and legacies. In this context, Bauman proves to be a strong critic of all kinds of ethno-nationalism and the romantic philosophy of the unique spirit of the ethnic nation *(Volksgeist)* and other cultural communities, which subsumed Montesquieu's general spirit of the laws under the concept of ethnic culture. He emphasises that ethnicity undeniably contributes to the identity of the most 'explosive communities' (Bauman 2000, 193). Nevertheless, he is far from simply contrasting the virtues of civil society and vices of ethnicity which is so typical of recent moral and political philosophy and cosmopolitan normative theory. Bauman, rather, accepts the sociological view that ethnic nationalism has always been an intrinsic part of modern democratic politics. The modern social order was marginalising and destroying the traditional communal forms of life in the name of a centralised, state-dominated and uniform life pattern. As Bauman points out:

> The war against the local, the irregular and the spontaneous was merciless, but the modern state and its educational arm seldom aimed at pouring out the child of the sacred together with the bathwater of local pluralism. Earnest efforts were made throughout the modern era to replace manifold communal gettings-together, in their much needed function of replenishing the reservoirs of sacred unity, with a centrally designed and controlled pantheon and calendar of festivities. As a rule, these were to become the focal points, symbols and the rituals of the new religion: that of nationalism (Bauman 1993, 135).

Ethnic nationalism thus became a central tendency of social and political mobilisation in the modern democratic state and the illusion of spontaneously shared national identity, history and political destiny came to its ultimate horror in the practice of totalitarian politics. In the totalitarian condition, the legal rational legitimacy of the modern state was accompanied by the culturally binding life and identity of the ethnic nation letting its individual members 'bask in the sun of eternity' (Bauman 1993, 138).

The modern era of nationalism and totalitarian politics may have come to its end, yet the current postmodern condition has brought to life a number of ethnic and cultural communities based on various tendencies towards social aggression and intolerance. Modern ethnic nationalism was assimilative and expansively aggressive because it sought to conquer ethnic foreigners and make them part of one nation. Current forms of nationalism, however, have transformed to 'ethnicism' based on:

> exclusion, non-coexistence with those who are culturally different, no expansion and no universalism. … The ethnic state cuts back its universalist roots and becomes oriented towards the interests and identities of whichever ethnic group is dominant in each area of the state apparatus (education, police, military, law, foreign policy) (Beck 2005, 259; for the concept of 'ethnicism', see Tamás 1996).

Under the disguise of the politics of identity, hostile ethnic and other cultural communities verbalise themselves 'in terms of incompatibility or unmixability of *cultures*, or of the self-defence of a form of life bequeathed by tradition' (Bauman 1993, 235).

A new kind of exclusionist otherness drawing on cultural identity and separatism emerges in the postmodern condition and the modern democratic state is weakened and threatened by various explosive communities. Bauman describes this form of communal life as the life of 'postmodern tribes' and concludes that the biggest political and social challenge lies in two apparently opposite but related effects:

> On the one hand, the sectarian fury of neotribal self-assertion, the resurgence of violence as the principal instrument of order-building, the feverish search for home truths hoped to fill the void of the deserted *agora*. On the other, the refusal by yesterday's rhetors of the *agora* to judge, discriminate, choose between choices: every choice goes, providing it is a choice, and each order is good, providing it is one of many and does not exclude other orders. Tolerance of the rhetors feeds on intolerance of the tribes. Intolerance of the tribes draws confidence from the tolerance of the rhetors (Bauman 1993, 238).

The postmodern political indifference to and desertion of the democratic public space of the *agora* is accompanied by the growing bellicosity of those attracted by this emptied space and their exclusionist ideologies of cultural uniqueness, homogeneity, and identity. Modern ethno-nationalist forms of violence, which used to be based on state institutions, change into the multi-tribal politics of cultural identity. Individual lives, collective identities and societies become liquid and our democratic *agora* is being built on increasingly shifting sands. Cosmopolitan calls are typically compromised by being pursued in the specifically modern and exclusive form of social engineering conducted in the name of one uniform pattern of 'rational' life. At the same time, one of the most dangerous alternatives to modernity is the cacophony of incomprehensible screaming by violent neo-tribes rushing to fill the space deserted by democratic politics.

If the European adventure has political meaning, it is a return to democratic politics that is in opposition to both exclusively modern 'rational' life and ethno-nationalist visions, and builds on unity

> which is *achieved*, and achieved daily anew, by confrontation, debate, negotiation and compromise between values, preferences and chosen ways of life and self-identifications of many and different, but always self-determining, members of the *polis* ... [T]his ... is the sole variant of unity ... which the conditions of liquid modernity render compatible, plausible and realistic ... (Bauman 2000, 178).

The European cultural and ethical heritage may be described as never-ending transgressive adventures and pursuits of otherness. Nevertheless, Bauman strongly supports the cosmopolitan project of civic and democratic politics at the level of both the nation state and the supra-national European Union. The modern distinction of *society (Gesellschaft)* and *community (Gemeinschaft)*, echoed in the tension between the *civic* and *ethnic* popular identity of the nation state, may have been substantially blurred in the postmodern political condition, yet continues to play an essential role in shaping European political identity and legitimising the project of constitutional and political integration of the continent.

The 'us' and 'them' distinction is redefined as 'universal' and 'particular' in modern society (Parsons 1967, 192–219). It specifies 'universal' as 'good' and approves 'particular' only if it can be linked to 'universals.' Within the context of European political integration, identity-building, and constitution-making, the 'universal/particular' distinction is reformulated as the 'cosmopolitan/national' political and moral distinction. European identity is considered cosmopolitan, transgressing the cultural identity differences among individual European nations. Therefore, the European Union's job is to keep the romantic spirits of different European nations outside the gate of European politics. Ethno-nationalist identities are contrasted with calls for Europe's global mission. Adherents of European unity and political integration keep confronting ethnic nationalism by emphasising Europe's cosmopolitan legacy.

The critique of European legality

However, these adherents also have to confront another structural irritation within the European Union – a growing gap between the idea of Europe and its economic, legal and political manifestation. Apart from old ethno-nationalist enemies, Europe's advocates increasingly criticise the Union's machinery and bureaucratic technical decision-making. According to committed Euro-enthusiasts, the Union now paradoxically obfuscates the ideal of the cosmopolitan 'everyone's Europe'. It is considered an obstacle to political integration and therefore apparently needs to be eliminated by further ethical humanisation.

A machine is a popular metaphor for the Union's political structure and legal system. A catalogue of legal rights is contrasted with human existence. The language of legality is treated as an example of dehumanising rationalism which needs to be politically counterbalanced by emotional attachment and the sense of identification, sharing and belonging. A spiritual sense of the cultural superiority of the European cosmopolitan legacy envisions a gradual cultural and political Europeanisation of national societies. The identity of Europe and the European Union is expected to transgress the instrumental rationality of legality and the common market economy. Advocates of a cosmopolitan Europe, such as Zygmunt Bauman, are highly critical of the formal concept of legality. Europe's identity apparently cannot be conveyed by the incomprehensible language of legality which, due to its fixation with words and political institutions, could bring the whole European project to a fatal end. From an ethical standpoint, legality is criticised as a technical tool and part of the failing instrumental rationality which dominates modern societies. According to this critical view, the Union's political decisions cannot be constantly obscured by an epistemological community of EU legal and administrative experts. As Bauman puts it:

> If the Maastricht Treaty, or the Accession Treaty that followed it, is the contemporary equivalent of the Declaration of the Rights of Man and of the Citizen, the American Declaration of Independence or the Communist Manifesto, then there seems little hope left for the next instalment of the European adventure. More specifically, for Europe retaining its fate/vocation of being the global yeast of shared global history ... (Bauman 2004, 24).

Europe and the European Union in its institutionalised form have to address urgent problems, crises, and tasks of global dimensions and therefore cannot be restricted to public law discourse.

In the same manner, Václav Havel, then President of the Czech Republic, sought to inspire European politicians and called for 'A Charter of European Identity' in his speech to the European Parliament on 8 March 1994. For Havel, Europe was to be defined as a community of values such as tolerance, humanity and fraternity which historically enhanced the political and moral evolution of democracy, freedom and responsibility. The Charter was supposed to become 'a definitive moral code for European citizens' (Havel 1994, 3) which could eventually result in the constitution of a political community of all European citizens and their ethical bonds and attachments. It was proposed as a single declaratory document that would be politically understandable and ethically appealing to the people of Europe.

Like so many moralists and intellectuals before him, Havel also critically commented on the instrumental rationality and techniques of modern social organisation when he compared the Maastricht Treaty and other political and legal documents of the EU to the workings of a perfect and ingenious modern machine missing 'a spiritual or moral or emotional dimension' (Havel 1994, 2). According to him, the European public law machine is merely an outcome of technical reason which entirely ignores the living realities of Europeans. The European Union is in danger of becoming a heartless iron cage of modernity incapable of inspiring a feeling of European togetherness and solidarity. In other words, Europe lacks the 'political charisma' which could legitimise the project of increasing political unification. So far, the Union's progressive integration has been a formal process of legalisation and the regulatory politics of numerous documents and norms. The machine of European institutions and regulations is expected to operate in the most efficient mode but the structure is too cold to allow any emotions of belonging, abstract solidarity and togetherness. A simple declaratory act or charter therefore should be an answer to the technical obscurity of European legal and economic rationality (for further analysis, see Přibáň 2007).

Criticisms of the instrumental rationality of the modern state and its legality are common in social and political theory. Organisational similarities between the state and business administration, highlighted by Weber (1983) and Kelsen (1929), have been criticised as dehumanising and depoliticising effects of instrumental reason. In his memorial Strasbourg speech addressing these undesired consequences of modernity, Havel added:

> The history of Europe is, in fact, the history of a constant searching and reshaping of its internal structures and the relationship of its parts. Today, if we talk about a single European civilization or about common European values, history, traditions, and destiny, what we are referring to is more the fruit of this tendency toward integration than its cause' (Havel 1994, 1).

This statement illustrates the reason behind criticisms of the Union's instrumental rationality and technical legalism – the search for legitimation of the European Union by cultural values and identity. According to Havel, it is important to support legitimation loops between European integration techniques and their cultural background and codify European cultural self-understanding by means of a single declaratory act.

Bauman, together with Havel and many others, also highlights the obscurity of technical legalistic language incapable of steering European citizens and peoples towards a feeling of political unity and collective identity. He thus inadvertently comments on what is commonly described as European governance by 'comitology' (Pedler and Schaefer 1996; Bradley 1997). This committee-based form of governance can hardly be described as either constitutional, or unconstitutional because it cannot be formulated and checked against a background of principles of legitimate democratic government, such as delegation and separation of power, checks and balances, etc. (Weiler 1999, 98). It consists of the exercise of administrative and regulative powers by representatives of member states, the Union's officials and the agents of a variety of advisory bodies sitting on different EU committees. The machine metaphor criticising the Union's existing structure and decision-making procedures is, therefore, a response to this deficit of political legitimacy and pursues the goal of establishing the symbolic political reference and the Union's legitimation code.

The legitimation of Europe by its culture?: remarks on instrumental and symbolic rationality

Criticisms of European legalism formulated by Bauman, Havel and others run the risk of overrating the political role and power of culture at the expense of everyday democratic politics and technical decision-making processes. They seem to suggest that cultural and intellectual history give direction to superficial politics, educate people to become 'valuable citizens', and legitimise institutions of representative democracy in terms of cultural aspirations – as if the modern liberal democratic state and its derivative supra-national institutions, such as the European Union, were not valuable themselves and needed further ethical, historical and cultural justification. The depiction of Europe as constant ethical searching and cultural reshaping, therefore, has been unsurprisingly and increasingly criticised as an obstacle to recognising and solving the real political problems of the continent (Judt 1996, 140).

Politics may depend on cultural symbols as expressions of collective unity but it also can easily be paralysed by the semantic structural limitations of these symbols. Instrumental legality and politics as a mere technique of power are favourite targets of moral criticisms. However, problem-recognition and conflict-resolution political mechanisms cannot ultimately be subjected to the system of symbolic cultural expressions and moral evaluations. The ethical ideal of 'Europe as humanity' cannot be fully grasped and implemented by European politics. The particularity of democratic politics can never accommodate the universality of cosmopolitan ethics.

Bauman's adventurous Europe and Havel's Europe of constant searching and reshaping may be examples of the unrealistic belief in the superiority of culture over the instrumental rationality of politics and legality. Nevertheless, they also persuasively show that any political project is accompanied by a search for legitimation by cultural symbols and values. These examples remind us that the concepts of 'legal integration', 'constitution-making', and 'legal order', apart from their technical meaning, are strong symbols and a point of departure for thinking about society itself. The concept of a legal system reflects the phenomena of social order, hierarchy, regularity, institutionalisation, etc. It still represents a way of thinking about power, government and state which symbolizes political unity, social solidarity, moral harmony and rational organization.[1] Recent discussions and disputes surrounding further European integration by constitution-making, therefore, can hardly avoid these symbolic reflections and criticisms.

Recurring reflections of European cultural identity and transgressing values, indeed, bring to mind Max Weber's classical distinction between formal and substantive law (Weber 1968, 655–8). Applying the distinction of instrumental,

1 For instance, the difference between repressive and restitutive elements in law significantly affected Durkheim's theory of modern society and his typology of mechanic and organic solidarity (Durkheim 1984, 24–5). Similarly, Herbert Spencer's evolutionary theory would be impossible without the classification of modern society as a contract-based collectivity which is different from pre-modern status-based societies (Spencer 1961). Modernity as a shift from status to contract appears in Henry Maine's seminal work on ancient law (Maine 1861).

purpose-oriented rationality and substantive, value-oriented rationality to the domain of law, legal reform and politics,[2] Weber perceived formal law as the totality of rules based on strictly legal logic without any reference to the social environment. Formal law is an expression of instrumental rationality and the disenchanted world of modern bureaucratic order which ensures the calculability of choices. Formal justice has to follow black-letter law's prescriptions and exclude other criteria of decision-making, such as compassion, strength, status, etc. On the other hand, substantive law reflects extra-juridical elements and accommodates moral, economic or traditional and religious criteria in the domain of positive law. It is based on substantive rationality which is defined by some ultimate values, be they equality, status or any other form of social justice. Unlike formal justice, substantive justice takes account of the social circumstances of legal regulation. The old distinction between law and equity thus has wide consequences: it creates the difference of legal expertise, the moral conflict between law and justice, and the political commitment of socially responsive legal reforms (for the importance of substantive/formal law distinction, see Freund 1968, 254–6).

The modern legal system accommodates both formal and substantive justice and thus regulates constant tensions arising from differences between calculable purposive ends and substantive value/belief commitments. Formal rationality and justice refer to the calculability of means and procedures while substantive rationality and justice refer to values as an end of social action. At the same time, the need for effective legal regulation is gradually transformed into the belief that legality is a social value, irrespective of its effects. Formal justice is transformed from a means to an end of social regulation and becomes a social value itself. Legal legitimacy therefore emerges as cultural sedimentation of law's formal rationality (Weber 1968, 215–23).

Apart from instrumental rationality, the modern legal system is also exposed to the demand of incorporating and directly symbolizing other substantive values which are treated as legitimate because they are recognised as absolutely binding and culturally valid. These values are primarily legitimised by their substantive rationality and not formal legality. The legal system is merely to reinforce and symbolize these substantive values and their social validity (Weber 1968, 815–6). The symbolic rationality of the constitution and any legal document or decision therefore draws on substantive rational legitimacy and expresses the moral authority of a political collectivity and its culture over individuals (for these Durkheimian elements in substantive rational legitimacy, see Durkheim 1953, 73).

The cultural legitimacy seeks to preserve the collective integrity and solidarity of a polity and present this preservation as itself a value (Parsons 1951, 97). Political institutions and laws are considered immediate expressions of a political society and its identity. In this expressive manner, Montesquieu, for instance, compared the

2 *Value*-rational action is a type of goal-oriented action different from the purposive (*zweckrational*) one. Unlike the instrumental rationality of purposive-rational action, people pursue values 'for their own sake' and irrespective of whether they mean any external success (for the role of a purposive-rational or instrumental orientation to utility satisfaction and an evaluative action-orientation in Weber's theory, see, for instance, Scaff 1989, 32–3).

British constitution with the work of Homer and called it the mirror of political liberty that should teach other nations a political lesson (Montesquieu 1989). Furthermore, it is expected that political institutions and laws as immediate expressive symbols and sources of cultural identity evolve into a set of moral dogmas which establishes belief systems and value orientations. Primary expressive symbolism is adjusted to mundane social reality and routinized by members of a collectivity. The symbolic power of constitutions cannot be only expressive: it has to become evaluative (Parsons 1951, 401–3). Expressive cultural symbols have to be manipulated and synthesised by moral judgements and converted into value-orientation patterns.

This transformation of expressive symbolism into its evaluative form is part of the process of what Max Weber had called the routinization of charisma and the disenchantment of the world. Modernity accommodates two distinct tendencies in modern culture: the tendency to become dogma and the concomitant tendency to consider any dogma as a problem in itself. These tendencies are, indeed, facilitated by legal norms and procedures. Laws and judicial decision-making, therefore, cannot be understood as a mere instrument for the circulation of political power or self-reference to the legal system: they also need to be analysed as an object of culture and tradition. They are both regulatory and symbolic, a useful tool of social control and a source of 'eternal truths' for a polity. Pragmatic legal tools and concepts, such as 'trust' or 'public work' are symbolized (Arnold 1962, 110), and symbols have the power to determine legal policies and suppress different ideologies and their symbolic universe. In this sense, Bauman's critique of the Union's legalist nature and Havel's call for a symbolic European charter inspiring the constitution of European charisma and the sense of abstract solidarity and identity are merely two of many examples of the differentiation between instrumental and symbolic rationality of modern society.

Postmodern ethics, the politics of ambivalence, and depoliticisation

Culture is a continual process of sustaining an identity through a moral conception of self (Bell 1979, 36, 248). In his project of postmodern ethics, Bauman warns against the organic neo-tribal politics of identity seeking to establish the ultimate cultural (in terms of race, ethnicity, religion, moral traditions, etc.) origins of political society and its laws. He is a powerful critic of tribal identity-based politics and the democratic state legitimised by popular modern nationalisms. He calls for more liquid ways of social and political spacing and symbolic expressions which would secure respect for otherness and promote togetherness and the sense of commonality. The cognitive space of modern rational order is to be both weakened and supplemented by aesthetic and moral spacing and the emerging common 'playground' structures:

> a homely order, a cosy order, an order which never hangs above the heads of the players as the laws of society or nature do, but one which is born ever anew, together with the players' willingness to obey it, and evaporates without sediment once that willingness peters out. This is what all order ought to be like. … We are all players. … (Bauman 1993, 172).

In his later work, Bauman continues analysing this postmodern liquidity as both an opportunity and a threat to the globalised societies and polity of Europe. His search for Europe's adventurous and transgressive identity indicates that neither the common market, nor the constitutional legalist model as a procedural and formal expression of political identity are sufficient stabilizers of the political community. Nevertheless, interpreting Bauman's notion of Europe as merely a cultural and controversial civilisational process would be misleading. According to Bauman, Europe is a cradle of modernity and modernity means the recognition of ambivalence (Bauman 1991). The political system of reflexive modern society can hardly be reduced to the symbolic politics of popular cultural self-images. Apart from simple rule-abiding strategies and political symbolism, it must accommodate the rule-altering ways of reflexive politics which are irreducible to legal procedures and the instrumental rationality of bureaucrats and other experts (Beck et al. 1994, 37). Politics as an ambivalent unity and tension between confrontation and compromise is the ultimate contribution of Europe to the emerging world society.

Europe's culture is politically ambiguous: it is the legitimate foundation of politics only because it can never be reduced to the technical rationality of rules and transgresses the political domain and its instrumental power logic. In this respect, Bauman and other adherents of reflexive social and political theory come surprisingly close to scholars such as Walter Benjamin and Carl Schmitt who also believed that politics ruled out the possibility of a pre-set, rule-fixed definition of sovereignty (Benjamin 1996; Schmitt 2005; for recent discussions of both philosophers, see Agamben 2005, 52–64). According to reflexive sociological and political theory, the state is not a central concept of today's politics because its unifying power is too weak to neutralise current political conflicts and the multiplicity of friend/enemy distinctions in contemporary societies. The rule of law is reformulated as the rule of men because law and politics are merely reflections of what is the ultimately contingent, complex, and unruly quality of individual and social life.

Critical social theory and legal studies can thus be easily inspired by these philosophers who claimed that human society can never be determined by rational (legal) rules and their application to individual situations and social circumstances. Liberal politics is criticised by both the left and right as an overly legalistic project of unjustifiably rationalistic politics. According to these views, modern parliamentary politics has been failing and the institution of parliament has become an empty machine processing public arguments and counter-arguments without taking democracy and its values into account (Schmitt 1985, 34–5). Although he accepts many such criticisms and shows a certain understanding of Schmitt's concept of politics as a never-ending chain of decisions temporarily recreating a judicial and political order out of the existing social chaos, Bauman's political ethos is, nevertheless, eventually closer to liberal universalism and different from decisionist theory. Like Schmitt and Benjamin, Bauman warns against turning the modern state into a huge industrial plant based on legalist thinking and the juridical normativism of the disenchanted political world. At the same time, he rejects the New Left's idea, inspired by Schmitt, Benjamin and others, that democracy negates liberalism and liberalism negates democracy. For Bauman, the conflictual nature of democratic politics has not lost its intellectual appeal and persuasiveness and still remains the best protection for civil rights and freedoms. The Kantian universe is inseparable from the Marxian concept of conflictual and dialectic politics.

Inspired by Benjamin and Schmitt, Bauman emphasises that the symbolic ethical problem of European identity needs to be examined against the depoliticising effects of economically and legally communicated integrative processes. The European Union's self-reflection historically lacks the political conception of democratic polemics, conflict and confrontation between different political agents and movements. The Union's generally neutralizing power permeates all levels and aspects of European politics. Its public law institutions are not established on the concepts of *polemos* or *hostis* (Schmitt 1996, 46–7). They, rather, draw on universalistic values and identity. The EU institutions build on a *depoliticised* concept of Europe and are thus under the constant threat of 'official lyricism and an increasingly distrustful popular indifference' (Touraine 2000, 204). For a long time, European integration, despite its clearly political meaning, has been presented in terms of economic prosperity, international safety, and legal regulation. In this context, Ulrich Beck comments that:

> Nowadays, … Europe is no longer the centre of the world, and a war between the major member states of the European Union, while not completely impossible, has become highly improbable at the very least. Europeans are a peaceable and prosperous set of people and tend to get upset about the poisons in their food (Beck 2005, 108).

As if public safety and living conditions dominated the European public domain and politics. Until the recent process of European constitution-making accompanied by national referenda in some member states to guarantee democratic legitimation, the very project of political unification used to be presented and progressed as a *politics of depoliticisation*.

Politics communicated through the logic of economy and law is a founding paradox of the European Union. Although Carl Schmitt's friend/enemy distinction should not be taken in an existential sense (and one should be aware of its possible political consequences), it is analytically valuable and illuminates the structural preconditions, achievements and limits of the European Union's political and legal systems. The EU's emerging public law system and constitutional framework are undoubtedly founded on demilitarized and depoliticised concepts and thus represent a coherent doctrine of liberal thought marginalising the political concepts of battle and enemy. The Union typically moves between ethics (moral and intellectual commitments in politics) and economics (free trade) and thus, using Schmitt's controversial concepts of political and legal theory, attempts 'to annihilate the political as a domain of conquering power and repression' (Schmitt 1996, 71).

The EU's strategy of establishing a system of permanent negotiations and compromise and substituting legal procedures for political struggles is certainly driven by the Union's goal of making national and international politics *safe*, a possibility which is categorically rejected by Schmitt. The Union's compromise-driven strategies may be only temporary, occasional, and never decisive in the sense of decision-making by the ultimate political sovereign. However, the depoliticisation of the EU's political domain and its transformation into neutral public law procedures clearly has some political significance and implications. Schmitt himself, indeed, was aware of this political function of liberalism and the political consequences of its tendency to neutralise and depoliticise the public domain (Schmitt 1996, 69). It may be argued that the European Union historically emerged as a depoliticising, yet profoundly political response to the unprecedented politics of local and universal genocides, extremely aggressive regionalisms, social-class discriminatory regimes, and their politically violent totalitarian ideologies.

There is even a 'Schmittian evidence' of the EU politics of depoliticisation: the 'Euroenthusiast/Eurosceptics' distinction has been commonly used as another term for the 'friend/enemy' distinction in European politics. Until the collapse of European constitution-making in 2005, most criticisms of ever-closer political union and integrative efforts had been immediately dismissed as anti-European and counterproductive. The Union's 'democratic deficit' was supplemented by European culture-based humanitarian legitimacy. The universalistic discourse of cosmopolitan Europe as humanity created the illusion of ideological humanitarian politics classifying all its opponents as disturbers and enemies of humanity (Schmitt 1996, 71–2). The European Union thus constituted a politically asymmetrical counter-concept of the enemy because universal humanity, by its definition, cannot have political enemies. Accordingly, all enemies would have to be considered enemies of the human race and, therefore, excluded from the domain of politics.

The liquid European people and building its identity

The Union's integration, based on the politics of depoliticisation, has primarily been a *legalistic project* criticised for its technical obscurity and lack of public accountability. The depoliticising effects of the instrumental rationality of European law and economics seem to eliminate the possibility of establishing a politics of democratic deliberation equally driven by consensus, compromise, and conflict between different political parties, groups, coalitions and informal movements. It is as if the systemic rationality of European laws and economics were creating the obscure reality of political institutions which could be described only as the most powerful machinery and, therefore, criticised from the perspective of cultural symbolism and metaphors: as if the true Europe existed behind the veil of the Union's techniques of economic and power regulations.

Indeed, European identity-building is a far more complex process than the constitution-making efforts, legal acts and cases of the EU. Close historical links between the nation and the state have been weakened by the transnationality of the EU and many in-between forms of political identification and legitimation currently support the project of European political and constitutional integration (Beck 2005, 204–5). Nevertheless, European cultural symbolism, the regulatory politics of 'comitology', and ethical calls cannot effectively substitute for the absence of a European *demos* and a European public sphere legitimising the European polity-in-waiting.

The fact that, at the European level, there is no European *demos* with the power to democratically legitimise the process of the Union's constitution-making, deliberate on its further political integration in public debate, and symbolically guarantee European political identity, has practical implications for the politics and law of both the EU and its member states. The absence of a European *demos* has even been used as an argument in disputes between European and member states' national institutions and legal systems.

In this context, the German Constitutional Court's Maastricht judgment concerning the divided sovereignty between the European and member state legal systems illustrates the technical legal consequences of the non-existence of a European people and the EC's lack of democratic legitimation. The Court's 'no *demos*' thesis (Weiler 1995, 219–58) used in the ruling can be interpreted in two different ways. According to a 'hard' nationalist version, there will never be a European *demos* which could guarantee as strong a feeling of collective identity – and therefore democratic legitimation – as modern ethnic European nations provide at the nation-state level. European democracy is impossible because there is no European people transformable into a political nation. According to the 'soft' version actually applied by the Court, this absence mainly indicates that democracy and constitutional rights guaranteed at the nation-state level cannot be compromised by supra-national structures (von Beyme 2001, 62–4).

The concept of *demos* and its absence at the European level, which is used in European legal and political debates on sovereignty and normative superiority by both Euroenthusiasts (as the goal to be gradually achieved by the process of constitution-making and further political integration) and Eurosceptics (as the reason to stop current attempts at further integration and constitution-making), is often presented as a *solid* political category and an essentialist identity concept even if it is not defined ethnically. It assumes a community integrating individual citizens into a whole composed of values and traditions. Ethnic nationalism and republican nationalism can paradoxically have similar exclusionary effects. The idea of the civil nation as a political unity free of ethnic meaning can, like ethno-nationalist notions of political society, speak the mythical language of historical roots, a genealogy of morals and values, and cultural commitments. Like ethno-nationalist fantasies of the people's historical destiny and uniqueness, the democratic republican concept of the nation can have cultural fundamentalist and communitarian foundations.

This transformation of the democratic nation into an organic community is critically analysed by Etienne Balibar as a paradox of 'republican communitarianism' according to which even a civic nation can construct a dangerously exclusive identity and attack any strangers and minorities in the name of its own political universalism (Balibar 2004, 64). Like Bauman and others, Balibar persuasively shows how universalist values can easily become neo-tribal expressions of exclusive and discriminatory particularisms. Although the European quest for its civil identity has been an effective tool in dismantling nation-state politics, too much European identity-building would amount to a social rigidity and cultural exclusion that is inconsistent with Europe's diversity, flexibility and cultural differences.

No wonder that enthusiastic calls for European federal statehood backed by a shared European identity are ever more dangerously confronted by reconfigured ethnic nationalism and the xenophobic populism of both the extreme left and right at member-state level. Euro-enthusiasts automatically label all critics of the EU statehood project as sceptical enemies of Europe and seek to exclude them from the European political debate. In the same manner, new political leaders calling for the preservation of the ethnic state label any EU politics as the myth of a united Europe threatening the political identity and communal bonds of the peoples of Europe and their nation states. While Euro-federalists dream of a European polity with strong communal (hopefully even national) bonds, new nationalists defending the ethnic state dream of the persistence of national cultures and peoples effectively insulated from supra-national European politics.

A European collective political identity based on strong cultural identification and civic communitarian fantasies could easily result in the emergence of Euro-chauvinism using the symbolic formula of 'the European people'. The very concept of European identity is not immune from neo-tribalism and political exclusionism. Calls for a European nation could easily repeat the fatal mistake of the modern age in which, according to Max Horkheimer, 'the nation has set itself up as the universal idol in place of the Most High' (Horkheimer 1994, 103). European identity, therefore, is susceptible to the nationalistic faith in 'one's own people' like any other form of modern nationalism. The most important European political questions, therefore, are: how much identity is a good thing in a large-scale economic, political and cultural unification of Europe, and how much unification can be pursued in the Union without the constituent democratic power?

These questions reflect a more general problem of European politics, namely, that the symbolisation of European political identity should be '*liquid*' (Bauman 2000) and disentangled from the notion of a common fate and historical reason solidified in charismatic acts and documents. In a critical reflection on Ernest Renan's concept of the nation as a soul constituted simultaneously by the past and the present, Philippe C. Schmitter raises the following questions:

> why should individuals (and, for that matter, organizations) in the Euro-polity have to be 'nationals' in some sense in order to act like citizens? Why could they not be loyal to a common set of institutions and political/legal principles rather than to some mystical charismatic founder or set of mythologized ancestors? Why could Renan's *plébiscite de tous les jours* not be about rights and procedures in the present, rather than sacrifices and glories of the past? (Schmitter 2001, 91).

Renan's frequently cited idea that a nation is a daily plebiscite (Renan 1996) is to be politicised by uprooting historical traditions and reinventing the art of protecting political rights and the conflictual character of liberal democracy.

The identity of the European *demos* would be impossible to formulate through the common political concepts of nationhood, sovereignty, and democratic state. Transforming Europe into a sovereign state and solidifying the European nation and nationalism would mean the end of Europe as an adventure. Paradoxically and contrary to Bauman's initial sweeping criticism of European legality, the main source of European political identity, instead of the overarching European cultural legacy, is the network of European legal regulations incorporating the concept of European citizenship and civil rights and freedoms. European identity may lack a common language and European traditions and cultures may draw on both negative and positive historical experiences, yet Europeans still can effectively identify with their rights and the existing post-Maastricht concept of European citizenship. The current trend of directly granting rights at the European level certainly weakens old communal loyalties without eradicating them and fully decoupling national and European citizenship.

Conclusion: towards a critical theory of European cosmopolitanism?

Bauman's critique of the EU's technical machinery and instrumental rationality is far from simply presenting the cultural and civilisational alternative of an unfinished and infinite adventure of Europe. Bauman is faithful to the legacy of the Frankfurt critical theory, especially Adorno and Horkheimer's dialectic of Enlightenment, and fully aware of the political risk of excluding all 'enemies' of Europe in the name of its civilisational mission or cultural legacy. He is critical of the communitarian myth of culture as the first precondition and legitimation of politics. The European legacy is the continent's cultural heterogeneity and incompleteness that is currently marked by the postmodern removal of boundaries and increasing liquidity.

Bauman, rather, elaborates on the idea of modernity suggested by Horkheimer and Adorno in their *Dialectic of Englightenment*, in which initially emancipatory reason – the driving force of social modernization – turns upon itself and becomes its own haunting spectre. Instead of the liberating emancipation of mankind by reason, the impersonal legal-rational bureaucracy builds up concentration camps and uses modern industrial and political technologies to imprison and exterminate those who are 'strangers' and different. As Horkheimer and Adorno rather provocatively stated, 'Enlightenment is totalitarian' (Horkheimer and Adorno 2002, 4) – the idea Bauman so persuasively elaborated in his *Modernity and the Holocaust* (1989).

European cosmopolitanism thus involves the internal paradox of the need for anti-foundationalist foundations for politics. A transcendental sense of Europe has its history and spatio-temporal limitations like all other human actions and artefacts in the world. While Habermas attempts to balance the expert-systems of politics and law with the public sphere of freely constructed democratic and rational will formation, Bauman has, on the contrary, been following the ambivalent character of modernity and modern reason. New ambivalent forms of social order are emerging and need to be comprehended by the reflexive postmodern ethics of interpretation and care for the other. Bauman's understanding of cosmopolitanism is not emancipatory in the sense of participatory democracy and its technology of bureaucratic modernity. Drawing on Adorno's critique of Nazi totalitarianism as technology, Bauman pursues a cosmopolitan pragmatics of interpreting and understanding the otherness and social complexity of non-identity (Lash 1994, 143–4). This pragmatics effectively eliminates communitarian elements of hermeneutics by emphasising the individual aesthetic aspect of postmodern ethics, diversity and the uniqueness of human lives 'in fragments' (Bauman 1995). In this sense, Bauman endorses Horkheimer's aesthetic-expressive individualism and warning against '[T]he decay of individual expressiveness, which is effected in home and school through the schematization of language' (Horkheimer 1994, 142). In our social condition, which has been fragmented by instrumental reason, one therefore has to recall Gadamer's hermeneutics and ethics of interpretation and shared meaning as the other European legacy that is inseparable from the Kantian cosmopolitan legacy of modernity.

European identity can consequently be symbolized only as a space of heterogeneity and permanent contestation of existing practices because it 'was a utopia at all moments in its history' (Bauman 2004, 36). This reflexive utopia, like any symbolic vision and moral dream, is everywhere and nowhere and thus successfully escapes any cultural and political definitions. There are no clear intellectual and political guidelines on how to live with social ambivalences. There is only an ethical effort to cope with them by the self-reflection and critique of our social and political condition.

The transgressive European culture and civilisation has one critical consequence – the impossibility of predetermining or even eliminating political change and dynamic. The liquid society is both more fragile and adventurous. Liquid politics is consequently both riskier and more open to democratic options and changes. In this condition, European citizenship and other legal categories cannot be subjected to a globalised cosmopolitan ethics of which the European Union would pretend to be an avant-garde supra-national organisation. Similarly, Europe is not a cosmopolitan political actor despite the normative efforts of the Convention during the constitution-making process. Contemporary united Europe still possesses only 'a provincial soul' (Beck 2005, 231). Bauman's depiction of cosmopolitan Europe as an adventure clearly shows that European politics can never be reduced either to the depoliticising European legality, or the universalist European culture. It, rather, feeds on cultural and legal antinomies and heterogeneities. The European Union historically emerged as a mixture of a market and a bureaucracy and currently operates as a hybrid political entity shaped by its member states and, at the same time, exercising enormous regulative power over these states and their citizens. The Union's transnational politics, therefore, is contradictory: it contributes to the resurgence of ethnic nationalisms, yet it also potentially strengthens the democratic governments of member states if the Union's transnational politics prove successful and beneficial. Politicians in the member states can effectively seek transnational European empowerment and thus even instrumentally contribute to the process of European identity-building outside the system of European constitutional law and political institutions.

In this sense, European identity-building has never been a dilemma of sharply divided cultural alternatives, European and national counter-policies, and contradicting legalisations but, rather, a process of supplementing and expanding one form of politics, political identity and its legal codification, over the other.

References

Agamben, G. (2005), *State of Exception* (Chicago: The University of Chicago Press).

Arnold, T. (1962), *The Symbols of Government* (New York: Harcourt Brace & World).

Balibar, E. (2004), *We, the People of Europe? Reflections on Transnational Citizenship* (Princeton: Princeton University Press).

Bauman, Z. (1989), *Modernity and the Holocaust* (Oxford: Blackwell Publishing).

Bauman, Z. (1991), *Modernity and Ambivalence* (Oxford: Blackwell Publishing).

Bauman, Z. (1993), *Postmodern Ethics* (Oxford: Blackwell Publishing).

Bauman, Z. (1995), *Life in Fragments: Essays in Postmodern Morality* (Oxford: Blackwell Publishing).

Bauman, Z. (1999), *In Search of Politics* (Cambridge: Polity Press).

Bauman, Z. (2000), *Liquid Modernity* (Cambridge: Polity Press).

Bauman, Z. (2004), *Europe: An Unfinished Adventure* (Cambridge: Polity Press).

Beck, U., Giddens, A., and Lash, S. (1994), *Reflexive Modernization: Politics, Tradition and Aesthetics in the Modern Social Order* (Cambridge: Polity Press).

Beck, U. (2005), *Power in the Global Age* (Cambridge: Polity Press).

Bell, D. (1979), *The Cultural Contradictions of Capitalism* (London: Heinemann).

Benhabib, S. (2002), *The Claims of Culture: Equality and Diversity in the Global Era* (Princeton, NJ: Princeton University Press).

Benjamin, W. (1996), 'Towards a Critique of Violence', in W. Benjamin, *Selected Writings*, vol. 1 (Cambridge, Mass.: Harvard University Press).

Bohman, J. and Lutz-Bachman, M. (eds.) (1997), *Perpetual Peace: Essays on Kant's Cosmopolitan Ideal* (Cambridge, Mass.: The MIT Press).

Bradley, K. (1997), 'The European Parliament and Comitology: On the Road to Nowhere?', *European Law Journal* 3, 273.

Durkheim, E. (1953), *Sociology and Philosophy* (London: Cohen & West).

Durkheim, E. (1984), *The Division of Labour in Society* (London: Macmillan).

Fasbender, B. (1998), 'The United Nations Charter as Constitution of the International Community' *Columbia Journal of Transnational Law* 37, 529–619.

Freund, J. (1968), *The Sociology of Max Weber* (Harmondsworth: Penguin).

Gadamer, H.-G. (1989), *Das Erbe Europas: Beiträge* (Frankfurt: Suhrkamp Verlag).

Habermas, J. (2001), *The Postnational Constellation: Political Essays* (Cambridge: Polity Press).

Havel, V. (1994), Speech in the European Parliament, Strasbourg, 8 March 1994, available at: <http://www.vaclavhavel.cz>.

Horkheimer, M. (1994), *Critique of Instrumental Reason: Lectures and Essays since the end of World War II* (New York: Continuum).

Horkheimer, M. and Adorno, T.W. (2002), *Dialectic of Enlightenment: Philosophical Fragments* (Stanford, Cal.: Stanford University Press).

Husserl, E. (1965), 'Philosophy and the Crisis of European Man', in *Phenomenology and the Crisis of Philosophy* (New York: Harper and Row), 149–92.

Husserl, E. (1970), 'Philosophy and the Crisis of European Humanity', in *The Crisis of European Sciences and Transcendental Phenomenology* (Evanston, Ill.: Northwestern University Press), 269–99.

Judt, T. (1996), *A Grand Illusion? An Essay on Europe* (New York: Hill and Wang).

Kagan, R. (2004), *Power and Paradise: America and Europe in the New World Order* (London: Atlantic Books).

Kant, I. (1971a), 'On the Common Saying: "This May be True in Theory, but it does not Apply in Practice"', in *Kant's Political Writings*, edited with an introduction and notes by H. Reiss, translated by H.B. Nisbet, (Cambridge: Cambridge University Press), 61–92.

Kant, I. (1971b), 'Perpetual Peace: A Philosophical Sketch', in *Kant's Political Writings*, edited with an introduction and notes by H. Reiss, translated by H.B. Nisbet, (Cambridge: Cambridge University Press), 93–130.

Kelsen, H. (1929), *Wesen und Wert der Demokratie* (Tübingen: J.C.B. Mohr Verlag).

Lash, S. (1994), 'Reflexivity and its Doubles: Structure, Aesthetics, Community', in U. Beck, A. Giddents, S. Lash, *Reflexive Modernization: Politics, Tradition and Aesthetics in the Modern Social Order* (Cambridge: Polity Press), 110–74.

Lepenies, W. (2006), *The Seduction of Culture in German History* (Princeton, NJ: Princeton University Press).

Maine, H. (1861), *Ancient Law* (London: John Murray).

Marx, K. and Engels, F. (2002), *The Communist Manifesto* (London: Penguin Books).

McCarthy, T. (2002), 'On Reconciling Cosmopolitan Unity and National Diversity' in P. De Greiff and C. Cronin (eds.), *Global Justice and Transnational Politics* (Cambridge: Mass., The MIT Press), 235–74.

Montesquieu, C. (1989), *The Spirit of the Laws* (Cambridge: Cambridge University Press).

Nietzsche, F. (2000), 'Beyond Good and Evil', in *Basic Writings of Nietzsche*, translated and edited by W. Kaufmann, introduction by P. Gay, (New York: The Modern Library Classics), 170–435.

Parsons, T. (1951), *The Social System* (London: Routledge).

Parsons, T. (1967), *Sociological Theory and Modern Society* (New York: Free Press).

Pedler, R.H. and Schaefer, G.F. (eds.) (1996), *Shaping European Law and Policy – The Role of Committees and Comitology in the Political Process* (Maastricht: European Centre for Public Affairs, European Institute of Public Administration).

Pomian, K. (1992), 'Europe et ses frontiéres', in *L' Europe retrouvée* (Neuchatel: Editions de la Baconiere).

Přibáň, J. (2007), 'Is There a Spirit of European Law?: Critical Remarks on the EU Constitution-making, Enlargement and Political Culture', in V. Gessner and D. Nelken (eds.), *European Ways of Law* (Oxford: Hart Publishing).

Renan, E. (1996), *Que'est-ce qu'une nation?/What Is a Nation?* (Toronto: Tapir Press).

Scaff, L.A. (1989), *Fleeing the Iron Cage: Culture, Politics, and Modernity in the Thought of Max Weber* (Berkeley, Cal.: University of California Press).

Schmitt, C. (1985), *The Crisis of Parliamentary Democracy* (Cambridge, Mass.: The MIT Press).

Schmitt, C. (1996), *The Concept of the Political* (Chicago: The University of Chicago Press).

Schmitt, C. (2005), *Political Theology: Four Chapters on the Concept of Sovereignty* (Chicago: The University of Chicago Press).

Schmitter, P.C. (2001), 'The Scope of Citizenship in a Democratized European Union', in K. Eder and B. Giesen (eds.), *European Citizenship between National Legacies and Postnational Projects* (Oxford: Oxford University Press), 86–121.

Schutz, A. (1997), 'The Twilight of the Global Polis: On Losing Paradigms, Environing Systems, and Observing World Society', in G. Teubner (ed.), *Global Law Without a State* (Aldershot: Dartmouth).

Spencer, H. (1961), *The Study of Sociology* (Ann Arbor: The University of Michigan Press).

Tamás, G.M. (1996), 'Ethnarchy and Ethno-Anarchism', *Social Research* 63, 147–90.

Touraine, A. (2000), *Can We Live Together? Equality and Difference* (Cambridge: Polity Press).

von Beyme, K. (2001), 'Citizenship and the European Union', in K. Eder and B. Giesen (eds.), *European Citizenship between National Legacies and Postnational Projects* (Oxford: Oxford University Press), 61–85.

Weber, M. (1968), *Economy and Society: An Outline of Interpretive Sociology, vol. II* (New York: Bedminster Press).

Weber, M. (1983), 'Parliament and Government in Newly Organized Germany', *Economy and Society* 4, 1381–462.

Weiler, J.H.H. (1995), 'Does Europe Need a Constitution? Reflections on Demos, Telos and the German Maastricht Decision', *European Law Journal* 1, 219–58.

Weiler, J.H.H. (1999), *The Constitution of Europe: 'Do the New Clothes have an Emperor?' and Other Essays on European Integration* (Cambridge: Cambridge University Press).

Chapter 8

Constitutional Identities in a Liquid Society

Vito Breda[1]

Introduction

What is national identity? What is its role in constitutional democracy? At first sight, the constitutional techniques which aspire to reduce the tension between cosmopolitanism and nationalism, most notably regionalism, federalism and devolution, appear not to have done so. Nationalist and regionalist movements are rising in the UK and in Europe. They are theoretically supported by authors, such as Canovan (1996) and Taylor (1992), who argue that national identities are normatively essential to the political stability of state-centred constitutional structures. The national community fosters the process of self-identification between individuals and law. This process can only be guaranteed within an autonomous constitutional structure which protects and promotes national social characteristics. On the other hand, cosmopolitan authors such as Habermas suggest that modern constitutions should be based exclusively on constitutional patriotism (Habermas 1999a). Constitutional patriotism is a set of post-national procedural norms which Habermas distils from a rational reading of the evolution of modern constitution making.

The implications of this quarrel are not limited to political science. At the constitutional level, the post-Westphalian principles of national sovereignty and state unity are challenged internally by regionalism and externally by cosmopolitanism. In this chapter, I will seek in Bauman's concept of 'liquid modernity' a new perspective on the constitutional debate over the role of national identity in modern democracy. According to his account, emerging regional movements are articulated social responses to global trends such as immigration and cultural uniformity which try to protect individuals' economic and political status in an unstable society (Bauman 2001). The complex interplay between these new ethnic communities and globalisation, Bauman argues, begs a new conceptual understanding of the role of identity in modern society. This new conceptual explanation, I argue, might help us to understand the constitutional role of ethnicity in modern society.

1 I am indebted to Jiří Přibáň and Richard Moorehead for their very helpful comments. Needless to say, responsibility for any error in the present work rests with the author. Lastly, I would like to thank Stefania Morandini for her help during the last stages of this chapter.

The chapter is in two parts. The first briefly discusses Bauman's concept of liquid modernity. In the second part, I argue that constitutional theorists such as Tully (1993) and Walker (2002) have sensed the effect of globalisation described in Bauman's analysis and have proposed new theoretical explanations of the role of identity in modern constitutional democracy.

Globalisation and identity: an analytical perspective

Constitutional theorists, more than any other legal experts, have traditionally referred to the work of sociologists and political scientists to explain or substantiate their normative claims (Přibáň 2006). The engineering and development of modern constitutional concepts such as freedom of association or political representation have been the results of dialectical debates between constitutional lawyers, sociologists, and moral philosophers. However, all constitutional attempts (e.g. federalism, regionalism, and devolution) to define the role of national identity in modern democracy appear to have enlarged the epistemic gulf between cosmopolitans, who consider nationalism as an ideology that threatens democracy, and those who consider the nation-state as the only possible form of stable political association.

Recently, Bauman's concept of 'liquid modernity' has shed new light on the role of globalisation which – I hope – will help us to understand the problematic relationship between constitutional democracy and national identity. The merit of this new approach is to place sociological and political analyses in a wider epistemic context (Bauman 2000). Bauman explains that globalisation has created the conditions for an unprecedented level of social *complexity* where all socio-political endeavours are interconnected. The effect of increased social complexity is particularly noticeable on the processes which drive identity and community making (Bauman 2000; 2001; 2001a). One of the reactions to globalisation, Bauman argues, is the desire to belong to a (social or ethnic) community which appears to provide a solid frame of reference. This desire for a more or less imagined national identity (for a general analysis of this point see, for instance, Anderson 1983) has theoretical and pragmatic implications (Bauman 2001, 89–109).

First, the process of seeking an identity reinforces the constitutional rhetoric which considers the political process as an exchange between individuals who already have something in common, notably a common ethnic heritage (Bauman 1999, 92). This process is supported by theorists such as Taylor (1992) who suggest that a polity cannot simply rely on a system of procedural rules but should also create a model of social cohesion. A homogeneous national population, Taylor continues, within state borders is the only guarantee of a substantive relation between democratic decision making and the legal system. This reasoning echoes Carl Schmitt's analysis of the relationship between nation and state. If logic cannot be the moral motivation which binds a community to its political decisions, Schmitt claims, then we have to assume that it is the sharing of national cultural characteristics which links people to institutions. Such an assumption (which pre-empts much of today's communitarianism) makes it possible to subvert the universal system of cosmopolitan values since democratic self-determination is based on ethnic homogeneity and not, as liberals want to believe, on political freedom (Schmitt 1976, 135).

Secondly, linking the idea of legal recognition of the role of a national community with institutional representation pragmatically modifies the interaction between national communities under the same constitutional umbrella and the interaction between nation-states. On the one hand, it equips nations and regions with a moral reason to act as individuals who struggle to protect their own private interest in a free market. On the other hand, it allows democratic states to behave in the international political arena according to the political template provided by the monarchy they have just superseded. This includes the idea of protecting the national community, with violence if necessary, which was previously associated with the defence of the crown.

The elusive myth of the uniform nation state underpinned by the Schmittian idea of 'my country, right or wrong' (Bauman 1997), combined with liberalism were historically part of an elite-driven project that converted ethnic diversity and individual freedom into a constitutionally engineered political community, notably the nation-state (Bauman 2001). Globalisation, Bauman continues, has revealed the fictitious nature of that arrangement by melting geopolitical divisions based on it. State borders cannot isolate national economies from international trading. After the world economic crisis of the 1920s, the necessity of limited control over national economies – in Keynesian terms – was favoured even by liberals who saw the devastating effects of a completely unrestrained economy. The consensus around the beneficial effects of limited state intervention in state economic internal policies gave rise to the implementation of redistributive policies which de facto guaranteed a degree of social justice. This had a paradoxical result on the uneasy relation between individual freedom and nation state. Redistributive policies which assure universal individual rights de jure, such as free education and healthcare, and so on, reinforced the linkage between liberal state and national population (Bauman 2001, 91–92). However, Bauman argues that states in a complex global economy market cannot guarantee the protection of their national policies without loosing their economic competitiveness (Bauman 1999, 170). This reduces the quantity of available recourses for national welfare systems and increases the level of social and economic instability. But these, Bauman argues, are the consequences of a process which originally set out to create a stable frame of reference for individuals in industrial societies, not in a complex globalised borderless economy.

The increased level of economic instability has re-awoken ethnic claims which appear to have preceded the formation of modern nation states. New ethnic communities have deconstructed old historical myths, created martyrs and new geopolitical borders. However, Bauman argues, the process of delegitimating nation-states, deconstructing national myths and inventing new ones is part of that globalisation process which increases social complexity and eventually propels – instead of reducing – social instability.

> The popular fascination with the issue of identity, aided, abetted and whipped up by politicians sniffing political (electoral) capital, as well as by the folk (one is tempted to say *völkisch*), mass-consumption, bowdlerized renditions of communitarian philosophy,

> may be a sui generis rational response to contemporary conditions; it may even 'make sense'. But it mislocates its own causes and in its therapeutic conclusions misses them by a wide margin. Militant assertion of group (local, territorial, limited) identity will do next to nothing to remove the source of insecurity which prompted it [...] Inviting inevitable frustration, it will, if anything, provide more reasons for its own continuing pugnacity (Bauman 1999, 197).

The desire for a community which empowers its members as part of a communal 'us' is not a solution to the problems which the nation state failed to address:it simply puts the issue/s under a different heading.

This representation of modern society as a complex landscape of multi-level interaction between indistinguishable social trends, which is in itself a ground-breaking critical account of the complex role of identity in modern society, is only the first part of Bauman's concept of liquid modernity. The second part describes the impact of globalisation at *epistemic* level. It contextualises narratives such as the ones proposed by nationalists and cosmopolitans which seek (solid) hierarchical theoretical structures in a globalised social environment.

Seen from this perspective, the term liquid modernity fulfils a double function – and incidentally reveals once more the originality of Bauman's account – by creating a *new narrative* and by setting a new distinct *historical context* which separates liquid from the old (solid) conception of modernity. A 'clear theoretical narrative' is crucial in any epistemic project since the use of general terms to describe issues changes in relation to the context in which these terms are used (Wittgenstein 1968, 83–85), yet it is in the social sciences where different variables contribute to a complex context that we should adopt a broad theoretical view (for a general analysis of this point, see, for instance, Tully 2002, 543).

An epistemic analysis: patriotism, communitarianism, and ethnicity in liquid modernity

In this section, I will adopt Bauman's critical approach for a brief account of cosmopolitanism, communitarianism, and liberal nationalism. In the past few decades, these schools of thought have significantly influenced the ongoing debate over the role of identity in modern democracy. This will provide the springboard for the second part of the chapter in which I will argue that the constitutional theories of Walker (2002) and Tully (1995; 2001) have sensed the change of scenario brought about by globalisation. These proposals suggest a new constitutional role for contemporary sub-national movements.

Habermas's cosmopolitan argument claims that the model of social cohesion, which binds citizens who are strangers to one another, should not derive from the sense of belonging to a national community but should, rather, spring from individual commitment to a constitution. He calls this model 'constitutional patriotism'. Citizens are obliged by legal norms only if they are allowed to participate in the communicative process which leads to legislative deliberation. He suggests that a society ruled in such a fashion will combine popular democracy and a Kantian theory of human rights. This linkage between law and the process of social integration around an autonomous system of moral statutes is guaranteed only if the democratic arena is completely open to social demands (Habermas 2001). In this representation of democracy, Habermas outlines a consensual theory of legitimacy, according to which constitutional norms can be legitimated only when social interests are discussed through the discursive channel of public debate. The prospect of achieving this cosmopolitan constitution, Habermas points out, depends on the procedural protection of the freedom to intervene in the political arena, and on the equality of the speakers. These two limits guarantee two things: individuals will be involved in the democratic process with the sole interest of disclosing personal reflections; and the openness of the public debate guarantees rational political decisions as the outcome of the activity of communicative persuasion.

This process, Habermas continues, might be endangered in the present conception of the nation state where state legitimacy is connected with a national community. If the relationship between state and nation is not well adjusted there are two possible consequences. First, the community might disintegrate and return to the form of democratic associations which historically preceded the national state. Every single element of these political associations is socially detached from the others and it is preoccupied by its ethnocentric search for a mythical natural population (a similar point is made in Bauman 2001, 103). This relentless search for a mythical origin drives apart the members of the association, with severe consequences (Habermas 1992, 2). The division of the former Yugoslavia is an example of this centrifugal process. Second, Habermas argues that linking the concept of nation to the political structure of the state might endanger the republican values on which the nation-state is based: '[T]he lesson to be learned from this sad history is obvious. The nation-state *must* [my emphasis] renounce the ambivalent potential that once propelled it' (Habermas 1999b, 117). The only normative solution to the risks associated with the traditional form of the nation-state is to renounce this irrational ambivalence and to change the actual structure of the state from nationalistic to patriotic (Habermas 1999b, 111).

Habermas has expanded his historical analysis (2001a), and his demands for a cosmopolitan constitution (2006), but has not introduced new elements into his conceptualisation of the patriotic state. The a priori exclusion of nationalism from the theoretical framework of the modern state provoked an array of direct and indirect critiques based on two different motivations: the inexactness of Habermas's account of the historical relation between nationalism and democracy (e.g., Canovan 1997), and the political instability of a state or a conglomerate of states such as the EU legally bound only by a constitutional agreement (e.g., Weiler 1999; 2001). In his reading of Habermas, however, Bauman does not contend either the aim of constitutional patriotism which is to move the concept of legality beyond formal legalism, nor the historical connection between nationalism and xenophobia. Instead he reveals the ontological limits of Habermas's (rigid) epistemic constructivism (for a general analysis of Habermas's political constructivism see, for instance, Estlund 1997 and Nino 1996) in a globalised society.

This move uncovers the normative limits of trying to protect republican values under a constitutional umbrella. Globalisation, Bauman explains, has dissolved at the international level the old conceptions of the protection of constitutionally guaranteed rights which Habermas claims in his constitutional patriotism (for a recent analysis of this point, see Anderson 2005). International organisations such as the UN, EU, WTO have taken over the role of guarantors of cosmopolitan values. This is so, even if the logic which underpins their actions is driven by strategic attitudes and utilitarian based policies. This multi-level interaction is an axiomatic element of a liquid modernity which rigid post-Kantian cosmopolitanism such as the one advocated by Habermas refuses to acknowledge. As Bauman says:

> A new consensus on citizenship ('constitutional patriotism', to deploy Jürgen Habermas's term) cannot be presently built, as it used to be built not-so-long before, on the assurances of constitutional protection against vagaries of the market that play havoc with social standing and sap the rights to social esteem and personal dignity (Bauman in this volume; a similar point is also made in Bauman 1999, 110).

However, Habermas, who so precisely criticises the historical incongruence of nationalist claims in a globalised society, overlooks the impact of globalisation at the international level. Strategic economic and sociological interplays dominate the international protection of rights and the conceptualisation of an ideal communicative democracy. It is precisely, as Bauman observes, this unwillingness to let go of a theoretical representation of legality superseded by globalisation which makes the claims of constitutional patriotism implausible.

Communitarian and liberal nationalism in liquid modernity

In Bauman's opinion, constitutional patriotism might have overlooked the normative effects of globalisation, yet the theoretical alternatives – notably, communitarianism and liberal nationalism – are similarly unconvincing. Communitarians (e.g., Taylor 1992) construct their theoretical niche on the cleavage created between cosmopolitanism and liberal nationalism. The main argument presented by communitarians is that democratic participation by itself cannot make people obey the decisions taken within the political arena. They argue that individuals are not to be considered simply members of the polity, but also conveyor of a concrete cultural heritage (a similar point is made in Renan 1996). These cultural elements create in the individual a set of obligations that lead the member to respect his/her cultural tradition. Because of this, a member of a national community appears to possess a unique form of commitment to the past and to the decisions taken within his/her community (Taylor 1989 and 1992). To guarantee the member's commitment to majority decisions, we need to share a sense of belonging which normatively precedes democratic legitimacy; this is provided by nationalism.

Communitarians were criticised for the internal and external unverifiability of their normative claims (for a recent critique, see Habermas 2005, 101–04). However, the logic of linking the shared social sense of belonging to the ethnically uniform national community, and then to the individual's loyalty to the law is problematic in a globalised society. There is no such thing as a uniform ethnic community within a modern state. Even the 27,000 residents of the republic of San Marino cannot claim ethnic homogeneity (NationMaster 2006). In Bauman's analysis, the pragmatic issue of setting the limits of the national community assumes relevance again at an epistemic level. By assuming a link between national community and democratic decisions, the nation-state a priori excludes those who refuse to conform to the given model of political association. It is not by chance, Bauman observes, that communitarians such as Taylor do not speak about the constitutional role of national communities (Bauman 2001, 139). The difficulties of 'translating' political analyses into rigid legal narratives, which is in itself a difficult task for any conceptual proposition (Přibáň 2006), would have magnified the epistemic limits of a theory which constructs a hierarchical chain of reasons based upon rigid sociological assumptions in a globalised society. In practice, a public lawyer would doubt whether community boundaries could be drawn and – if that were possible – would ask who would have the task of designating them in a social context where communal identities are constantly altered by immigration and the emergence of new sub-national movements.

By contrast with communitarianism, the proposals of liberal nationalists such as Smith (1971; 1986; and 1992) appear to be – at least for constitutional theorists – more attractive. For instance, MacCormick directly refers to Smith's analysis supporting his case for national self-determination (MacCormick 1991; 1995; and 1999). The merit of Smith's proposal is its divergence from the ideology and nationalism of Renan (1996). 'For an "ethnocentric" nationalist both power and values inhere in his cultural group [...] my group is the vessel of wisdom, beauty, holiness, and culture; hence power automatically belongs to my group' (Smith 1971, 158). By contrast, liberal nationalism considers a nation as an ensemble of different groups. This kind of 'polycentric' nationalism perceives the existence of other nationalities as equal and tries to join different nations in a family of nations.

This last form of nationalism appeared after the republican revival which followed the American and French revolutions and it is related to a theoretical mutation in the sociological nature of nationalism. Polycentric liberal nationalism – which Smith associates with modern democratic nationalism – has three features which differentiate this sociological phenomenon from the old ethnocentric nationalism. First, liberal nationalism is an autonomous political movement which does not need to link itself to divinity – as ethnocentric nationalism does – to demand the protection of its political rights. Secondly, it claims that each nation has its own peculiar sociological characteristics. Nationalists demand the protection of these cultural features. Given that these sociological aspects are different, different nations have different claims. This point is crucial for supporters of regional movements who demand constitutional recognition of their national identity. Thirdly, liberal nationalism recognises the existence of equal rights among different nations. Smith explains that the acknowledgment of the existence of other groups with their own claims makes liberal nationalism respectful of pluralism (Smith 1971, 171). Polycentric nationalism, Smith continues, supports an idea of world order in which liberty depends on the dialectic equilibrium between the development of national identities and democracy, each of which makes its own contribution to humanity by expressing its own cultural character in a state of its own (Smith 1971, 171).

At first sight, Bauman appears to agree with Smith's analytical account of the role of nationalism in modern constitutional democracy. Individuals in a liberal society interact with each other, and this process takes place within a national community which becomes an element of the democratic procedure. This is so, Bauman argues, even if the relationship between the two theoretical perspectives is problematic.

> The conflict inside the pattern of the republic is always there, and the danger of striking a wrong kind of compromise or of venturing too far in making room for one principle and unduly constraining the other is always lurking in the wings. And yet the two principles are like two legs – the republic would not walk straight without either (Bauman 1999, 166).

However, he makes clear that the political success of nationalism and the development of modern constitutional democracy are normatively unrelated.

> Apart from operating on the same ground and aspiring to be the principal adhesive which binds and holds together the same population, republic and nation differ from each other in virtually every other respect. Each one, being doomed to the company of the other (Bauman 1999, 163).

The identity-seeking process which supports modern nationalism, he argues, was an articulate attempt to create an orderly mass society, whereas constitutional democracy represents the aspirations of creating a political space where claims are mediated by the democratic process.

> Time and again after a long period of peaceful coexistence it once more flares into the open for one reason or another; it does so, for instance, today in Europe, where the eminently expandable republics rush into the European Union while the eminently unstretchable nations stay behind and lean over backwards to hold the escaping republics back (Bauman 1999, 163).

The dilemma, Bauman observes, which the polycentric nation state cannot solve is that, on the one hand, citizens are in a contractual partnership with the liberal set of principles embedded in the democratic constitution, yet on the other hand, they are organic members of the national community which has a democratically unquestionable system of values.

> Nationalism proclaimed the nation itself, the living legacy of long and tortuous history, to be a good in its own right – and not just one good among many others, but the supreme good, one that dwarfs and subordinates all other goods. (Bauman 1999, 165).

Bauman points out the radical difference between ethnic identities, which preceded the formation of modern nation states, and sub-national and tribal communities which claim ethnic credentials in a globalised society. Modern constitutional democracies are – Bauman agrees with Smith – the result of a political bargain between different ethnic groups and liberal values protected by the state. The nation state emerged from the bargaining process which saw ethnic groups relinquish their parochial claims in exchange for the constitutional protection of rights.

> Building the modern state consisted in replacing the old loyalties to the parish, to the neighbourhood community or to the artisan guild by new citizen-style loyalties to the

> abstract and distant totality of the nation and the laws of the land. [...] The constructing and servicing of the modern order required managers and teachers. The era of state- and-nation-building had to be, and was, a time of direct engagement between the rulers and the ruled (Bauman 2001, 127).

However, global interrelations have revealed the limits of the nation state. The state cannot guarantee the protection of rights and this has stimulated a quest for new regional and local protections. These new sub-national communities claim an affiliation of those which preceded the formation of the modern state – and in certain cases they share the same geographical setting – but they are part of a new social phenomenon which is fomented by globalisation and cannot be accommodated in Smith's analysis.

> Insecurity (among the immigrant as much as among the native population) tends to transform multiculturality into 'multicommunitarianism'. Profound or trifling, salient or hardly noticeable cultural differences are used as building materials in the frenzied construction of defensive walls and missile launching pads. 'Culture' becomes a synonym for a besieged fortress, and in fortresses under siege the inhabitants are required to manifest their unswerving loyalty daily and to abstain from any hob-nobbing with outsiders (Bauman 2001, 141).

The origin of new national communities is no longer due to an engagement between ethnic and enlightenment values (well described by Smith); instead, it is the product of globalisation, or better, a by-product of it. 'Nowadays community is sought as a shelter from the gathering tides of global turbulence – tides originating as a rule in faraway places which no locality can control on its own (Bauman 2001, 142). However, the attempt to shape new identities on the basis of the medieval association which preceded the state is impossible. 'The construction of walled-up communities ... instead of aiming at the sources of insecurity, it channels attention and energy away from them' (Bauman 2001, 143). This inadequacy is sensed by community members, but they are forced to linger within the boundaries of their new chosen identity till a new, more attractive group appears.

> The main, and most nerve-breaking, worry is not how to find a place inside a solid frame of social class or category and, having found it, how best to guard it and avoid eviction. What makes one worry it is the suspicion that the hard-won framework will be soon be torn apart or melted (Bauman 2001, 126).

These cycles of community formations cannot be explained by Smith's account of the role of nationalism in modern society. Let me clarify this point with an example. Since 1991 an Italian political party, the Lega Nord has put forward a claim for an independent Northern Italy. The political party created *ex novo* a nation (Padania), a historical past loosely connected with the confederation of free city-states that defeated the troops of the Emperor Barbarossa (Battle of Legnago, 1176), and a set of symbols. Both name and historical past were constructed through a selective reading of medieval history which could not pass the most basic test of congruence. For instance, the original Lega included cities from central Italy. Despite its precarious ethnic foundation, the Lega Nord won the administrative election in

Milan, the economic heart of the country (1992), and then (1997) joined a coalition which won power nationally. If we exclude the brief parenthesis (seven months) of Prodi's executive, the Lega Nord has been the third most influential political party within Berlusconi's coalition on the Italian executive between 1997 and the 2006 parliamentary election. However, in the past few years the league has lost most of its political impetus. Diatribes over the geopolitical boundaries of the self-proclaimed Northern Italian republic, support for a controversial constitutional reform of the regional system, and the emergence of new ethnic groups within the original Lega have fragmented an already geographically localised political movement.

Obviously, the case of Lega Nord in Italy cannot be compared with other ethnic communities which have a more substantial historical base (such as the Scottish, the Welsh, or the Basque) but it is exactly that historical idiosyncrasy which makes the Lega an archetype of identity formation in a globalised society (for other examples of new tribalism, see Bauman 1993, 238).

Constitutional identities in a liquid society

Bauman's analysis is multi-faceted. On the one hand, it describes modern globalised society as a complex multi-level interaction between dynamic identities. On the other hand, liquid modernity explains the effect of this complexity at an epistemic level. In this section, I will adopt Bauman's epistemic account in order to shed new light on the role of national identity in modern constitutional democracy.

However, in preparation for this analysis, some points need to be clarified. First, Bauman's theory of liquid modernity is not, and was never intended to be, a constitutional theory which suggests an alternative constitutional template for a globalised polity. Instead, the term liquid modernity includes a series of reflections on the recent developments of modern society. Concepts such as community and identity are analysed by Bauman to 'make sense' of their increased popularity. It is this reflective process which reveals the limits of theoretical perspectives such as ethnic nationalism, communitarianiam, and cosmopolitanism which foment the constitutional debate over the role of nationalism in modern democracy. Second, the debate is not whether national identity is a sociological phenomenon that threatens democracy, as suggested by cosmopolitans or the guarantor of political stability as suggested by nationalists. In this chapter the issue discussed is, rather, this: has modern constitutional theory sensed the sociological changes brought about by globalisation in the role of national identity in modern democracy?

The short answer to this question is affirmative. Authors such as Tierney (2004, 2005), Tully (2001; 2002a), and Walker (2002) have recently questioned the myths surrounding the concept of national sovereignty and criticised legal narratives which neglect, or unreasonably simplify, the role of national identities in modern constitutional democracy. Even if these authors do not refer directly – as far as I know – to Bauman's concept of liquid modernity, their analyses adopt the same epistemic structure. First, they describe analytically the new level of social complexity which characterises modern globalised societies. Then, they point out the theoretical limits of current constitutional conceptions.

For instance, in his theorisation of constitutional pluralism, Walker argues that constitutional narratives require a new structural dimension which acknowledges the developments of new socio-political identities (Walker 2002, 354). At first sight, Walker observes, demanding constitutional recognition of identities which demand unilateral secession or independence appears counter-intuitive. If these claims manage to attract enough political support they may dissolve the very constitutional system which has recognised them. However, placing theoretical claims in a democratic arena reveals their structural coherence and supports the democratic process that legitimates constitutional norms.

Like Bauman's analysis of the role of community (Bauman 1993; 2001), Walker's concept of constitutional pluralism does not substantively acknowledge cultural diversity, which simply gives the problematic relations between ethnicity and democracy a different label; rather, it points out the dynamic effect of identity formation at normative level. This move reveals the limits of constitutional theories which fail to question the relationship (this point is also made by Canovan 1996) between liberal values and national sovereignty.

Walker's work is particularly illuminating at a European level. The collapse of the constitutional treaty and the subsequent extended period of reflection has created the conditions for a renewed constitutional debate on the feasibility of such a project. On the one hand constitutional theorists, such as MacCormick (1999) and Weiler (2001), argue that European constitutional norms can be mediated only within the civic network of liberal institutions which pragmatically underpin the constitutional model they aspire to supersede, notably, the template of the sovereign nation state. On the other hand, political theorists such as Habermas (see, for instance, Habermas 2003) argue that a European constitution should be based on the republican values which politically and culturally defined European common culture. However, Neil Walker (2007) argues that both European political theorists and public law lawyers overlook the integrative role of the process of constitutional law making in modern democracies.

Tully's analysis (1995) of the relationship between constitutional theory and identity formation follows even more closely the methodological structure proposed by Bauman. He describes the complex process of identity formation adopted by Native Canadians as interplay between traditional beliefs and modern legal concepts. The sociological structures of these tribal identities, which historically preceded the constitutional formation of the Canadian Federation, are rapidly adapting to the new legal scenario. Tully argues that this process is not acknowledged at theoretical and constitutional level (2001). The process of identity formation is overlooked by those who consider the formation of new national identity the first step towards segregation, but this fear is unproved (a similar point is argued in Tierney 2005, 162). The relationship between identity and democracy – Tully conceives – creates a tension between those who demand recognition of their national identity and those who refuse this claim on the ground that it is theoretically incompatible with a constitutional state.

> Consequently, multinational democracy appears to run against the prevailing norms of legitimacy for a single–nation democracy and it is condemned as unreasonable or

> abnormal by both the defenders of the status quo and the proponents of secession (Tully 2001, 3).

However, Tully – like Bauman – reflects on the counter-factuality of this theoretical position. The most common political demand of modern national groups is not independence and state sovereignty, as widely assumed, but the acknowledgment of changed socio-political circumstances. The connection between independence, which in the modern world is a chimera for any state, Renan's ethnic homogeneity (1996), and national aspirations is due to the overlapping of meaning between nation and state sovereignty.

> This classic understanding of the freedom of self-determination has been called into question and discredited by the persistence of struggles for recognition in the very societies which were until recently legitimated by it, for the struggles demonstrate that the constitution is not acceptable for all. As a result, the question of the freedom of self-determination is raised anew. It is raised in the context of multinational societies whose members have passed through the experience of struggles over recognition and learned that these do not admit a definitive solution (Tully 2001, 6).

Even if this belief is historically inaccurate, individuals have the tendency to understand democracy as a technical apparatus for finding political solutions within a single national community. The misunderstanding of the relationship between a national population and democracy transforms the constitutional systems of modern states into an 'empire of uniformity' (a similar point is made by Hardt and Negri 2000, chapters 1–3; see, also, Christodoulidis 1998). Modern constitutionalism and the concept of popular sovereignty eliminate cultural diversity as a constitutive aspect of politics (Tully 1995, 63). Tully observes that an unreasonable denial of the role of national identities in a globalised society is particularly evident in the liberal interpretation of cosmopolitanism. Liberalism considers the constitutional recognition of a national identity to be theoretically inconsistent with the principle of equality. 'Modern constitutionalism developed over the last four centuries around two main forms of recognition: the equality of independent, self-governing nation-states and the equality of individual citizens' (Tully 2001, 15). In a legal system in which all individuals are equal, there is little space for the political claims of a group which asserts to be different.

> When forms of multinational federalism are advanced as solutions to some of the demands of cultural recognition, they appear 'ad hoc', even as a threat to democracy, equality and liberty, rather than as forms of recognition that can be explained and justified in accordance with the principles of constitutionalism (Tully 2001, 15).

However, the institutional attempt to channel the process of identity recognition into a rigid legal structure or the a priori ruling out of claims related to the protection of national identities transforms a constitutional theory into a homogenising ideology which exploits and destroys cultural diversity.

Again, like Bauman, Tully does not support the substantive claims of ethnic communities, nor rigid cosmopolitanism; rather, he contextualises ongoing constitutional debates on the role of sub-national and ethnic identities. This procedure reveals their internal epistemic incongruence which – and this is a peculiar element of constitutional theory – begs the question of their democratic coherence.

> The principle of democracy (or popular sovereignty) requires that, although the people or the peoples who comprise a political association are subject to the constitutional system, they, or their representatives, must also impose the general system on themselves in order to be sovereign and free, and thus for the association to be *democratically* legitimate. The sovereign people or peoples 'impose' the constitutional system on themselves by means of having a say over the principles, rules and procedures through the exchange of public reasons in the democratic practice of deliberation (Tully 2002, 205).

A constitution, Tully argues, should consider the recognition of cultural diversity to be part of the democratic practice of contesting and understanding previous cultural and theoretical assumptions.

> A contemporary constitution can recognise cultural diversity if it is received as what might be called a 'form of accommodation' of cultural diversity. A constitution should be seen as a form of activity, an intercultural dialogue in which culturally diverse sovereign citizens of contemporary societies negotiated agreement on their forms of association over time in accordance with the three conventions of mutual recognition, consent, and cultural continuity (Tully 2001, 31).

If we insert the concept of a nation-state into a globalised society, the demands of national groups become expressions of political freedom which might be channelled into constitutional norms. But democracy is perpetuated by the practice of making decisions which leads to the formation of constitutional rules, not by norms. It is precisely for this reason that rigid constitutional techniques such as federalism, confederation, and regionalism do not represent a solution to the problematic relationship between the concept of nation, democracy, and legal system.

> It [the question of freedom] is raised in the context of multinational societies whose members have passed through the experience of struggles over recognition and learned that these do not admit a definitive solution (and so cannot be accommodated within the classic understanding of self-determination). Rather, these contexts constitute an enduring dimension of modern politics: the public disclosure of misrecognized identities and the demand that the other members acknowledge these and respond (Tully 2001, 6).

Again, Tully does not solve the debate regarding the substantive relationship – or lack of it – between liberal values and nationalism, nor does he discuss the role of constitutional norms in a globalised society; rather, he contextualises constitutional conceptions which attempt to confine dynamic social entities within rigid legal frames. The recognition of national identities already occurs in many constitutional democracies, such as Canada, Belgium, Switzerland, Spain and the UK, but its normative impact in modern democracies is limited to proposed constitutional answers, such as the adoption of a federal system or devolution (for a detailed critical analysis of the role of sub-national constitutional movements, see, for instance, Tierney 2004). Instead, the acknowledgement of national identities, Tully argues, should be considered a general obligation for any democratic community which wants to maintain the linkage between legal system and people(s).

However, the process of recognition of national identities is problematic; how can modern constitutional democracy accommodate ethnocentric political claims? Could we allow nationalistic demands in a public debate that discriminated against women or immigrants? Can a national identity use the political arena for articulating anti-democratic political demands? This is a delicate issue since a debate about racist claims made by a national group can divide a community regardless of political approval. The Lega Nord has used the protection of political freedom in a relentless campaign against the inhabitants of southern Italy who are portrayed as lazy and dishonest. Should we allow these political claims in a modern constitutional democracy? There are no easy constitutional answers to this problem. However, Bauman's theorisation of liquid modernity might indirectly suggest a gambit. If Bauman is correct, the process of communal identity formation is an endless multi-phase cycle closely related to globalisation trends. The constitutional aspirations of new sub-national communities increase the mediating interest of individuals disillusioned by their present communal identity, and that, in turn, might quickly swell the ranks of sub-national movements.

Conclusion

Bauman's hermeneutic analysis of the socio-political effects of globalisation is illuminating. With his concept of liquid modernity, he minutely defines the interrelationships between apparently unrelated social phenomena. According to his account, emerging regional movements are responses to globalised trends, such as the consolidation of English as new *lingua franca*, and immigration which has melted old social and moral frames of reference. Geopolitical borders are washed away by world-wide policies decided by international organisations and uncontrolled economic trends. These axiological elements of modernity, Bauman argues, provide the conditions for a social sense of anxiety. Social and political theories cannot be based on rigid normative definitions. For instance, in his analysis of the emerging role of communitarianism, Bauman makes clear the incongruence of communitarian normative claims based on the notion of a socially coherent and closed community. This process of contextualising theoretical claims, I argue, brings a fresh perspective to the ongoing debate on the role of national identity in modern constitutional democracy.

Constitutional theories proposed by authors such as Walker and Tully have sensed the new normative scenario brought by globalisation and have suggested new conceptual analyses of the role of cultural diversity in modern society. Even if these new constitutional theories do not refer directly to Bauman's work, they share, first, a critique of past rigid conceptions of modernity which, in the case of constitutional law, have the tendency to entrench legal formalism, and second, a vision of society as a complex interplay of different socio-political elements. By questioning basic socio-political assumptions such as territorial sovereignty and ethnic uniformity, these authors also reveal a new democratic dimension to the debate on the role of identity in modern constitutional theory. A democratic constitution has to recognise cultural diversity and the social entities which represent it. That recognition, as Tully argues, is a logical requirement of any democratic debate which assumes normative significance in a discussion of the role of sub-national, ethnic or tribal identities in modern constitutional democracy. Tully's idea is innovative but it is also risky. It opens the political debate to ethnic claims which – if they generate enough of a political consensus – might endanger the democratic stability of a polity. It is a danger unavoidable in Bauman's conceptualisation of liquid society.

References

Anderson, B. (1983), *Imagined Communities: Reflections on the Origin and Spread of Nationalism* (London: Verso).

Anderson, G.W. (2005), *Constitutional Rights After Globalization* (Oxford: Hart).

Arendt, H. (1958), *The Origins of Totalitarianism* (London: G. Allen & Unwin).

Arendt H. and Charles R. (1958a), *The Human Condition* (Chicago: University of Chicago Press).

Bauman, Z. (1993), *Postmodern Ethics* (Oxford: Blackwell Publishing).

Bauman, Z. (1997), 'Right or Wrong – My Country', in *Argument*, 39, 327–330.

Bauman, Z. (1999), *In Search of Politics* (Cambridge: Polity Press).

Bauman, Z. (2000), *Liquid Modernity* (Cambridge: Polity Press).

Bauman, Z. (2001), *Community: Seeking Safety in an Insecure World* (Cambridge: Polity Press).

Bauman, Z. (2001a), 'Identity in the globalising world', in *Social Anthropology*, 9/12, 121–130.

Bauman, Z. (2007), 'Uncertainty and Other Liquid-Modern Fears', in J. Přibáň (ed.), *Liquid Society and Its Law* (Aldershot: Ashgate).

Breda, V. (2004), 'The Incoherence of the Patriotic State: A Critique of Constitutional Patriotism', in *Res Publica*, 10, 247–265.

Breda, V. (2006), 'A European Constitution in a Multinational Europe or a Multinational Constitution for Europe?', in *European Law Journal*, 12, 330–344.

Christodoulidis, E. (1998), *Law and Reflexive Politics* (Dordrecht: Kluwer).

Canovan, M. (1996), *Nationhood and Political Theory* (Cheltenham: Edward Elgar).

Canovan M. (1997), *Patriotism Is Not Enough* (Exeter: University of Exeter Press).

Eco, U. (1994), 'Apocalypse Postponed', in R. Lumley (ed.), *Perspectives* (London: British Film Institute).

Estlund, D. (1997), 'Beyond Fairness and Deliberation', in J. Bohman and W. Rehg (eds.), *Deliberative Democracy: Essays on Reason and Politics* (Cambridge, Mass.: MIT Press).

Freud, S. (1917), 'The Taboo of Virginity', in *S.E. XI*, 191–208.

Gellner, E. (1998), *Nationalism* (London: Phoenix).

Habermas, J. (1976), *Legitimation Crisis* (London: Heinemann).

Habermas, J. (1992), 'Citizenship and National Identity: Some Reflections on the Future of Europe', in *Praxis International*, 12:1, 1–19.

Habermas, J. (1996), *Between Facts and Norms: Contributions to a Discourse Theory of Law and Democracy* (Cambridge: Polity).

Habermas, J. (1996), 'The European Nation State. Its Achievements and Its Limitations', in *Ratio Juris*, 9, 125–137.

Habermas, J. (1998), 'The European Nation-State: On the Past and Future of Sovereignty and Citizenship', in *Public Culture*, 10, 397-416.

Habermas, J. (1999a), 'The European Nation-State and the Pressures of Globalization', in *New Left Review*, 1/235, 46–59.

Habermas, J. (1999b), *The Inclusion of the Other: Studies in Political Theory*, edited with an introduction by P. De Greiff (Cambridge: Polity).

Habermas, J. (2001), 'Constitutional Democracy: A Paradoxical Union of Contradictory Principles?', in *Political Theory*, 29, 766–781.

Habermas, J. (2001a), *The Postnational Constellation*, trans. and edited by M. Pensky (Cambridge: Polity).

Habermas, J. (2003), 'Toward a Cosmopolitan Europe', in *Journal of Democracy*, 14, 86–100.

Habermas, J. (2006), *The West Divided* (Cambridge, Polity).

Hardt, M. and Negri, A. (2000), *Empire* (Cambridge, Mass.: Harvard University Press).

Ignatieff, M. (1994), *Blood and Belonging: Journeys into the New Nationalism* (London: Vintage).

MacCormick, N. (1991), 'Is Nationalism Philosophically Credible?', in W. Twining et al. (eds.), *Issues of Self-determination* (Aberdeen: Aberdeen University Press).

MacCormick, N. (1995), 'What Place for Nationalism in the Modern World?', in S. Caney et al. (eds.), *National rights and international obligations* (Newcastle-upon-Tyne: Westview Press) 34–52.

MacCormick, N. (1999), *Questioning Sovereignty. Law, State and Nation in the European Commonwealth* (Oxford: Oxford University Press).

NationMaster, (2006), *Encyclopaedia: Demographics of San Marino* (available at: http://www.nationmaster.com/encyclopedia/Demographics-of-San-Marino).

Nino C.S. (1996), *The Constitution of Deliberative Democracy* (New Haven: Yale University Press).

Pÿibáÿ, J. (2006), 'The Time of Constitution-Making: On the Differentiation of the Legal, Political and Moral Systems and Temporality of Constitutional Symbolism', in *Ratio Juris*, 19:4, 456–78.

Rawls, J. (1993), *Political Liberalism* (New York: Columbia University Press).

Renan, E. (1996), *Que'est-ce qu'une nation?/What Is a Nation?* (Toronto: Tapir Press).

Schmitt, C. (1976), *The Concept of the Political*, edited by G. Schwab and L. Strauss (New Brunswick, N.J.: Rutgers University Press).

Smith A.D. (1971), *Theories of Nationalism* (London: Duckworth).

Smith, A.D. (1981), *The Ethnic Revival* (Cambridge: Cambridge University Press).

Smith, A.D. (1986), *The Ethnic Origins of Nations* (Oxford: Basil Blackwell).

Smith, A.D. (1992), *Ethnicity and Nationalism* (New York: E.J. Brill).

Taylor, C. (1989), 'The Liberal-Communitarian Debate', in N.L. Rosenblum (ed.), *Liberalism and the Moral Life* (Cambridge, Mass.: Harvard University Press).

Taylor, C. (1992), *Multiculturalism and 'The Politics of Recognition'*, edited by A. Gutmann (Princeton: Princeton University Press).

Tully, J. (1995), *Strange Multiplicity: Constitutionalism in an Age of Diversity* (Cambridge: Cambridge University Press).

Tully, J. (2001), 'Introduction', in J. Tully et al., *Multinational Democracies* (Cambridge: Cambridge University Press).

Tully, J. (2002) 'Political Philosophy as a Critical Activity', in *Political Theory*, 30:4, 533–55.

Tully, J. (2002a), 'The Unfreedom of the Moderns in Comparison to Their Ideals of Constitutional Democracy', in *Modern Law Review*, 65:2, 204–228 .

Tierney, S. (2004), *Constitutional Law and National Pluralism* (Oxford: Oxford University Press).

Walker, N. (2002), 'The Idea of Constitutional Pluralism', in *Modern Law Review*, 65:3, 317–59.

Walker, N. (2005), 'The Migration of Constitutional Ideas and the Migration of the Constitutional Idea: The Case of the EU', (EUI Law Working Paper No. 2005/11).

Walker, N. (2007), 'Post-Constituent Constitutionalism', in M. Loughlin and N. Walker (eds.), *The Paradox of Constitutionalism* (Oxford: Oxford University Press).

Walzer, M. (1983), *Spheres of Justice: A Defense of Pluralism and Equality* (New York: Basic Books).

Weiler, J.H.H. (1999), *The Constitution of Europe: Do the New Clothes Have an Emperor? and other Essays on European Integration* (Cambridge: Cambridge University Press).

Weiler, J.H.H. (2001), 'The Promised Constitutional Land', in *Kings College Law Journal*, 12:1, 5–16.

Wittgenstein, L. and Anscombe, G.E.M. (1968), *Philosophical Investigations* (Oxford: Blackwell).

PART V
LIQUIDITY OF SOCIAL INCLUSION POLICIES, MIGRATIONS AND INTEGRATIONS

Chapter 9

The Liquidity and Solidity of Contemporary Social Reality: The Example of Social Inclusion Policies[1]

Pierre Guibentif

In his recent book, *Europe: An Unfinished Adventure*, Zygmunt Bauman puts forward a definition of the European way of practising culture, which would serve admirably as a programme for the present chapter:

> First it was the 'world out there' which was transferred from the penumbra of *zuhanden* into the searchlight and spotlight of *vorhanden* – but thereafter the act of transfer itself was subjected to the same operation (Bauman 2004, 11).

My purpose here, indeed, is to discuss some observations gathered in the course of research I have carried out, using the concept of 'liquidity' formulated by Bauman, and, at the same time, to discuss this concept itself, reflecting what impact it has had on my way of looking at the contemporary social world.

There are two reasons for adopting this approach to Bauman's work. A general reason, which has guided my work as a sociologist for several years, is the assumption that one of the main challenges faced by our discipline nowadays is to feed theory back into the empirical work. Ambitious theoretical proposals are available, shaped already in narrow contact with empirical researches. The development of both these theoretical elements and the practice of empirical research depends upon our ability to preserve the connection between these two levels of scientific activity. One way of doing this is to extract descriptive concepts from the theories available (Guibentif 2001b) – or to couple some interpretive concepts with the descriptive concepts best suited to such coupling (Guibentif 1995) – and to apply them to new data. Benefits are twofold: the operation may shed new light on these data; it also may supply arguments for a critical discussion of the theoretical input.

A second motive is related specifically to Zygmunt Bauman's interpretation of our time. To make things clear from the outset, my deep conviction is that his recent reflections both on the impact of the current societal 'fluidification' and the corresponding emergence of the category of 'human waste' give a very accurate account of our time, and call for urgent debate and action. However, I see our primary role as sociologists in supplying information on the facts or, in terms Bauman probably

1 I warmly thank Richard Wall for his careful language editing of this chapter.

would accept, in giving these facts an adequate status of reality, in making them *vorhanden*. Debate is another issue, and is, obviously, not a specifically sociological task. In other words, the most appropriate tribute we can pay, as sociologists, to Bauman's thesis of the 'liquidity' of our time is to analyse on a concrete empirical level what, in our contemporary social world deserves to be described as 'liquid'; and what precisely this qualification means.

I shall start with a general introduction to the concept (I), followed by a presentation, based on that concept, of a concrete social context (II), and finally by some more evaluative thoughts on the concept (III).

Liquidity-solidity as a concept and as a metaphor

After some years of in-depth discussion of our current time, Zygmunt Bauman was led to consider the word 'liquid' as most appropriate to formulate a synthetic qualification of it.[2] The word seemed strong enough to him to be used not just as one among many adjectives in his discourse, but as the crucial term in the title of several books, such as: *Liquid Modernity* (2000) and *Liquid Love* (2003). In the meanwhile, many commentators gratefully adopted the word.

Now that I am attempting to reuse the word for my own sociological work, it is worth questioning its status in the writings of Zygmunt Bauman. What justifies this discussion, beyond the need to introduce the analysis of socio-legal phenomena in the second part of this chapter, is that Bauman's success in launching the notion of 'liquidity' gives us a striking opportunity to reflect how we sociologists think, write and debate.

Arguably, the status of 'liquidity' in Bauman's work is twofold. On the one hand, it operates as a concept; on the other hand, as a metaphor.

Let us briefly recall what concepts are: words, the meaning of which has been shaped by specialists in such a way as to make them fit for a use as far as possible not conditioned by their 'common' meaning, mainly by mechanisms such as explicit

---

2 For earlier attempts to qualify the current time, see for instance Bauman (1998b, ch. 2). The appearance of the word 'liquid' in 2000 is a good example of the way Bauman produces notions in the very process of writing. In terms of comparative sociological theorizing, he does this in a manner which is different from Bourdieu (1985), who develops his concepts in the course of the fieldwork, or Luhmann (1981), in whose work concepts emerge as a result of new connections between other, pre-existing concepts. As a result of his 'discursive' way of developing concepts, Bauman uses not only the word 'liquidity', but also 'fluidity' (explicit on this alternative: Bauman 2000, 2). Let us remember that the very first words of *Liquid Modernity* (Bauman 2000, 1) are, actually: '"Fluidity" is the quality of liquids and gases.' To make a detailed account of Bauman's thought on modern 'liquidity' (for an early use of the liquidity metaphor see, for instance, Bauman 1993, 117; see, also, Bauman 1998a, 156, where a quotation includes the phrase 'fluid conditions of generalized anomie') and to take the best possible advantages of the proposed metaphor, it could be worth discussing the differences between the two wordings. However, I will not tackle this discussion in the present chapter. I shall use, in principle, the words 'liquid' and 'liquidity', but I shall prefer 'fluidification'. I felt it was more accurate to use the adjective 'fluid' in some cases where the positive potential of modern society was to be highlighted.

definition and relation to other concepts. The most important features of concepts, however, are their functions. With their efforts to tame the meaning of the words they use, specialists (in our case sociologists) endeavour to create a language which enables them to produce new narratives of the world, not conditioned by our immediate experience. In the field of social sciences, more specific functions may be identified. The calling of the social sciences is to produce new visions of social reality on the basis of observation, interpretations of their results, and critical discussion of these interpretations. In these activities, concepts play basically three different roles: they help to designate elements of reality, thereby orienting the scientist's view of the facts to be observed (descriptive concepts); they help to connect different phenomena observed within a broader interpretive scheme (interpretive concepts); they identify positions in the debate between different interpretations (identifying concepts).

In general terms, the words 'liquidity' or 'fluidity', as opposed to 'solidity', refer to a common-sense notion in relation to their usage in common language. The notion becomes conceptual when it is joined to another, which common sense would not readily associate with it: the notion, not of a substance like water or oil, or, indeed, air or iron, but of a period of time, modernity. The concept of 'liquid modernity' is produced within the framework of a model of the recent evolution of mankind, represented as a succession of two phases: 'solid modernity' and 'liquid modernity'. By using these words, Bauman, as we know, wants, first of all, to break up a monolithic notion of 'modernity' that might exist as part of (modern?) common sense, and, secondly, to escape, in the realm of the language of specialists (sociologists, philosophers), from the connotations of the modernity/postmodernity dichotomy; in other words, to escape notions such as those which posit a radical shift between the two periods, or a contrast in evaluative terms. The adjectives 'solid' and 'liquid' separate two phases of the same longer period, and, a priori, neither of the two suggests the idea of something 'better'.

So we have here the making of a vocabulary which seeks to create a language independent of others. This is definitely a characteristic of concepts. Beyond this first 'test of conceptuality' we can now try to categorize the concepts of 'liquid' and 'solid modernity' according to the typology introduced above. Taking apart their identifying function (as things stand at the moment, given the visibility of Zygmunt Bauman's work, they easily identify a discourse as inspired by, or seeking to develop Bauman's intuitions), to what extent may they be considered as interpretive or descriptive concepts?

As already stated, the reference to liquid and solid modernity evokes a model of recent historical development. In this sense, they may inspire the interpretation of local phenomena, which may be considered as typical of one of the two phases identified. However, we have to recognize that their interpretive potential, in the narrower sense of the phrase, is rather limited. Nothing is suggested that would explain the differences between the two periods, or the transition from one to the other. We shall have to come back to this point in the third part of this chapter.

As such, the phrases 'solid modernity' and 'liquid modernity' are unlikely to guide concrete empirical research. On the other hand, 'solidity' and 'liquidity', as characterizing more specific phenomena, could play a role in the business of observation. Actually, this is quite a specific role: they do not orient the view of the researcher towards specific phenomena (as would be the case for concepts like 'organization', 'nuclear family', 'profession', and so on) but programme an operation of measuring phenomena on a specific scale, which goes from 'solid' to 'liquid', just as one can measure phenomena according to their level of 'differentiation' (Guibentif 2001b), or by applying the two scales of the 'grid-group table' of Mary Douglas (among other sources, Douglas and Ney 1998, 100).[3] However, if we are to accept these descriptive versions of the concepts of 'solidity' and 'liquidity', some methodological questions have now to be tackled. What do we mean by 'solid' and 'liquid', since both words are admittedly used in a metaphorical sense, and have lost their obvious literal meaning? And, as soon as new definitions are available, the question will be: what are the possible empirical indicators of the levels of liquidity/solidity? These are the questions we will have to handle throughout the second part of this chapter.

The full understanding of a concept requires its analysis as part of a broader conceptual network. Such a network of concepts may be more or less coherent and be conceived of as forming a unity. Efforts in the direction of such coherence and unity correspond to what we used to call 'theoretical work' and, as far as such work succeeds, its results are called 'theories'. Zygmunt Bauman avoids such wording. According to his views, 'theory', as an order of concepts, typically belongs to solid modernity, 'theoretical efforts' being a kind of gardening of ideas, always tempted by 'legislative' ambitions. He definitely prefers a more 'fluid' way of dealing with ideas and concepts. But despite this liquidity, some links are emphasized.

The main relationship in this conceptual world, obviously, is the one set by the opposition between 'solid modernity' and 'liquid modernity'. Bauman gives more substance to this opposition mainly by making it correspond to another opposition, between work and consumption. Furthermore, he discusses in some detail the current period, relating 'liquidity' in particular to growing 'insecurity' and 'individualization'.

The set of concepts very briefly recalled above forms a coherent whole which may be described as a theory of modernity. It is more difficult to link other concepts, crucial in the development of Bauman's thought, to these theoretical elements. On several occasions Bauman insists on the relevance of humanity, beyond society. Trying to relate both lines of thought, we are led to the following question: does the transition from solid to liquid modernity correspond to changes in the way society deals with humanity? Or, in more general terms, to changes in the relationship between society and humanity?

---

3 In a more detailed account of the diversity of sociological concepts, one would have to distinguish the kind of scale created by these concepts: 'independent scales', in the sense that they are likely to be applied to different social phenomena, and scales inherent to certain concepts, targeting a specific phenomenon. To quote a well-known example of a concept of the first type: the identification of 'poverty' requires the previous definition of levels of income or wealth, and the later measurement of concrete economic data; an example of a concept of the second type is conflict, where a scale of conflict's intensity cannot be constructed without reference to the notion of conflict itself.

In its first formulation, the question suggests the following answer: in both periods, what is at stake is the reduction of the unpredictable 'human impulse'. In the solid phase, this reduction was the result of a strong normative framework, set up by detailed legislation, implemented by heavy administrative structures. In such a setting, people had to fulfil specialized duties, not as human beings but as 'officials' and, in acting in such settings, they addressed not human beings, primarily, but issues to be solved. In the second, current phase, people seem to be more important than issues, and their lives to be more a matter of personal experience than of professional or functional performance.[4] But, on the other hand, the scope of personal experience seems to have shrunk in the course of the individualization process, and new categories of 'specific others' are made available, helping us to reduce the impulses likely to be triggered by experience of the others' situation.

In its second formulation, the question seems, at first glance, easier to answer with regard to 'liquid modernity'. On the one hand, Bauman observes how the liquidity of today's social arrangements does hamper the establishment of 'human bonds'. On the other hand, humanity seems also to be characterized as unpredictable, by something 'chaotic', and the dynamics made possible by these features are to be preserved against what Bauman sometimes calls 'ossification'. The 'fluid' settings of our time may be considered, at first glance, as more appropriate to these dynamics than the rigid institutions of the first type of modernity.

So the concept of 'liquidity' is to be related to a complex construct of notions, some of which – those regarding the difference between solid and liquid modernity – seek mainly to produce a suggestive view of our time; in this sense they are more descriptive tools. Others – those introducing the notion of 'human' – seem likely to provide some foundation for an interpretation or even an evaluation of that same historical period. Given the 'loose coupling' – in Goffman's words (1981, 11), rather than Luhmann's concept – of all these concepts, it makes sense to compare the thought of Bauman with observations gathered in particular empirical fields in relation to the concept of 'liquidity' and not, from the outset, with any kind of broader theory. We should never lose sight, however – and this was the purpose of this introduction – of the broader context of thought in which the notion emerged.

'Liquidity', however, is also a metaphor. A feature of social reality is designated by referring to an experience we have from another realm of reality, in this case, the physical world. In the work of Zygmunt Bauman this is one metaphor among countless others. Indeed, the frequency and diversity of metaphorical constructions in his writings is impressive. To quote just a few examples, some of the most eloquent: individuals, in solid modernity located in relation to each other like 'Lego or Meccano assembly pieces' (Bauman 1995, 153); places of employment feeling like 'camping

4 One is tempted here to add 'again', in allusion to a presumptive pre-modern phase in which the adiaphorizing mechanisms of modernity would not yet have reduced the human dimension in social relationships. But it would be rash to assume such an idyllic vision of pre-modern social togetherness. In any event, one would have to take into account the relevance of personal status, which heavily conditioned any impulse likely to arise in concrete face-to-face relations. A free person probably viewed the 'face' of a slave in a completely different way from that of a peer.

sites' (Bauman 2000, 149); the human world being at risk of 'ossification' (Bauman 2001, 13); culture fulfilling the function of a 'repair workshop' (Bauman 2004, 12).

Compared with other authors, Bauman is certainly one of those who make the most intensive use of metaphors. It challenges us, actually, to revise and enlarge the classical typology of sociological metaphors once proposed by Brown (1977): machines, organisms, language, dramas, and games. This may be related to other aspects of his way of working as sociologist, but also to the notion of society that underpins his writings.

Regarding his way of working let us remember that Bauman is, first of all, a writer. Among the typical activities of sociologists, this is certainly the one to which he has devoted most of his efforts, especially in recent years. Moreover, it is through the very process of writing that he intends to give strength to his ideas, much more than through the treatment of data,[5] or by shaping notions in the course of debates with other authors, or working to construct a coherent set of relations between concepts. In doing so, Bauman acknowledges one feature in particular of the current state of our discipline. Data are available, but their volume and mode of management make them unfit to supply the words of specialists with meanings likely to be understood by lay persons. With his commitment to metaphors, Bauman hopes to re-establish the links between sociological reflection and public debate.

Bauman's way of using metaphors in his writing may also be related to the relevance he gives to metaphors as a mechanism operating in social reality. Let us consider the following statement:

> In other words, bonds and partnerships tend to be viewed and treated as things meant to be *consumed*, not produced; they are subject to the same criteria of evaluation as all other objects of consumption. (Bauman 2000, 163; emphasis by Bauman.)

The idea underpinning the interpretation of social reality formulated here is that some realms of human activity may give rise to categories and attitudes likely to be transplanted to other realms of activities. Such an interpretation is grounded on several assumptions. First, that human activity, or at least part of it, requires semantic means that are unlikely to be found in the situation itself. This is a point on which Bauman insists on many occasions, notably by recalling Heidegger's distinction between *zuhanden* and *vorhanden*, and by developing his concept of culture. Things in 'the world out there', as well as my own behaviour, have to make sense to me. And that meaning has somehow to be created, which needs more than just one occasional event. Secondly, that these meanings of the world and of our acts may vary according to different types of situation. Up to that point, there is a close parallel between Bauman and Bourdieu, to whom practice requires the *habitus*, and the *habitus* is produced by *fields* which correspond to limited areas of social activity, and which actually come about in the very process of that limitation (among

5 It has to be noted, however, that his crucial work, *Modernity and the Holocaust* (1989), has as its explicit purpose the in-depth discussion of findings collected in the course of previous research carried out by fellow social scientists in order to 'feed them back into the mainstream of our discipline' (Bauman 1989, xiii). In that case, the work consisted precisely of dealing with observations.

other sources, Bourdieu 1985). What Bauman adds to that picture is the following hypothesis: in a social world where individuals often have to switch from one field to the other, they may take with them some of the cultural tools linked to one of these fields and reuse them in another field. Arguably, this may happen all the time when there is in one field a shortage of cultural tools, either because the activity is new, or because the field undergoes profound changes, challenging the relevance of the cultural tools developed under other historical conditions (as is the case today in the workplace). And the process will certainly be assisted by the fact that, in another field, strong and currently efficient categories are available (as with the consumer market today). Most important, obviously, are the effects of such a process. Indeed, the transplantation of categories means that a practice tends to be experienced not 'for itself' but through the prism (one more metaphor) of categories that are biased or at least conditioned by their origins.

Bauman pays special attention to some of these cases. Those in which categories originally shaped in a relationship between man and objects are imported into fields where they frame relations between different human beings. This is exactly what happens when a human encounter is tackled in terms of consumption, or, in the extreme case rightly pointed out by Bauman: when the destiny of a person is managed in terms coined in the context of waste recycling.

Impressed by the way these transfers of categories act upon our perception of social reality, Zygmunt Bauman attempts to take advantage, within the framework of the relationship with his readers, of a mechanism similar to these 'real existing metaphors', making extensive use of rhetorical metaphors.

Having discussed now these two roles of the notion of 'liquidity', both as a concept and a metaphor, one question remains: how do these two roles relate to one another? This is not an innocent question, since the metaphor draws its impact from the way it infuses the force of common-sense notions into the sociological discourse, while the concept draws its descriptive and interpretive potential from the distance it establishes between these two realms. We shall come back to it in the third part of this essay, after having carried out a practical application of the concept.

The concepts of 'liquidity' and 'solidity' applied to the field of social inclusion policies

We shall now attempt to use 'liquidity' and 'solidity' as descriptive concepts, that is, as tools for observing today's social world.

In his account of the liquid aspects of contemporary social world, Bauman considers mainly the life of individuals, in their private relations with other individuals, and at their workplace (Bauman 2000, 2003). The realm of individuals' experience certainly deserves priority in the analysis, considering the process of individualization that he rightly highlights in many of his recent papers (Bauman 2001). But individuals' experience is just one aspect of social reality. It has even been argued that it is not part of it, according to the provocative thesis of Niklas Luhmann (1984/1995, 255). Even if we do not go that far in challenging the individual dimension, we shall have to recognize that there is, in any event, another dimension, which could be called the organizational dimension.[6] In a summary account of Bauman's recent work, it could be said that, while he offers a thorough analysis of what happens at the individual level with the transition to liquid modernity, his analysis of the organizational dimension focuses on the period before that transition. This is one of the main issues of *Modernity and the Holocaust* (Bauman 1989). This is also his concern in his recent studies of the social state (Bauman 1998b, ch. 3; 2004, 74). So the field in which Bauman's thesis of contemporary 'liquidity' deserves further analysis is that of organizations after that transition. This is what I shall attempt to do here, analysing a domain which connects in many aspects directly to topics addressed in Zygmunt Bauman's recent books, namely, European policies of social inclusion.

The subject can be linked to Bauman's work in three ways. First, these policies address, precisely, people experiencing the contemporary liquidity of social bonds. In this sense, their object is also the main object of Zygmunt Bauman's sociology. Secondly, it confronts us with examples of a new generation of social policies, developed in the course of the transformation of the 'solid' social state. This gives us the opportunity to work further on the lines initiated by Bauman with his analysis of the social state, examining how it evolves in current 'liquid' times. Thirdly, it offers additional material for reflection on the role of Europe today.

Our question will be whether these policies confirm the 'liquidity' of our contemporary society. More specifically, we shall have to distinguish different aspects of these policies, provided that it is possible to measure levels of 'liquidity' in all these different aspects, thus paving the way to a global assessment of the liquidity of the society in which these policies are carried out. Obviously, a crucial methodological question is to specify indicators of what is called 'liquidity'. We assume, however, that this discussion has to be tackled not in abstract and general terms, but separately in relation to those particular aspects of the field under observation, where we may find a more solid ground for a truly methodological discussion.

In approaching the field to which the concepts of 'liquidity' are to be applied, we shall adopt the following division. First, there is what we could call an active side: people and organizations playing a role in the implementation of inclusion policies. Then there is a passive side: society as an object of these policies. Here a further distinction is needed. On the one hand, there is the social world that social policy aims to create or reinforce, in other words, society as a project. On the other hand, there is 'real' society, that is, the situations 'out there', as encountered by the agents of social policy, as they are before implementation of that policy, or as they become as a result of these policies. Finally, we shall examine in greater detail legislation, as one of the tools used by the active players in order to obtain some results on the passive side.

6 In the socio-legal field, the contrast between organizations and individuals has been emphasized in particular by Belley (2002). His discussion of this contrast draws upon the work of authors inspired by a systemist approach, like Teubner (1997).

(a) Agencies involved

Let us first remember the complex settings of the entities involved in the implementation of the policies concerned. By definition, implementing European policies of social inclusion brings together the European member states and the public agencies they comprise. Then we have European entities, playing a role in the definition and supervision of modes of cooperation between these states and public entities. The entity that dominates the scene here is the European Commission. Apart from this set of public entities, there is a universe of private entities, acting on their own initiative or in partnership with public entities. Such partnerships may work on the European, national or local level.

To characterize this domain of analysis, two modes of definition are available. On the one hand, we have what sociologists call structures, that is, a complex mix of legal definitions, effectively recognized, identifying single entities or relations between them, and material means, effectively available to these entities or circulating between them. On the other hand, strategies are being pursued and forces are used with a view to obtaining results, which reveals what sociologists usually call actors. The way in which these two aspects are linked is not discussed here. Let us just make one simple point: the legally defined entities do not necessarily correspond to actors. They may become actors under certain circumstances (for example, private associations – NGOs – acting as representatives of stakeholders). But they may also just provide the playing field for many different actors (which is usually the case for states). In a more specific hypothesis, they may form the field where several actors emerge in a particular relationship: an obvious example is the European Council, where the strategies of different governments meet.

What could be the concrete content of the concepts of 'liquidity' and 'solidity' in this domain? In the first place, it may refer to the durability of the entities: the longer they have been in existence, the more 'solid' the universe they form; the shorter, the more 'liquid'. It could also measure the durability of the relations between them. More subtly, it could be applied to the internal structures of the entities or to the more or less strict definition of their relationships with each other.

Let us first consider the simplest indicator of 'liquidity-solidity', the duration of entities. According to the twofold definition adopted here, we should examine successively the level of structures (formally existing entities) and the level of the actors.

As far as formally recognized entities are concerned, what we observe is a rather solid reality. States and the public agencies they include still play an important role. Some public agencies may be dismantled and others created, but a more detailed look on the ground reveals that, in many cases, new names are applied to previously existing entities, taking over their staff and facilities.[7] Some signs of 'liquidity' may,

7 Examples of the re-qualification of existing entities may easily be found in the field of social security agencies. In the case of Portugal, see the case of the regional agencies, renamed and submitted successively to different legal frameworks (Guibentif 1997, 230, 233). For another example, see the creation of the new French *Agence nationale de l'accueil des étrangers et des migrations* (ANAEM) (Guibentif 2005, 21).

however, be noted. Within the state administration, new kinds of 'commissions' or 'task forces' are created, which are conceived of, from the outset, as temporary or are supposed to function without their own staff and facilities. Examples of these are: the 'Contact and Assessment Teams' created for implementing the English rough-sleeping strategy, 'multidisciplinary teams run by the voluntary sector but with statutory involvement' (Vranken 2004, 21); an NGO operating at national level involving in its activity field social workers belonging to the municipalities in the Czech Republic (Minev 2005, 20). There is no doubt that such entities are becoming more frequent. A more significant trend towards 'liquidity' is the involvement of private entities. These entities, indeed, are perhaps easier to set up and more likely to disappear in the short run.

One phenomenon that is not easy to qualify by using a 'liquid-solid' scale is the emergence of new professions. 'Project managers' in agencies operating in cooperation with the European Commission; *social assessors* (*auditeurs sociaux*) newly trained in France in order to conduct social check-ups of the situation of new immigrants (Guibentif 2005, 18); *field social workers* in the Czech Republic (Minev 2005, 21), and so on. On the one hand, these new professions have in common a vocation to create bridges with more traditional professional practices, research, social service, legal advice, and so on. In this sense, they may allow some 'fluidification' in the cooperative arrangements between these other professions. On the other hand, however, they create new instances of solidity, by giving rise to new professional identities, or by imposing new constraints on the exercise of other professions.

It is more difficult to assess the development of relationships between entities. If we regard as solid a relationship that is subject to fixed principles and routines, there might be some trend towards 'liquidity'. If, on the other hand, we consider criteria such as the number of statutory players involved, or the steps to be performed in the carrying out of some activity, what we observe has rather 'solid' features. Where formerly a national public agency was in charge of public assistance tasks, designed according to locally identified needs, and had wide margins of discretion, we now find procedures which not only involve stricter governmental controls on the activity of that agency, but also require that local partnerships with private stakeholders be developed and, most interestingly, an evaluation ('peer review') of the activity of that agency by representatives of the administration of other European member-states. The 'peer review procedures', on the other hand, are subject to very detailed rules, imposing on all participants precise tasks of analysing, reporting, discussing, summarizing, and so on.

Regarding the actors in the field, we shall limit the present discussion to their number and durability. Consideration of relations between them would go well beyond the limited framework of this chapter. What we observe in terms of existing players confirms what observers of the current process of globalization already have pointed out: if years ago, under what Bauman calls solid modernity, social policies were designed by officials, working in a context dominated by the tensions between competing claims and the plans of employers organizations and trade unions, we now see a fuzzy picture in which numerous interest groups are present: professional organizations, consulting agencies, and so on, blurring the old divide between two opposing positions (World Commission 2004, 567ff.). Liquidification, we may say. Yes indeed. However, the increase in the number of these players is related to the rather solid design of European procedures for consultation and evaluation, which favours the creation of stakeholders' representations, and gives them a status as entities and acknowledges their arguments.

Moreover, the notion of fluidification may hide another phenomenon. If the great 'solid' divide is challenged by recent developments, this does not at all mean that tensions and conflicts disappear. The increasing number of players may give rise to new kinds of conflicts or divergences. Two examples: those reported in the case of the United Kingdom between new entities created by the government and some voluntary groups (which organize 'soup runs' making sleeping rough, dare one say, less unattractive: Vranken 2004, 25); or, in France, those opposing locally operating private associations and the state-run service for the reception of newly arrived migrants (Guibentif 2005, 41). Here the notion of a 'new pluralism' may be more appropriate than that of 'liquidity'.

To conclude this section, what we observe is not so much a process of general liquidification but, rather, new moments of solidification which permit new trends in fluidification to develop. We shall come back to this statement after having looked at other aspects of the field under analysis.

(b) Society as a project guiding social policies

Social policies are guided by a certain notion of society, or, to use the more abstract and apt phrase frequently used by Zygmunt Bauman, of social togetherness. The first and most explicit feature of that social togetherness is the one their designation explicitly refers to: what these policies are supposed to bring about is an 'inclusive society'. This notion actually creates a paradox. Indeed, at the very moment we present ourselves as inclusive, we recognize the relevance of the notion of exclusion. In more concrete terms, inclusion policies do aim to re-include people, re-establishing society as a whole, hosting all human beings. But by the way they formulate this aim and carry out measures to achieve it, they identify – 'make real' – the situation of exclusion. An attempt to escape the paradox is the use of the notion of 'risk of exclusion': nobody is actually excluded, but some of us require help, or else they will effectively be excluded. But still, such a discourse makes it possible to establish a divide between two categories of people, those included and those (at risk of being) excluded. The divide is both a symbolic one (there are categories made available to make it *vorhanden*) and a concrete one: people may or not be subject to inclusive social policy measures, to being targeted by such measures, and to being thereby officially recognized as at risk of being excluded. So one hardly can deny that an inclusive society is also always an exclusive one (Guibentif 2001a, 264).

What can be said about such an inclusive/exclusive society in terms of 'liquidity'? First of all, it confirms the portrait of liquid society drawn by Zygmunt Bauman, who relates the fluidification of social bonds to the emergence of the category of human waste (Bauman 2004, 77; Bauman 2007). This category is supposed to cover all those who have turned out to be no longer able to contribute to either production or consumption. As it is not possible for western societies to export them to other regions of the globe, we have to live with them. Since we cannot simply throw them away, we do our best to recycle them.

We could go further in discussing this notion of society in terms of solidity/liquidity. Since we are here discussing the general features of an 'image' of society, we shall, for the time being, use a very simple criterion for liquidity and solidity: what is likely to move in the picture? What are the fixed elements? Applying this criterion, we are led to an appreciation that is actually less cynical than the one of society recycling its human waste: society, more or less liquid in its core regions (we shall come back to this part of the picture in a moment) is conceived of as being surrounded by solid mechanisms which prevent people from falling outside society. This is precisely the idea conveyed by another metaphor familiar to politicians – the 'safety net'. As a matter of fact, inclusion mechanisms may be considered as 'solid' walls preventing people from falling outside society. The question that is left unanswered by this picture is the way people 'touching' these walls or 'safety nets' are treated. A general discourse cannot in fact tell us more than this about 'inclusion'. A more detailed picture appears when the operation of these nets and walls are evaluated, and this is what we shall examine in the next section. The general image that is most consistently offered to public opinion concerning these outer edges of society does not relate to the protective mechanisms themselves but, rather, to the people who benefit from them. And on that point, little is done to distance reality from Bauman's horrifying notion of human waste: people who reach these regions of society are presumed not to work because of their lack of skills, of flexibility, of will; or even worse, because they were attracted by the benefits that are within reach of those who are clever enough to cheat the welfare administration.

So there is a serious ambiguity: does the construction of those solid 'walls' or 'safety nets' reveal the human impulse spread through a collectivity that cares for those at risk of falling apart? Or the punitive instinct of the same collectivity addressing alleged 'freeloaders'? This ambivalence is felt by all those who hesitate to describe our states as social or security states.

A more detailed analysis of immigration policies reveals a further interesting aspect of the picture. What is at stake here is no longer the periphery but the centre of society where immigrants are supposed to be welcomed. Here we have to stress one crucial point: we are not discussing the 'reality of immigration out there', but the official rationale for some of the policies addressing them. In recent years, the main issue in immigration policies, at the national as well as the European level, has been the *integration* of migrants. The assumption underlying these policies is that concrete steps can be taken to make immigrants members of the host societies. Let us remember these steps which reveal, in rather concrete terms, a substantive notion of society. According to the current consensus in Europe (Niessen and Schibel 2004), the main integration measures are language training and civic education. What is a 'society' of which you are a member from the moment you speak a certain language and have assimilated some 'basic values'? It is a very specific kind of human togetherness just ensuring acceptable conditions for interaction and thus supplying the ground on which more demanding cooperative arrangements may be negotiated or implemented. To reconstruct such a notion of society should not lead us to underestimate what we have found. Indeed, such an elementary but, even so, substantive social fabric may create favourable conditions for the development of the most diverse and sophisticated undertakings and, for individuals who need to engage successively with different undertakings of this sort, provide them with minimal tools to assist with the transition between them.

The 'society' which is aimed at by such integration measures has all the characteristics of a 'liquid society'. One question worth asking here, however, concerns the location of such a society in time. According to Bauman, 'liquidity' is a feature of the recent 'second' phase of modernity. But society, in the above-reconstructed sense, is a phenomenon already observed by, among others, Georg Simmel. Confronting these two locations in time could lead to the following model of modern society: since early modernity there would have been a trend towards the differentiation of such a basic social fabric, loosely integrated, in this sense 'liquid' for a long time – actually strongly favoured by the development of industrial and commercial urban areas, and, parallel to that trend, the formation of new types of organization or togetherness – from the factory to the nuclear family which, for some decades, were quite 'solid'. These organizations and forms of togetherness underwent drastic changes in recent times, step by step liquefying those regions of the social fabric to which they formerly gave solidity. In other words, 'society', if there is a precise meaning to this concept, always was liquid; other levels of togetherness, on the other hand, are now in the course of being liquefied.

Admittedly, however, this is not the only concept of integration – and of society – European politicians refer to. A more ambitious concept exists, too. It conceives of integration as the result of economic, political, cultural and social inclusion (Spencer 2003). One could call it a communitarian concept, as opposed to a more liberal concept. Integration, in this sense, does not only involve providing individuals with the basic tools needed to join in more differentiated activities; it will be attained when the individual is included in those activities. Society is not just the background fabric in which more differentiated sets of social relations will develop; it is the whole set of social relations. So there is nowadays, in the European public sphere, a competition between two imaginary societies, one more liquid and the other more solid. Which brings us back to what has already been observed at the level of existing actors in the field (the two phenomena are obviously linked: the different models of society are invoked by different actors): the plurality of positions and the tension between them.

Given the competition between these two models of society, one could question Castoriadis's statement that Bauman likes to quote, namely that society has ceased to question itself (Bauman 2000, 22). Here we have, indeed, a question that addresses society. But if society is the object of the question, who asks the question? In very concrete terms, European experts in matters of social integration. Under these circumstances, we probably have to admit, again, that Castoriadis is right. On the one hand, experts' debates used to take place far from public awareness. So it is not society which asks the question. Actually experts do not represent society, but, on the contrary, speak instead of lay people whose opinion loses its legitimacy from the moment expert opinion is sought. On the other hand, the experts' role is not to ask, but to answer questions.[8]

This brings us back to the notion of 'liquidity' and to a contrast implicit in Zygmunt Bauman's work. 'Fluidification' of social relations may go along with the 'solidification' of some of the notions we use to qualify those social settings. So, we witness increasing 'liquidity' but at the same time we learn that 'there is no alternative' (Bauman 2004, 73, 78, 128), a rather 'solid' statement.

(c) Society as a result of social policies

Social policies in action do produce, as they are carried out, 'society', by compiling data and giving visibility to certain facts. Inclusion policies, as defined today, that is, those 'targeting' the situations of the people most at risk of exclusion, give visibility to a specific region of society: its 'margins', all that goes on close to the 'safety nets' or 'walls' surrounding it. Procedures such as 'peer reviews in the field of social inclusion policies', the results of which are available to the public, give a detailed account of what is going on in this region of society.[9]

Again, we must first give a more precise definition of what is solid or liquid here. On a first and factual level, we may take as our point of departure the broad definition of society underlying social policies: a set of individuals,[10] some of them in need of help, others better off. What could be called the 'liquidity' or 'solidity' of such a reality is the level of structuring of the relations between these individuals.

---

8 In a meeting about the integration of newly arrived migrants, I was told by a representative of one of the participating countries that 'integration' had recently been defined in a European expert meeting. The information was helpful. But to see the concept of 'integration' no longer open to sociological discussion, but taken over by European policy-making processes was, on the other hand, an intriguing experience of a concept's 'ossification' (Bauman 2001, 13). One could object here that sociologists are experts too. Indeed, they may act as experts in certain procedures but in general terms, the calling of sociology is not to supply experts, but to maintain a space for professionally trained data gathering and discussion of research results always open, however, to lay attention and permanently questioning its relationship to debates in the public sphere.

9 See, in particular: http://www.peer-review-social-inclusion.net/peer/en/index_html (last accessed November 2005). The summary reports of the different individual peer review procedures were also published as books.

10 Here we must note the considerable distance that exists between this concept of society and several sociological concepts that insist precisely on the difference between individual experience and social reality. The most radical is the systemic model put forward by Luhmann, already quoted. Zygmunt Bauman establishes a distinction worth comparing with the distinction between social communication and individual perception, even if its theoretical context and its aim are radically different: the distinction between society and humanity which underlies oppositions such as 'end-oriented, rational action' versus 'mutual assistance, solidarity, reciprocal respect' (Bauman 1989, 28) or 'ethical negotiation and consensus' versus 'personal morality' (Bauman 1993, 34). Actually, what is most relevant for sociology is not the gap between political and sociological concepts, but the gap within sociology itself between these more abstract concepts and the more concrete notion of grouping individuals that is also, often implicitly, used by sociologists themselves.

Here different criteria may compete: one criterion is that, in a given relationship, objectives and roles may be more or less precisely defined; another, not necessarily corresponding to the first, is the durability of the relationship. In connection with the definition of objectives and roles, another difference may – or may not – be related to a scale from liquid to solid: these objectives and roles may be more or less explicit, or, using the vocabulary of Mary Douglas, more or less institutionalized (1986, 46). The more consistent the formal definition, the more solid the reality it addresses is likely to be, since it will be more costly to reinvent, in practice, alternative objectives and roles. But at the same time, a clear, explicit definition also makes possible a clear rejection, in this sense: it allows more liquidity. We shall have to come back to this mixed appreciation. Let us, for the time being, accept the following simplifying criteria: the more institutionalized, the more solid, unless there are concrete indications that rejection of the institution is a viable alternative.

If we use the criterion of the level of structuring of the relationships under observation, we have to recognize that there are rather solid elements of the social fabric here. The roles of the professionals active in the field, as well as of the beneficiaries of the measures, are quite precisely defined. And a specific notion, frequently used in the design of social inclusion measures mirrors this idea of solidity quite well: the notion of pathways.[11] Beneficiaries of the measures are supposed to follow, as far as possible, pre-installed tracks. Another indicator of a fairly high level of solidity is the fact that people who have 'entered' a measure are likely to remain there for some time. The identification of this well-known 'poverty trap' has led to the design of sophisticated measures aimed at encouraging effective reintegration of the people to whom the measures are addressed into work-life balance, access to decent housing, and so on. Nevertheless, many people remain in situations of 'exclusion' for a long time (Vranken 2004, 22; Nicaise and Meinema 2004, 21; where one finds the almost Baumanian metaphor: 'the programme reached the hard core of the social assistance population').

This brings us back to the picture of a society surrounded by solid mechanisms, details of which are revealed in particular by evaluation procedures. In a pessimistic appreciation, these solid mechanisms of inclusion might be compared to the solid 'tightly closed containers' built up by our contemporary security states (Bauman 2007). Together with other, more punitive mechanisms, they would participate in the separation of liquid society from what Bauman calls human waste.

One objection to this picture is suggested by the analysis of integration policies aimed at migrants. Indeed, in this field 'pathways' are created not only for the 'excluded', but for all newcomers, with the objective of preventing exclusion. One could argue that immigrants, as strangers, are close to the category of people likely

11 For the relevance of the concept of pathways in the design of social inclusion policies, see Vranken (2004, 25); see, also, the Executive Summary of the Final Report 2004 of the peer review in the field of social inclusion programmes, by the INBAS/NIZW/European Centre Consortium, available at http://www.peer-review-social-inclusion.net/peer/en/general_information/exec_sum2004 (last accessed November 2004): 'Pathway approaches based on the assessment of the individual capabilities of clients and accommodating to their needs and potential pay attention to the long-term social inclusion process.'

to be submitted to tight 'solid' control measures. Another interpretation is that this treatment of all immigrants reveals a broader trend towards the creation of detailed 'pathways' for very different categories of people. This is at least what a look at national education systems suggests, where students are nowadays committed to follow detailed training programmes at least until their PhD. Or else, in a completely different field, the way people are channelled by physical devices in large stores, museums or, even more obviously, in airports.

Another trend that has to be mentioned here is the reinforcement of mechanisms of data collection on people subject to inclusion measures, and on the functioning of the agencies implementing inclusion policies, in relation to the development of internal and external evaluation procedures. Such data gathering requires procedures which burden the persons concerned with considerable constraints. In this sense, it may be considered as contributing to the solidification of the social fabric. The fact that this information exists may also condition the activity of people in a sense that could correspond to rather solid limitations.

(d) A tool for implementing social policies: legislation

In the attempt to apply Bauman's concept of liquidity to concrete social settings, we first looked at who is acting there, then at the projects orienting their activities, and at the results of these activities. An additional element of the social setting under analysis is the kind of tools used for carrying out these activities. As a sociologist of law, I pay special attention, among these instruments, to the law, and it is the law that will be discussed here. However, law is, obviously, not the only instrument available to social action. This was recognized decades ago even by law specialists, whose attention was focused on instruments specifically aimed at guiding social behaviour. These long established reflections on other tools which guide social action come under the heading of 'legal pluralism' (Simon 1998). Jurists themselves (a profession far older than our modern notion of law) have over the centuries applied different instruments to the handling of the cases submitted to them (Hespanha 2002).[12] As far as state activity is concerned, law was, for a long time, regarded as the main instrument (see the importance of law schools in the training of higher civil servants, or the relevance given to the notion of the *Rule of Law/Rechtsstaat/Etat de droit*). Recent research, however, at the crossroads between sociology of law and public policy studies, highlights the diversity of the instruments used by state agencies (Peters and Van Nispen 1998; Lascoumes and Le Galés 2004). Indeed, any public policy also uses material equipment, professions, procedures, and so on, as well as financial means. Law may play a role in the constitution of all these instruments, but in such a varying way that the recognition of their diversity is an indispensable first step in any reflection on the activity of the state.

This means that, in tackling the tools of social activity, we should widen the scope of our scrutiny. It would also be interesting to analyse why observers of the state's activity have for so long had their attention captured by the law, and why so

12 In this chapter, Hespanha revisits the transformation in history of the jurists' role on the basis of the main theses of Bauman (1987).

little attention has been paid to other instruments. The concrete division of function between the different instruments and its changes over time would also merit study. In the present essay, however, we shall restrict ourselves to the law, assuming that legislation is not only used as a tool for the activities of state agencies, but also for guiding citizens in their relations with these agencies, as well as shaping the image of the activity concerned in the eyes of a broader public.

Social policies, at a national as well as European level, are structured by detailed legislation. As relevant authors in socio-legal studies have pointed out, legislation is currently undergoing profound changes, changes that are also visible in the social area. Let us briefly recall the two main trends. One concerns the focus of legal production. In a process of 'decentralization of legality' (Přibáň 2001, 121), the legal 'order' ceased to be structured beneath one sole and unquestionable central reference, the national constitution. International and supranational standards and norms have acquired increased relevance (among many others, Teubner 1997; Roberts 1998; 2005). New agencies producing such norms appear, such as the WTO or regional entities like NAFTA or the MERCOSUR (López Ayllón and Fix-Fierro 1999). Numerous trans-national operations oblige courts and public agencies to deal with norms originated by different national orders (Gessner and Cem Budak 1999). The other trend concerns the nature of the norms. Apart from statutory law, enacted by the state, other forms of normativity are gaining in importance, such as the rules enacted by autonomous regulatory agencies, contractual arrangements negotiated between state agencies and relevant private actors, codes of conduct, and so on (among others, Belley 2002).

In the domain of social inclusion policies, both trends are observable. Since the beginning of the twentieth century, efforts have been made to give social rights international recognition and to create and strengthen agencies supervising the action of states in the social field. These efforts led to the foundation of the ILO, and, more recently, among other developments, have shaped the action of the Council of Europe. Direct interference between international norms produced under the auspices of these organizations and national law, however, has been rare. It has taken place mainly in a domain which is limited, although relevant for many people, namely, the rules coordinating social security legislation which seek to protect migrants in particular (Guibentif 1998). Apart from this domain, it was taken for granted, notably within the European Union, that social issues, and thereby social law, were the exclusive competence of the member states. Prospects for harmonization, and later for convergence of the different systems of social protection across the Union, gave rise to only limited efforts in the form of mere comparisons between these systems. This has changed since the Amsterdam Treaty came into force. With the recognition of a European citizenship and the assumption that economic integration must be accompanied by a Europe-wide effort against its negative social side-effects, closer cooperation between European states in the social domain was needed.[13]

The main instrument chosen at European level to give a new impetus to cooperation between the member-states of the EU was the so-called Open Method

13 For more detailed references to the political and legal background of current European inclusion policies, see Guibentif (2005, 14).

of Coordination. This brings us to the other change in social legislation. The Open Method of Coordination consists of developing procedures in which the member states report their policies to the other members and to the European Commission, compare the objectives and results of these policies, derive from this comparison common goals, and identify 'best practices' that demonstrate particular efficiency in the achievement of these goals. These procedures are framed, contrary to traditional international instruments, such as those of the ILO, not by norms giving expression to general principles in the form of recognized rights for individuals, but by procedural rules defining how the comparison, evaluation, goal-setting, and so on, takes place, and by substantive reports giving a periodic public account of the results of the procedures.[14] A more detailed analysis of these procedures reveals that their management is entrusted to private entities independent from states as well as from the organs of the EU, chosen on the basis of public calls for tender. The rules governing the procedures, therefore, are a combination of principles laid down in the initial calls for tender, later specified in the contracts signed between the European Commission and the entities chosen for the management of the procedures, and finally translated into concrete guidelines for those involved in the procedures, produced and disseminated by these entities.[15]

On a national level as well, as the outcome of these procedures reveals, statutory law is no longer the main normative instrument. Governments make extensive use of internal administrative guidelines for running their own agencies, and a significant part of the work is entrusted to private entities on the basis of bilateral agreements or other kinds of action programmes.

Zygmunt Bauman's concept of 'liquidity' fits in perfectly with these developments in the law, at least, as far as substantive rules are concerned defining targets and specifying benefits. Such rules are subject to frequent changes or even abandoned or deemed to have no direct relevance.[16] This fluidification is strongly linked to the changes in the *medium* of the law: it is no longer to be found just in statutory law but also in contracts, action programmes, internal guidelines, and so on. In more general terms, what recent socio-legal scholarship has called 'post-modern law' could aptly be named 'liquid law', a wording actually close to the already familiar metaphor of 'soft law' (Trubek and Trubek, 2005).

It seems advisable, however, to make one reservation in connection with this labelling. While rules governing procedures may frequently change, they are also becoming more numerous and complex. Time and role constraints for those involved

---

14 See, in particular, the *Joint Report by the Commission and the Council on Social Inclusion*, 5 March 2004.

15 For an example, see the *Operational Guide* for the peer review procedures in the field of social inclusion, available at http://www.peer-review-social-inclusion.net/peer/en/general_information (last accessed November 2005).

16 An interesting question is the relationship between the benchmarks worked out in the framework of the Open Method of Coordination and the levels of social protection to which states have committed themselves in signing the ILO conventions, such as Convention No. 102 on social security. From a European perspective it makes sense to favour the former. Should this mean that the social rights recognized under the auspices of the ILO lose their concrete relevance?

in these procedures (as already noted under section (a) above) are increasing. Here, the physical metaphor of a scale from solid to liquid does not really help. Or if we try to work it out, perhaps we should say that what is being constructed are rather solid machines, even if their pieces are multiple and small, subject to frequent change, and they work on well-lubricated bearings. And even if the aims of their methods of operation are not solidly formulated, they act according to targets (notably those permanently reformulated in evaluation procedures) defined far beyond the reach of most people involved or concerned.[17]

Back to the concept of 'liquidity': potential for its use

A possible conclusion to the analysis sketched out in the previous section might look something like this: if we look into the details, our modernity is far less liquid than the provocative thesis of Zygmunt Bauman suggests. But this would be a simplistic answer to a simplistic reading of Bauman. To go further along such lines, we should compare the observations discussed here with those likely to be gathered in other fields. And we would be wise also to take into account all the nuances in Bauman's thought. The more feasible alternative, it seems to me, is to evaluate the outcome of the concepts of 'liquidity' and 'solidity' in the discussion of concrete social settings.

What we did was to derive from Bauman's interpretation of late modernity a descriptive concept, enabling us to make a specific description of our observations. More precisely, the descriptive concept consists of a scale from more 'solid' to more 'liquid', whereas the precise meaning of 'solid' and 'liquid', both adjectives used in a metaphorical sense, would still have to be worked out for all different aspects of the reality under scrutiny. A first appreciation is that the metaphor allows a suggestive comparative treatment of very different aspects of reality (actors, actions, purposes, results, tools). Interestingly, it is the work of giving different concrete meanings to one strong metaphor that creates the conditions for a careful differentiation of the various dimensions or aspects of the object and, by the same token, a consistent perspective on these different dimensions or aspects. So the metaphor is useful – a criterion of appreciation rightly emphasized by Nelken (2001, 274) – to the extent that it makes our descriptive efforts more coherent.

Considering the picture of social reality that the application of the 'solid-liquid' scale produces, let us make one comment on what it shows, one on the reflections this picture calls for, and one about what is not in the picture or, at least, not rendered quite visible.

The most consistent statement that could be drawn from the observations discussed is that we always find combinations of liquidity and solidity. It seems that 'social life' requires both. The simple case of language confirms it: there is no verbal communication without signs, the meaning of which cannot be changed by those actually involved in the communication. Under these circumstances, the question

17 The continuation of this discussion should take into account, in particular, the considerable scholarly work already produced on the Open Method of Coordination. (See, for example, Chalmers and Lodge 2003; Dehousse 2004; Trubek and Trubek 2005.)

is not, in the first place, how liquid or solid a social setting is. Actually the very measuring of such an 'overall' or 'mean' solidity or liquidity level would raise tricky methodological questions. The question is how more solid elements relate to more liquid elements; whether the level of solidity/liquidity of these different elements varies; and whether there are relations between these variations; and eventually – a more demanding appreciation – to what extent it is possible, in a social grouping, to act upon the level of solidity/liquidity of its elements. For example, one could measure the pace of evolution of languages transformations in their vocabulary, syntax, and so on, and compare it with the pace of thematic evolution in differentiated domains where this language is used (literature, sciences).

Findings discussed here suggest possible compensation mechanisms. Players in the procedures of evaluating inclusion policies are more diverse and changing; on the other hand, the legal status of the entities involved, the kind of contract to be signed with the Commission, the specialized tasks to be allocated from 'project management' to 'web-mastering' are more precisely defined. Or in the field of the law: substantive law becomes more liquid, procedural law more solid. And these compensation mechanisms are activated deliberately: the institution of 'quasi-markets' allows liquidity on the level of the service providers, which have to be numerous and compete with each other (Glennerster and Le Grand 1995). It also creates solidity, requiring the entities to adopt a certain legal status. But the most solid new element is the market itself, which will be extremely difficult to dismantle, given the consequences that would follow if a state were to disappoint the expectations of globally operating shareholders.

As a physical metaphor, the 'solid-liquid' scale looks at first glance rather *wertneutral*. Nevertheless, it may be worthwhile to evaluate the realities it addresses. This is what Zygmunt Bauman actually does. His account of late modernity is, successively, mainly positive in the early 1990s (for instance in Bauman 1993) when he highlights the new possibilities opened up by the end of the Cold War. The appreciation becomes predominantly negative in the late 1990s when he observes the general 'dilution' of social bonds and the fate of those unable to cope with the uncertainty brought about by that dilution. These two appreciations reveal the ambivalence of 'liquidity'. On the one hand, in all its forms (mutability of the law, open role definitions, possibilities of forming new groupings, and so on), it may favour what could be named 'creativity'; on the other hand, it may also make social relationships more difficult or even impossible (by diluting the symbols available to give expression to them, reducing the attention one pays to another, and so on). It is worthwhile for sociologists to measure these two opposite effects. Indeed 'creativity of social activity' and 'fragility of social bonds' may be two acceptable criteria for a truly sociological evaluation of a given social context, allowing the sociologist to go beyond mere factual reporting, but without entering the field of moral or political appreciation. Preventing the ossification of concepts or routines says nothing about the moral value of new practices which might be invented as a result. Preventing the dilution of social bonds says nothing about the human quality of the bonds maintained. But there may be a minimum of social cohesion necessary for human togetherness, as well as a minimum margin for inventiveness. The sociologist is in a good position to assess whether, in a given context, there is a risk of falling below these minimum levels, and to draw the attention of his or her fellow citizens to the urgency of a political and moral debate.

A last word on what the 'liquid-solid' scale may lead us to neglect, in particular as an effect of the physical metaphor. If there is a difference between physical substance and human relations, it lies in the fact that a social fabric is a medium where different actors may emerge, all pursuing their own purposes and thus likely to come into conflict with one another. It is true that 'liquid society' has been individualized to a level at which the formation of groups in conflictual opposition has become improbable.[18] So conflicts may no longer be at the top of the sociological agenda where Lewis Coser and Ralf Dahrendorf wanted to place them some years ago. But we have to ensure that our instruments remain sensitive to their possible emergence, and to the formation of actors in them. This is the condition that allows us to identify and evaluate the force and social impact of social movements of all kinds on a timely basis; and perhaps to take some steps towards a more precise identification of the forces causing the current trends of fluidification/solidification, the point at which, in my view, the work of Zygmunt Bauman most needs to be continued.

References

Bauman, Z. (1987), *Legislators and Interpreters* (Cambridge: Polity).

Bauman, Z. (1989), *Modernity and the Holocaust* (Cambridge: Polity).

Bauman, Z. (1993), *Postmodern Ethics* (Oxford: Blackwell Publishing).

Bauman, Z. (1995), *Life in Fragments. Essays in Postmodern Morality* (Oxford: Oxford University Press).

Bauman, Z. (1998a), *In Search of Politics* (Cambridge: Polity).

Bauman, Z. (1998b), *Work, Consumerism and the New Poor* (Buckingham: Open University Press).

Bauman, Z. (2000), *Liquid Modernity* (Cambridge: Polity).

Bauman, Z. (2001), *The Individualized Society* (Cambridge: Polity).

Bauman, Z. (2003), *Liquid Love* (Oxford: Blackwell Publishing).

Bauman, Z. (2004), *Europe, An Unfinished Adventure* (Cambridge: Polity).

Bauman, Z. (2007), 'Uncertainty and Other Liquid-Modern Fears', in this volume.

Brown, R. (1977), *A Poetic for Sociology* (Cambridge: Cambridge University Press).

Belley, J.-G. (2002), 'Le pluralisme juridique comme doctrine de la science du droit' [Legal Pluralism as a doctrine for jurisprudence], in J. Kellerhals, D. Manaï and R. Roth (eds.), *Pour un droit pluriel. Études offertes au professeur Jean-François Perrin* (Geneva/Basel/München: Helbing and Lichtenhahn), 135–65.

Bourdieu, P. (1985), 'The genesis of the concepts of Habitus and Field', *Sociocriticism II*/2, 11–24.

18 See the difference between the recent riots in France and the student revolt in May 1968.

Chalmers, D. and Lodge, M. (2003), *The Open Method of Co-ordination and The European Welfare State* (London: ESRC Centre for the Analysis of Risk and Regulation, LSE).

Dehousse, R. (2005), 'La méthode ouverte de coordination. Quand l'instrument tient lieu de politique' ['The Open Method of Co-Ordination. When instruments take the place of politics'] in P. Lascoumes and P. Le Galès (eds.), *Gouverner par les instruments* (Paris: Presses Universitaires de Sciences-Po), 331–56.

Douglas, M. (1986), *How Institutions Think* (New York: Syracuse University Press).

Douglas, M. and Ney, S. 1998, *Missing Persons. A Critique of the Social Sciences* (Berkeley: University of California Press).

Gessner, V. and Cem Budak, A. (eds.) (1998), *Emerging Legal Certainty. Empirical Studies on the Globalization of Law* (Aldershot: Dartmouth).

Glennerster, H. and Le Grand, J. (1995), 'The development of quasi-markets in welfare provision', in A.M. Guillemard, J. Lewis, S. Ringen and R. Salais (eds.), *Comparing social welfare systems in Europe – vol. 1 – Oxford Conference* (Paris: MIRE), 277–294.

Goffman, E. (1981), 'The Interaction Order', *American Sociological Review* 48, 1–17.

Guibentif, P. (1996), 'Approaching the Production of Law through Habermas's Concept of Communicative Action' in M. Deflem (ed.), *Habermas, Modernity and Law* (London: Sage), 45–70.

Guibentif, P. (1997), 'The Transformation of the Portuguese Social Security System' in Rhodes, M. (ed.), *Southern European Welfare States – Between Crisis and Reform* (London: Frank Cass), 219–39.

Guibentif, P. (1998), 'Cross-Border Legal Issues Arising from International Migrations : The Case of Portugal', in V. Gessner and A. Cem Budak (eds.), *Emerging Legal Certainty. Empirical Studies on the Globalization of Law* (Aldershot: Dartmouth), 241–82.

Guibentif, P. (2001a), 'Minimum Income and Basic Income – Meeting the Challenge of Social Exclusion', in *Policies and Instruments to Fight Poverty in the European Union: The Guarantee of a Minimum Income* (Lisbon: Instituto para o Desenvolvimento Social), 257–71.

Guibentif, P. (2001b), 'La théorie des systèmes et l'étude de la communication juridique quotidienne' [Systems theory and the study of everyday legal communication], *Droit et Société* 47, 123–53.

Guibentif, P. (2005), *Reception and Integration of New Migrants – Synthesis Report Peer Review in the Field of Social Inclusion Policies* (Brussels: INBAS/European Centre/NIZW, on behalf of the European Commission, DG Employment and Social Affairs), also at http://www.peer-review-social-inclusion.net/peer/en/Review_DB/show_peer_review_single?peer_review_key=17andyear=2004 (last accessed November 2005).

Hespanha, A. (2002), 'Os juristas como couteiros. A ordem na Europa ocidental dos inícios da idade moderna' [The jurists as gamekeepers. The order in Western Europe at the beginning of the Modern Age], *Análise Social* 161, 1183–1268.

Lascoumes, P. and Le Galès, P. (2004), 'L'action publique saisie par ses instruments' [Public action grasped by its instruments], in Lascoumes, P. and Le Galès, P. (eds.), *Gouverner par les instruments* (Paris: Les Presses de Sciences Politique), 11–44.

López Ayllon, S. and Fix-Fierro, H. (1999), 'Communication between Legal Cultures: The Case of NAFTA's Chapter 19 Binational Panels', in Perret, L. (ed.), *The Evolution of Free Trade in the Americas* (Montreal: Wilson and Lafleur), 3–48.

Luhmann, N. (1981), 'Kommunikation mit Zettelkästen: ein Erfahrungsbericht' ['Communication with index card boxes. A report based on experience'], in Baier, H. et al. (eds.), *Öffentliche Meinung und sozialer Wandel: Für Elisabeth Noelle-Neumann* (Opladen: Westdeutscher Verlag), 222–8.

Luhmann, N. (1984/1995), *Social Systems* (Stanford: Stanford University Press). [orig. publ. Frankfurt: Suhrkamp, 1984].

Nelken, D. (2001), 'Beyond the Metaphor of Legal Transplants? Consequences of Autopoietic Theory for the Study of Cross-Cultural Legal Adaptation', in J. Přibáň and D. Nelken (eds.), *Law's New Boundaries. The Consequences of Legal Autopoiesis* (Aldershot: Ashgate), 265–302.

Minev, D. (2005), *Field Social Work Programmes in Neighbourhoods Threatened by Social Exclusion*: Synthesis Report (Offenbach-am-Main: INBAS).

Nicaise, I. and Meinema, T. (2004), *Experiments in Social Activation in the Netherlands*: Synthesis Report (Offenbach-am-Main: INBAS).

Niessen, J. and Schibel, Y. (2004), *Handbook on Integration*, Luxembourg, European Commission, available at http://europa.eu.int/comm/justice_home/doc_centre/immigration/integration/doc_immigration_integration_fr.htm (last accessed November 2005).

Peters, B. and Van Nispen, F. ed. (1998), *Public Policy Instruments. Evaluating the Tools of Public Administration* (Cheltenham: Edward Elgar).

Přibáň, J. (2001), 'Legitimation Between the Noise of Politics and the Order of Law', in J. Přibáň and D. Nelken (eds.), *Law's New Boundaries. The Consequences of Legal Autopoiesis* (Aldershot: Ashgate), 104–22.

Roberts, S. (1998), 'Against Legal Pluralism', *Journal of Legal Pluralism* 42, 95–106.

Roberts, S. (2005), 'After Government? On Representing Law without the State', *Modern Law Review* 68, 1ff.

Spencer, S. (2003), 'The Challenges of Integration for the EU', *Migration Information Source* (Washington DC: Migration Policy Institute) available at http://www.migrationinformation.org/Feature/display.cfm?ID=170 (accessed November 2005).

Teubner, G. (1997), '"Global Bukovina": Legal Pluralism in the World Society', in G. Teubner (ed.), *Global Law Without A State* (Aldershot: Dartmouth), 3–28.

Trubek, D. and Trubek, L. (2005), 'The Open Method of Co-ordination and the Debate over "Hard" and "Soft" Law', in J. Zeitlin and P. Pochet with L. Magnusson (eds.), *The Open Method of Co-ordination in Action. The European Employment and Social Inclusion Strategies* (Bern: Peter Lang).

Vranken, J. (2004), *The English Rough Sleeping Strategy in a European Context*: Synthesis Report (Offenbach-am-Main: INBAS).

World Commission on the Social Dimension of Globalization 2004, *A Fair Globalization. Creating Opportunities For All*, Geneva, ILO, 2004.

Chapter 10

Liquid Modernity and the Integration of Young Immigrants in Italy[1]

David Nelken

Introduction

One of the central themes of Bauman's *Liquid Modernity* (as well as many of his other recent books) is the search for identity, which he describes as ' the ongoing struggle to arrest or slow down the flow, to solidify the fluid, to give form to the formless and friable stuff of life' (Bauman 2000, 82). If this is a challenge for all those living in post-modern times, it is doubly so for immigrant groups (Sayad 2002), many of whom come from pre-modern societies in search of modern life-chances to find themselves caught up in the changes of post-modernity. Immigrants are said to be the epitome of the post-modern condition yet also its perfect scapegoats (Baumann 2004). On the one hand we are all strangers now: 'Liquid' modernity has led to the 'melting' of previously 'solid' bonds of collective identity into the less determined, more vicarious forms of 'individually conducted life policies' (Bauman 2000, 6). We are 'witnessing', suggests Bauman, 'the revenge of nomadism over the principle of territoriality and settlement' (Bauman 2000, 13). On the other hand, immigrants are repeatedly used as the 'dangerous supplement' that defines what a society has in common (Catanzaro and Nelken 2003), and Gypsies and travellers are often treated as the least desirable people with whom to interact. Many members of the host societies, and of immigrant groups themselves, seek security by seeking to stabilise or essentialise their differences; 'ethnicity more than any other kind of postulated identity', argues Bauman, is the first choice when it comes to the withdrawal from the frightening polyphonic space where no one knows how to talk to anyone else' (Bauman 2000, 107). But, paradoxically, this means that difference is not a given; even non-negotiable obligations have to be chosen, in a world where 'we shop around for identities to make or unmake at will, or so it seems' (Bauman 2000, 83).

The value of these provocative insights into the sociology of identity, however, does not exempt us from the need to pay careful attention to empirical variation in the construction of difference and the way this changes over time and place, within as well as between societies. This chapter will focus on the identities chosen by the children of immigrant parents in Italy, a country where large-scale immigration is a recent phenomena. But at least some of its findings may be of relevance even in

1 In memory of one of the victims of the July 2005 London bombings, Benedetta Caccia of Norwich, who was engaged to be married to Fiaz Bhatti.

countries with more long-standing experience of immigration. In fact, when I first designed a research project on his topic I did not imagine just how politically salient the identity of young people from second or third generation immigrant backgrounds in Europe was going to become. In the UK, the London bombings of July 2005 were experienced by many people as particularly shocking because they were carried out by young people who in many cases seemed to be well-integrated into the society. Feelings were fanned by newspaper opinion-surveys carried out after the attacks that reported that 21 per cent of those polled amongst some immigrant groups said they would not be willing to help the police catch the bombers and no more than 12 per cent thought of themselves as principally British. Did this put in doubt the British approach of permitting a fair degree of pluralism amongst different communities and ethnic groups? In France, in the same year, rioting by young men in the *banlieue* of the large cities went on for weeks and was widely seen as a protest against the failure of the type of integration promised by the more rigorous assimilationist French model (Favell 1998). Italy has not witnessed such conflicts and there are still relatively few second-generation immigrants in the sense of children born in Italy from parents settled there. But an increasing proportion of young people in Italian schools (now around 10 per cent) are from families with recent immigrant backgrounds immigrants, and this proportion will grow if the low native Italian birth-rate does not change. What integration is or should mean is likely to become as contested as it is in countries with longer histories of immigration.

The meanings of integration

In these debates, in Italy as elsewhere, one term that plays a central role in both political and academic discussion about the implications of immigration is that of the need to successfully 'integrate' immigrant groups (Ciarloni 2000). But not all of those who use this term mean the same things by it; in particular it is not always made clear how, if at all, integration differs from assimilation (Recchi and Allam 2002), where the condition of acceptance is that the others become as far as possible 'like us'. Philosophical discussions of the appropriate relationships between majority and minority cultures offer one important route to understanding what is at stake in talking about integration.[2] They are especially valuable in exploring such normative questions as how to balance the obligation of liberal societies to safeguard the rights of their minority groups at the same time as protecting the rights of individuals within such minority groups.[3] But merely theoretical debates about the competing virtues of, say, multiculturalism and 'plural equalities' will tell us little about the changing realities of integration on the ground. In the academic literature in Italy for example, there is still too big a gap between, on the one hand, theoretical discussions of integration as a goal (discussions which are often highly abstract and over-

2 For examples of the extensive literature see Kymlicka (1995), Parekh (2000) and Benhabib (2002).

3 Liberal polities are distinctive in the emphasis they place on giving the individual the right to leave his or her group. But in some groups in these same societies all meaning and honour comes from belonging to and respecting the mutual obligations of the group.

idealistic), and, on the other, over-localised empirical descriptions of immigrant groups (where scholars simply employ their own taken-for-granted ideas about what represents realistic levels of integration).

What is needed is more 'middle range theory' and related empirical research geared to explaining variations in degrees and types of inclusion experienced and pursued by different groups and individuals, and the implications these variations have for different possible ideals of integration. But such research is not easy. In particular it treads a thin line between either underestimating or else over-essentialising the complexity and specificity of immigrant identities and of confounding intergroup and intragroup differences. Some valuable studies concentrating on differences between immigrant groups can already be found in the Italian literature, from the first attempts to understand the phenomenon of immigration (for instance, IRES 1991), to more recent updates (Pollini 2000; Cologna and Breveglieri 2003). But, while the IRES study insisted that it was 'profoundly misleading to think of immigrants as bearing a solidified and distinct identity, one which could be reduced to a given nationality or ethnic group ... religion, language and culture can be mixed together in an infinite variety of possibilities and situations ' (IRES 1991, 10; my translation), the more recent Cologna and Breveglieri study uses headings such as 'the confused lives of young Ethiopians' and talks of 'the Egyptian families' even though the majority of their sample were Egyptian Copts (my translations).

It is important not to assume that the attractions of integration are necessarily the same for the host society and for members of the different immigrant[4] groups who are being asked to integrate. Theoretical discussions of integration must therefore be enriched by empirical enquiry that allows the views and experiences of immigrants themselves to be heard, as this research tries to do. This is not because immigrants themselves can provide *the* 'solution' to the question of what represents successful integration with the host society. Apart from anything else, immigrants, of course, do not speak with *one* voice. There are differences of economic interests, status, loyalties, and values between groups and within groups, as well as amongst individuals. The ideas of religious traditionalists are not those of laymen, those of men not necessarily those of women, those of parents not always those of children. But this makes it all the more necessary to try to understand these different points of view. In this research I give particular attention to the voice of young people.

In both everyday public discussion and media reporting enormous energy is devoted to symbolic issues such as whether the crucifix should continue to be fixed to the walls of public institutions. But the significance of this issue is almost certainly greater for the host community than it is for the immigrant communities. Much more typical everyday problems for immigrant families have to do with the tensions

4 For simplicity I will speak throughout this chapter of 'immigrants' without further specification. As used in most academic writings as well as public debate this term is used to cover economic migrants, exiles, refugees, guest workers, tourists, traders, transnational migrants and even long standing minorities. But, for many purposes, it would be essential to make further distinctions between these categories and also examine their relationship. For example the problem of the so-called 'second generation' has much to do with what happens when immigrants become, and see themselves as becoming, established minorities.

surrounding the appropriate role for girls caught between traditional cultures and the different ways of the Italian of the same age group. Increasingly, this type of situation is also beginning to be reported by the media. But it tends to be used as yet another illustration of what is wrong with the culture immigrants bring with them, rather than understood as an aspect of common conflicts between the generations, which are especially likely between first and second generation immigrants. This is seen clearly in the way one widely read Italian newspaper reported the following recent case.

According to the newspaper, Pakistani parents, living in Prato, a medium sized town near Florence with one of the largest proportions of immigrants in the country, had just had their parental rights (and passports) withdrawn. The decision was taken on the basis of the response provided by the Juvenile court to a report of parental abuse by a school Headmaster.[5] The 17 year old daughter in the case had appealed to the Headmaster alleging that her father had stopped her mixing with her Italian friends, beat her and her older sister, kept her home from school, and tried to persuade her to get married in Pakistan.[6] This case, despite being, or, better, just because it was an extreme one, was used by the newspaper as an opportunity to remind its readers why immigrants must learn to adjust to the (superior) Italian way of life. It entitled its report 'I don't want to wear a Chador. Help me: She is taken out of her father's control.'[7] By the side of its headline it explained, 'Freedom of behaviour. The case of Sara presents us yet again with the question of how far we need to respect the practices of foreigners who live in Italy. These should be sacrosanct only as far as they do not undermine the traditions of this country and personal freedoms.' The report itself described the girl's 'rebellion' as involving no more than 'a touch of make-up, jeans, girlfriends, books', and it wrote, with what was intended to be obvious irony, of the 'temptations of the western world.' It ended by quoting the Headmaster who is alleged to have said: 'Prato is a town that is able to welcome foreigners and integrate them – this is its greatness. But we must not confuse tolerance with hypocritical 'anything goes'.' (my translation). Whatever the truth(s) of this particular family conflict, the report also serves to reassure the paper's readers of their cultural superiority *in general* (*our* tradition of personal freedom as compared to *their* lack of such a history) as revealed by the way oppressive immigrant parents try to deprive their children of their fundamental rights.

Cases of this sort do occur and, apart from any necessary legal action, they raise genuine problems of the sort for which the philosophical literature tries to give guidance.[8] But they are exceptional and it is their very exceptionality that explains why they reach the attention of the courts and media. They will for that very reason not be representative of more common and less extreme situations of problems of

---

5 *Il Resto di Carlino*, 20 December 2004, 13.

6 The Headmaster is said to have told this story at the provincial congress of the Democratic Left Political Party (the leading party in his region).

7 The legal basis for the court's action was not explained in the report. As the girl concerned was beyond the age of official school leaving age the grounds probably had to do with the father's alleged violence, or the enforced segregation at home.

8 See supra n. 2.

integration. By contrast, the research which will be discussed in this chapter, based on 100 interviews with young immigrants coming from Moroccan, Chinese, Albanian and Gypsy backgrounds, was designed to provide insights into their experience of subjective integration, including the extent to which they feel caught between family expectations and those of Italian society more generally.[9]

In an earlier discussion of the larger project from which this chapter is drawn, I first located this empirical research into the experiences of young immigrants in Emilia Romagna and the Marche regions of Italy into a larger theoretical context. I discussed what is meant by objective and subjective integration, examined the definition of subjective integration, the variables which can affect it, the dynamics of integration as an ongoing process, and the way integration is affected by globalisation and recent changes in ways of thinking about the problem of multiple identities (Nelken 2005). For reasons of space I shall present here only that part of the theoretical discussion that has most bearing on Bauman's ideas about identity in 'liquid' modernity. I shall then refer to the interview material[10] that tells us something about how these young people construct their identities under these conditions.

Theorising cultural navigation

Many of those writing about culture, and not just Bauman, claim that social change has undermined older ways of thinking about identity. Culture can no longer be treated as 'out there' and determining, well-bounded, integrated and securely rooted in time and space. The new vocabulary they use speaks instead of hybridity, liminality, uprooting, in-betweenness, border zones, diasporas and fragmentation (for instance, see Papastergiadis 2000). Identities emerge and are shaped within dynamic fields of force that include the home country, the host society, the community and family relationships, and larger globalising trends and fashions. They are inevitably 'the unfinished, and always only partly realized, outcomes of practices of differentiation, negotiation, accommodation, and conflict, rather than of effective cultural doping or successful individual maturation in stable encompassing contexts' (Stuart Hall, quoted in Staring, Van der Land, Tak and Kalb 1997). Individuals are seen as not only following traditions but also as blurring, changing and inventing them. Caught in potential contradictions between the dictates of different identities, individuals can select the occasions in which they treat such scripts as binding on them. Researchers in the UK for example report that 'national, ethnic and religious identities intersect

9 The project was financed by the Italian Ministry for the Universities and relies on semi-structured interviews with 100 young immigrants carried out by a number of research assistants using an interview schedule that I developed. A small comparative project into identities of young immigrants in Wales was carried out with the assistance of Jonathon Scourfield and Sean O'Neill of Cardiff University.

10 It should be born in mind that interview data like any other is itself produced as a result of social processes, starting with the interview situation and ending with the selection work of the writer. In addition, as Bauman argues, interviews 'do not reveal selves but create them' (Bauman 2000, 84).

and individuals can 'play' with one or all of them, in specific social interactions' (Scourfield and Davis 2002, cf. Scourfield and Davies 2005).

Some of the most knowledgeable of current commentators on the politics of immigration are tempted to celebrate hybridity as one of the 'defences of the weak'. Favell, for example, argues that the refusal of assimilation is a strength. It puts in doubt that 'belonging is an unquestionable good, indeed a necessary precondition for meaningful and effective political action and representation within any given society, or social situation'. On the contrary, he argues, the whole point of the 'post-national' space that has opened up, 'beyond' the integrating nation state, is that this can reveal 'resources of power and cultural action, to be found by refusing (or, better, playing with) the logic of belonging; by rejecting, countering or evading social norms that are imposed and enforced on newcomers and outsiders when they are integrated' (Favell 2002, 220).

On the other hand, these ideas should not be taken to represent the mainstream. We should not rule out *a priori* the possibility that many still aspire to 'successful individual maturation in stable encompassing contexts' (Hall in Staring, Van der Land, Tak and Kalb 1997). As against those who welcome hybridity there are many more who fear it. And, when they see advantages from doing so, members of both host societies and minority groups stand ready to transform 'differences' into 'essences', often with tragic consequences. To be successfully asserted, identity depends on power and the nation state retains considerable power in this sphere. By contrast, work in the cultural studies tradition often implies too much 'free-floating', innovative talent on the part of what are almost always subordinate communities. Since much of the creativity of diaspora communities is in any case directed to the goals of chauvinist nationalism, ethnicity and religion back home, this again confirms that what many people seem to want is fixed centres rather than hybridity. What seems undeniable, in any case, is the need to place any study of subjective integration in the context of the increasing significance of the relationships immigrants have with members of their groups in other places than the host society. As Papastergiadis puts it: 'in diasporic community identity is produced through the constant negotiation between past and present, here and elsewhere, absence and presence, self and other' (2000, 159).

A recently published article that brings this out well is an account by Sissel Ostberg of Pakistani youth growing up in Norway (Ostberg 2003).[11] Using the method of participant observation, Ostberg followed a group of Norwegian/Pakistani adolescents over an extended period. The young people he studied were strongly linked at the same time both to their school and to their part of town (though many aimed to live one day outside the Pakistani ghetto), as well as to a global network

11 Ostberg's study, because it also deals with Pakistani youngsters, can help us put the type of situation revealed (and denounced) by the *Resto di Carlino* newspaper at the beginning of this chapter into a wider context. For example the pattern of going back to Pakistan for marriage partners is here made to seem 'normal'. Norway and Italy (for all their differences) may also have a number of relevant features in common. In both countries immigration is relatively recent, does not come from former colonies, and has to integrate into what had previously been a highly homogenous society.

of relatives both back in Pakistan and in other parts of the Pakistani diaspora such as England. Interestingly, though, while all the young people he talked to felt an attachment to Pakistan, none of them actually wanted to live there. In part this was because they positively identified with the country in which they had grown up and in part (but the two are connected) because they disliked things about Pakistan such as the heat and the corruption, and believed that it is more difficult there to discuss things with teachers.

Ostberg's research methods of following the group over time were especially apt for studying the dynamics of evolving identity. He found that, as they grew older, the youngsters tended to have more Pakistani rather than native Norwegian friends, claiming to share more interests with them. In particular, Ostberg describes in detail the way these youngsters negotiated religious identity and gender, ethnicity and social boundaries and the changing degree of their participation in Islamic practices such as prayers, fasting and pilgrimage. Though they saw other religions as not so different from their own, they now said they wanted more knowledge of their own traditions. For all these youngsters, prayer and fasting now assumed more importance as they tried harder than they had as children to understand the significance of such practices for themselves.

As they grew to adulthood these young people (like all adolescents) explored and tested boundaries, learning through processes of negotiation which were permeable and which were not. In this process some boundaries were changed or rejected. For instance, when it came to partying, there was some bending of boundaries. Similarly they sometimes distinguished Islamic from merely Pakistani traditions, with the latter being the easier to re-negotiate, oppose or even reject. But many restrictions were eventually internalised and accepted. What typically takes place, Ostberg says, is a shift from unthinking obedience to negotiations about how to be authentically oneself within the tradition. He sees this process as both a 'dis–integration' of previous social forms as well as the willing acceptance of new demands, controls and constraints.[12] One girl who chose to begin wearing a headscarf found this to be a way of more truly expressing herself. She said that it would now feel strange not to dress in this way even though friends within and outside her own group continued to make comments. (While her parents approved, her sisters did not follow her example.) But there were also some examples of what Ostberg calls innovations within the boundaries of tradition.[13] Some girls got to know their future arranged marriage partners better by chatting on the Internet. Faced with an arranged marriage with her cousin in Pakistan, one girl understood that her family would be angry if she did not go through with it. She responded by negotiating with her parents so as to postpone marriage till after she had obtained her professional qualifications.

12 But the small size of Ostberg's sample makes it difficult to know how far such a 'successful' pattern of cultural reproduction amongst Pakistani youth can be generalised to other times and places, and how far it is specific to a given generation or given immigrant group.

13 See Lapassade (1998) for a somewhat similar discussion of what he calls 'deviant conformity', when describing how Maghreb girls marry from their own group, but do the choosing of partners themselves.

As this suggests, both family contexts and personality differences were central to the ways these youngsters handled their identities. Family life in a relational and hierarchical sense very much shaped individuals' choices. There was a heavy burden on children to justify the emigration by raising the family status (through educational achievement and consequent better employment opportunities). Not surprisingly, as Ostberg remarks, 'gender is at the core of the ethnicity issue'. Crucial issues in these families revolved round the extent of prohibitions on mixing with the other sex, or the appropriateness of going back to Pakistan to get married. The most rigid boundaries had to do with relating to those of the other sex and not drinking alcohol. Parents were stricter towards girls' behaviour because of the way rumours would spread. It was acceptable for girls to talk to boys at school but not in leisure time, and it was out of the question for them to have boyfriends. But the ruling against going to discos applied also to boys, even if they generally enjoyed more freedom than girls. In terms of their place in the family the voices of young people, including girls, were more taken into account as they grew older. But the highest values still included deference to the wishes of elders and the acceptance of arranged marriages, values that, he argues, are in contradiction to the values of ethnic Norwegians.

Ostberg argues that the immigrants he studied did not have hyphenated or creolised identities – they did not see themselves as 'Pakistani-Norwegians'. When asked to describe their identity(ies) they said that they were both Pakistani and Norwegian, but that they were more Pakistanis. Although their identity was in some ways both changeable and fluid – it also showed an underlying stability. Ostberg calls this way of handling different identities 'cultural navigation' because it suggests that while such youngsters do relate beyond their cultural boundaries both socially and culturally, they are not aiming at fully integrating two or more identities but rather express an 'integrated plural identity' that shifts according to the context or situation. Thus, typically, they listened to both Western *and* Asian music, and dressed, on different occasions, in either style of clothes. More, they did not perceive any contradiction between wearing the hijab and listening to techno music. Watching 'soaps' by satellite from Pakistan had its importance, but in their own everyday life they did not think in ethnic categories. Choosing a video depended on how they were feeling, not on whether it was a Hindu or American one. At the same time, when in Hungary for her studies, one of the youngsters said that she could express herself not only as a Norwegian, but also as an Asian, as when dressing up for religious festivals with (real) Asian flatmates. On the other hand, they were perhaps more self-conscious than many youngsters. This was a result not only, as he suggests, of the reflexivity typical of late modernity and the general soul searching characteristic of adolescence, but probably also of being a member of a Muslim minority. (He does not discuss how wider developments in the world impacted on the evolution of identity. This is only partially justified by the fact that his research pre-dates the 9/11 attack on the World Trade Centre.) Ostberg shows us how youngsters reconciled finding their own individual paths in life with their choice to maintain their traditions. On the basis of his observations, he concludes that in general this process of testing the limits – and discovering the restrictions required by Islamic tradition tended to strengthen ethnic identity.

Finding identity(ies)

What then of the Italian sample? There were interesting differences in the way the young people belonging to the four groups sampled related to the host society. The Albanians, for example, were the most individualistic. Belying their public image, they included some very cosmopolitan youngsters, looking as far as the USA for future career opportunities. They were keen to participate in the wider Italian society given the chance, even to the extent of assimilating. The Moroccans, partly because of the sampling method used, included contrasting groups of traditionally-minded youngsters and others who were keen to enter fully into Italian life and lifestyle. The Chinese girls presented themselves as claiming to be fully open to their host society but also as largely accepting of the role allocated to them by their families. The Gypsies were the most closed of the groups but also those most convinced that the wider society was closed to them. In all the groups there were differences between the approved roles of young men and young women. In some groups, such as the Moroccans, girls were being particularly discouraged from mixing, but in others, such as the Gypsies, the women played the main role as mediators between their society and the outside world.

The approach to integration was shaped to a large extent by each youngster's group of reference and immediate family. But our interviews also revealed considerable differences amongst individuals within each of the groups. Most of the young immigrants living in these two regions of Italy apparently managed to live at ease with their multiple identities and did not find themselves forced to make zero-sum choices. But, as Ostberg (2002) notes, this does not mean that they thought of themselves as Chinese-Italians or as Morrocan-Italians etc. This terminology is not yet current in Italian society and perhaps may never be. The lack of a defined 'hyphenated identity' did not seem to constitute any obstacle to young people drawing, as needed, on both their identities. As Ostberg also found, the responses to the interview questions showed that most youngsters dealt with their plural identity by opting for different cultural behaviours according to the situation or circumstances. They placed greater or lesser emphasis on one or the other of their identities at different times and for different purposes. They behaved one way with their parents, another with their friends, did one thing at home, another when going out, behaved one way in Italy, in another way when they returned to their parent's home country. Religion or culture could assume an importance at a festival or wedding that it would not otherwise have. For some of these young people, above all for some Albanians, even religious identity itself could be treated as situational. The following extract from an interview with one Albanian girl suggests a level of flexibility that the institutional religious authorities might have difficulty in accepting.[14]

> What religion are you?
>
> Here I am Catholic; there I am Muslim.
>
> How does that work?

---

14 The attitude to religion of some Albanians (whatever one thinks of it) must be understood against a background of fifty years of state-enforced atheism.

When I came to Italy I got baptised.

Why did you get baptised?

Because, back in Albania, I was the girlfriend of a boy who was 24 years old and a Christian. We often went to church and I felt the desire to do so regularly. I felt free there, when I prayed. So when I arrived here I got myself baptised.

But is it better to be Muslim or Catholic?

Well, for me it's not as if there are ten different Gods. God is one and I believe in God. Therefore you can be either a Christian or a Muslim. It's equally good. Here when I go to Church I have more freedom. Muslim women on the other hand should cover up, though as a matter of fact in Albania we didn't do so.

Did you keep the fast of Ramadan in Albania?

Yes I did so for four years. But I didn't do so because I had to, because they told me to do so. I did so because, living with my grandmother, I felt sorry for her when she got up at 4 in the morning and had to eat all by herself. I did it only for that reason.

Having had a richer life experience than most of the young people of their age meant that the interviewees were often able to describe both the advantages and disadvantages of the different cultures they had experienced. In answer to the question whether Italian boys were spoilt one Albanian girl respondent agreed:

Yes, they are too much 'mummy's boys'. At least the ones I have got to know have been.

Explain what you mean.

Italian young men are frightened to make decisions for themselves even if they are thirty years old.

And Albanians?

No, I would say they are more mature.

But she then quickly went on to mention that, from her point of view, Albanian boys had other vices.

...But the Albanians are pretty nasty (stronzi) – excuse the term –

Why?

If they have a relationship with a girl and then the relationship ends, if they then see you around they will tell everyone that they have been with you and what you did together.

This 'seeing both sides' was particularly likely in the responses given by girl interviewees with respect to the condition of women in Italy as compared to their home countries and home cultures:

Is it better to be a young woman in Italy or in Albania?

Here they have too much freedom, and I don't like that

And there?

They are too closed-minded.

Seeing both sides did not mean that these youngsters were unable to make choices for themselves. In all of these groups in their cultures of origin women had a different social status and more restricted role. But many girls appreciated the fact that Italy offered them more chances of equality than they would have had otherwise had, and they made it clear that they intended to make use of these opportunities. At the same time, however, some of the young people also acknowledged that they (and/or their parents) might have to draw the line against going out with, or marrying, youngsters from a different group to their own. Many of the Moroccans in particular said they would only like to marry those who shared their religion or were willing to convert. Chinese girls said they had little time for socialising. They tended to say that there was no problem in theory about marrying out, but that, in practice, Italian boys would have difficulty in becoming part of the demanding life and work habits of Chinese families.

There was also little doubt that many of these young people were only too aware of the wider developments which influence the way they are viewed by the host society, and make them willing or unwilling representatives of other people's conflicts and projections. Gypsies, Moroccans and Albanians all said they had come across popular hostility to their social groups. Only a small minority of the young people reported cases of open hostility or discrimination as having happened to them personally. Specifically, however, many of the Gypsies did say that they had had bad experiences at school, and some Moroccans too made comments about the difficulty shown in accommodating religious differences at school. (If anything, the problem with integration at school may be less the extent of prejudice than the fact that schools are not preparing these young people for the realities of life outside, including the 'structural' and other types of discrimination they may encounter later. For example, hardly any of the young immigrants we interviewed appeared to know what was meant by talking of getting a post with the help of a 'racommandazione' – the intervention of a sponsor). Few of these young people spoke of problems with the police. In addition, the evidence from the questions about deviant conduct included in the last part of the interview schedule actually suggested that these young immigrants were less prepared to tolerate common forms of low-level deviance than Italians of the same age.

Three stories of conflicted identities[15]

I have suggested so far that most of the young people interviewed seemed to have a relatively unproblematic approach to living with their identity(ies). But even such a small sample of interviews (collected in such relatively well-off and well-organised regions of Italy) did throw up examples of more complicated responses to multiple identities. I have chosen the following three cases as good illustrations of such reactions. It is not by chance that all three cases involve young women; interviews with all four groups confirmed that it is they who are the ones most likely to be caught in the tensions between the old and the new, the here and the there,

15 These excellent interviews were all carried out by Tamara Riccialdelli.

the wishes of parents and the desires of youth. Two of these interviews were with young women from Moroccan backgrounds, and the other with a youngster from an Albanian background. The extracts from the first interview illustrate how one response to the challenge of subjective integration may be to abandon the old and adopt the new, those taken from the second shows how another response may be to reject the new and seek to recreate the 'old', while the quotations taken from the last, least resolved case, shows a young woman still struggling to find a place for both her identities.

The first interview involved a young Moroccan woman who had decided to leave home and live with an Italian lorry driver. The decision to make such a drastic choice came to light when the interviewee was asked whether her relationship with her parents was going smoothly. To this she replied:

> Well, my mother still has a conflictual relationship with my man, perhaps because she sees him as someone who took me away from home, though that is not true.
>
> Is he Moroccan or Italian?
> No, he's Italian.
>
> Was that… is that a problem for your mother?
>
> No, the fact that we got together? No, because my mother is quite open minded from that point of view. My dad doesn't live with us and probably he would not have accepted the fact that I was going out with a man … but perhaps. Many things can be accepted if they are not done obviously in public, if they are … my mother no, she has always accepted it, now anyway. When I was smaller it was more of a problem, but little by little as I grew up, mum, ... I have lived these things, I've had pain over them, mum tried to stop them, but now, for my other sisters I can see is more accepting of it. My twelve year old little sister, the other day, talked of her first boyfriend and mum took the news without reacting. In my case when I was twelve I spoke about my first boyfriend and my mother told me, 'no, you are going back to Morocco to get married'! It's clear, I suppose, that the first children have the hardest time over this. And in my case all the more so because we had just moved from another country where probably things were done differently... But the problem is not so much that he is Italian but that I've gone to live with him, and we're not married and these sort of things.
>
> How did your mother deal with the situation? Can you tell me what happened when you came home and said I'm going out regularly with someone…?
>
> Well, I had always gone out with Italian boys. ... never Moroccans. Not because I've got anything against Moroccans, it's simply that if you live in another country you're going to met obviously a high number of Italians and anyway, in my opinion, the Moroccans you met around here are really low-life. Not because they are Moroccans. I am Moroccan and when they say to me 'How long have you lived here? 13 years. Well you're an Italian by now 'I reply NO I'm here for 13 years but I'll always be a Moroccan and I want it to be that way. I can't stand people who deny their origins or ... I have relatives in particular an aunt who says 'I've lived in France and then I've lived in Italy ... I've never ever actually lived in Morocco, 'If we're the first to be ashamed of our origins then there is all the more reason why people will come along and say 'ah you're a Moroccan' – thinking that this is offensive. There are even people that when you tell them you come from Morocco reply 'ah you're a Moroccan'. Excuse me. That's how you say it, 'I don't mean to offend you'. Well that's like saying 'Oh so you are Italian, no offence meant'. That's because we're in the habit of using certain terms as if they were insults.

What exactly was the problem that, according to you, led your mother to throw you out?

Oh yes, well, I wasn't studying at school, in fact I didn't even go there – a bit like my sister – I went out on the town at night time, staying out as late as possible and coming back at midday, or later. Perhaps for that reason. Then once , he was a lorry driver and, since I knew my mother would have said no, I went away with him for two days because that's how long his trips are. Then I came home again. When I'd gone off with him I hadn't said anything. Then I'd phoned home the next day, 'Mum' … 'Oh no this time don't bother to come home'. That time was it ... but afterwards, I'm quite proud and so I said 'Right I'm not going to come home ever!' My sister called me up and said 'what are you doing, stupid, come back, you know what mum is like in certain moments'. Mum was a bit shaken from that point of view, but me, I was proud I took my things and left there and then.

How did your boyfriend's family treat you when you arrived at their home?

They took me in without any problems. In fact they were great really, given that they accepted someone who wasn't a member of their family just like that. It's not as if I was their daughter or cousin … only their son's girlfriend. I am sure they did it for their son, because they behaved towards me as if I had been just any 'Maria' or 'Carla'. Ok they are doing it for their son, but all in all I felt ok there. Certainly it's a difficult situation. Now it's getting easier though because we're building another storey to the house where we can go and live together. I'm already living on top by myself. And when he gets back from work to sleep he comes upstairs to me. Now we're going to make a kitchen, and buy the furniture, were going to make our own furniture because he delivers furniture so we'll buy it from the deposit. The bed has arrived, but we're waiting for the mattress, slowly we are getting it together.

Were your parents already separated when all this happened?

When I left home? Yes, my dad and mum were separated. It seems like it's been forever.

Did they come together to Italy?

Yes, and then that's where the problems started in my opinion. In part because above all ... because it wasn't possible ... I don't know ... mum, the women here, the women have more freedom that's a fact isn't it? So they begin to dress differently they start a little to open up, not so much my mother, I've never seen her open up she'd rather be dead, but a little distance grew up between them and then my dad was an export-import merchant, and spent months at a time in Morocco and so she began to make friends with other women ... I'd never seen her get carried away, perhaps after they were separated but never before ... and perhaps men don't manage , maybe they are not sufficiently intelligent to follow the women, to allow them perhaps to open up mentally a little. According to me, if this process can be lived through by both partners together, the husband sees his wife changing but also that that is true of others, if they do this together then they could stay married. But it often happens that one goes ahead, and the other is more attached to older ways of doing things. I can understand, it is important to hold on to one's roots, but open up a little is not a bad thing either! See what the others can offer you. Recognise that which is good; that which you don't like you don't have to take. But you shouldn't reject what's different just because it's different…

The second case offers a contrasting example to the first. As the extract from the interview shows, this young Moroccan woman is as determined to stay within the bounds of her culture as the former young woman was to leave it.

Is there anything you have copied from Italian ways of behaving that your parents don't appreciate?

No, I haven't taken anything.

Why? Because you don't like their way of behaving, because you're not interested?

I'm not interested, I don't like their ways, Boh!

What is it that you don't like?

Me? Well, to start with, I don't have any Italian friends, and I don't know a lot about their ways... or what I might be able to learn from Italians ways.

Why don't you have Italian friends? Did you not want to get know them – or did they exclude you?

Well, I have a closed character. If people don't speak to me I can go without speaking to them even for a year. Have you understood? I'm just too shy, that's my character. I have problems in being the one to start a relationship, I've got a closed character, I'm made like that.

But is this, according to you, connected to the fact that you are Moroccan, or is it just something about you as an individual?

No it's just me. Even in class in Morocco I didn't have many friends because I am a closed type of person. Others had lots of friends. In fact I know a Moroccan girl who has many Italian friends ... It's just that my personality doesn't help me.

Could this depend on the fact that you belong to a large family and spend a lot of time with them?

Yes.

Do you spend most of your time with your brothers and sisters?

Yes.

Do you go out with your sister?

Yes.

Why do you like staying with your family?

Because they understand me better.

You are able to open up more with them?

Not really, because I have this type of character, I don't talk much. Ok I do speak a bit at home but then I can't make friends with Italians because well, I don't know, I feel as if they are bad types. Both. Bad not in the sense that… I don't know how to explain it.

Please try.

Bad in the sense that they have never tried to help me.

How could they have helped you?

Neither at elementary school or in school now. Well, here a bit, but in elementary school not at all. Worse, they used to make fun of me, and that was before I wore the foulard. I've only been wearing it the last year or two, not for very long. They made fun of me. Because they realised that I didn't know Italian very well they wrote words that had one meaning and told me only about the other meaning.

They said one word and told you it had another meaning?

Yes, for example they would say this means tree when really it meant flower. Really the opposite.

But you told me before that, when you had the support teacher, you used to speak a lot, so much so that they had to move you from where you were sitting.

Ok, but my classmate then was also a Moroccan.

Did you speak in Arabic?

Yes, because she too had just arrived so I asked her about everything.

So you don't trust Italians?

As I said before, I don't have Italian friends so I can't say.

But you wanted to get to know some?

Its not that I didn't want to, my character didn't help me and nor did they make any effort.

Why, two years ago, did you decide to wear the Foulard?

Because my religion tells me to do so.

At home do you all wear it?

Only my mother and I.

Not your older sister?

No.

Why not?

Because she is not ready, yet. Inside she doesn't feel ready.

When is the age when one should wear it?

It should be worn from seven years old. But I didn't do so at that age because I hadn't understood the matter very well. Then when I began to read the Koran, and read other books, and listen to cassettes, then that's when I put it on.

Did anything change in your relationship with others after you started wearing it?

Not really. I could say that people out of curiosity were more likely to ask me questions – so these questions actually helped me. I got a bit closer to my schoolmates last year because of their questions… and in the end I made friends with of an Italian girl, but then our paths separated and I don't see her anymore. She lives in another town.

Did changing to high school recently mean that you had to start everything all over again with friends?

No, because I did have one friend, as I told you before, who was from the Congo. And we both enrolled in the same school …

At this point I have to ask you a series of questions about what you have in common with Italian girls on the one hand and Moroccan girls on the other. I think I've understood that you feel that you don't have anything in common with the Italians?

That's right.

What do you have in common with the Moroccans that you don't have with the Italians?

Language, yes language. And the same country of origin. The same way of thinking.

Tell me about your way of thinking, why is it different?

Somewhat different, but not totally so. But with the Italian girls here what do I have in common? With Moroccans I share the hope of returning to Morocco, to do something first here and then go back… I don't mean all the Moroccan girls think like that, I'm speaking more or less about the ones I've got to know.

What about ways of dressing, with whom do you feel you have most in common?

Neither group.

Why?

Because I wear long dresses. But the other Moroccans I know dress differently, like the Italians.

The other Moroccans dress like Italians while you have maintained the Moroccan way of dressing?

More than Moroccan, Islamic. Let's say that we are obliged to wear long dresses.

What do you mean by a long dress?

Something that covers the body.

What music do you listen to?

Calm music, Arabic music of the 1960's.

Is your way of spending your free time more like that of the Italians or more like the Moroccans?

Italian girls go out every afternoon.

And the Moroccans?

This friend I had then I knew only at school so I don't know what she did in the afternoons.

Is your way of passing the time the same here as it was in Morocco?

No, it's different. There I spent more time with my friends.

Why not the same here?

Perhaps because the friend I have here lives a bit far from my house. I go round to her if I'm free in the afternoon. It's not that I never go out.

But after supper, only on Saturdays?

No, I don't go out then.

Not even on Saturdays?

No, because we get home late in the afternoon so …

You told me that you go out with parents on Saturdays.

Yes, we go shopping.

You always go out with them that day?

No, sometimes with my sister.

And Sunday?

No, on Sundays I stay at home … sometimes our cousins come round.

Does the fact that you are a Moroccan help you in facing life's problems?

That depends on other people. Because there are people who simply because they see you as Moroccan... boh! I don't know what they think of me...except that when I go out wearing my foulard lots of people stare at me.

What effect does that have on you?

On the one hand I feel proud, on the other had it shows such ignorance, excuse the word, people who stare at you like I've come from another planet. Not everyone though.

Could it be because they see you as someone different?

Yes but to stare so much! Looking is OK but such fixed staring is not right don't you think?

Did anyone say anything to you, or did you ever overhear any comments?

No, never. It's better not to hear them.

What effect would it have on you?

First of all I would turn away and laugh at them and then I'd just keep on walking. I'd make them feel ignorant and that's all. I wouldn't say a word, just keep going.

So you speak Arabic?

Yes. Arabic. The Moroccan language doesn't exist. When people say Moroccan perhaps they mean dialect, in which case they should really say 'do you speak the Moroccan dialect?'. With Arabic one means the written language, the formal language.

You said you speak Arabic at home.

Yes.

On what other occasions do you speak it then?

Every time I meet someone who speaks Arabic/Moroccan. Most of the time where I come from we speak Arabic in dialect, not so much as it is when it is written.

So when do you speak Italian?

At school and a little at home.

With whom do you speak it at home?

With my brother when I have to explain homework to him because he doesn't understand much, and then when I have to tell the time to my brother and sister.

The younger ones?

Yes.

It's easier for you to speak Italian with them?

Yes it's easier.

Do they know Arabic?

I think so.

Would your parents be willing to consider you go getting together with a boy who doesn't belong to your group?

No, and I wouldn't want to do so either.

Why not?

Let's say they would have to at least be Arab, though I would prefer it if they were Moroccan.

So at least Arab, but better if he was Moroccan?

Yes, because that way at least he would know my customs, understand my culture, more or less.

And if you got to know an Italian boy who wanted to learn your culture?

Well, he'd first of all have to be a Muslim.

Therefore: Muslim, Arabic and best of all Moroccan?

And you wouldn't go out even with a boy who wasn't Muslim?

No, I wouldn't dream of it.

Because I don't like the way boys from here behave – they seem girlish to me… in their way of walking, talking, the language they use…

So an Arab man is more virile?

Yes, The Italians seem like girls.

Because of how they dress?

For the way they walk, how they behave, one of my friends says the same thing, it's not just me, in fact two of my friends…

What makes a Moroccan male different from this?

I wouldn't know how to explain it (she laughs) he is more in the truth, let's say ... – he's more, looks more to the future.

He's more down to earth?

What does that mean?

He pays more attention to everyday realities, worries more about the family, the house, work, whilst Italian males think more about how to have a good time?

Yes, but they too think about having a good time but don't exaggerate. Here for example they think only about travelling and having money without needing to work.

They are irresponsible?

Yes, I prefer men who are more grown up.

The third and final case takes us to the heart of the difficulty facing those who decide that they need to renegotiate their identities. As the interview proceeds we see the problem of building a plural identity when both identities present themselves as self-sufficient, and where in addition your parents want you to preserve the more fragile one. The difficulties here are perhaps in part connected to the specificities of Albanian identity as well as to the relatively brief period in which this girl has lived in Italy.

At the outset of the interview she explained that she mixed only with Italians. So, consistently, when asked to comment on the question 'When you are in need can you always count on someone from your own group?' she replied:

> If only there was such a person. This is the point for me because I really believe if I could have a (female) Albanian friend in my town, that would be great. But seeing as that is not the case it's not worth thinking about.

She went on to explain, however, that the problem was not actually finding any Albanians.

It's not that there are no Albanians, and bear in mind that I'm Albanian when I say this … but some of the ones who you find round here don't seem to me trustworthy people.

And how can you tell that?

From their attitudes and behaviour. For example there were a few Albanian young men who came up to me and my sister joking … you know, showing off, saying various swearwords and other things to make us go with them. Then one of them said something in Albanese which meant more or less, 'Phew! Look at her !' which made us feel bad. He said something like 'Look at that cutie, I'd really dig doing it with her' and I shouted back, 'Look here I've already got a boyfriend' and he answered 'Sorry! But how did you understand what I was saying? So I told him 'You're just stupid. I'm Albanese too.' Apart from this which was annoying, that is to say, this sort of behaviour is generally really annoying because most people consider Albania a country that isn't good for much, but that is not true from my point of view.

But according to you what is it about those boys, those about whom you say 'I don't like the ones I've met'?

No, those I try to avoid, but not because they are Albanese, and now that I live in Italy I think I'm 'who knows what'. On the contrary, it would be very good if I did mix with people from my own nation, who can understand me better … if I have problems, and other things. The problem is, I really don't like the few I have known so far and that's why I keep out of their way.

In answer to the question whether she felt she had more in common with Albanians or Italians she replied.

> If you ask me that, then I would say Albanians … It's something that comes naturally to me, love for the mother country. I adore my country even though I hear it so often criticised. Many of my friends, before, four years ago, when I arrived, said, 'you should be ashamed of being Albanese.' And I felt awful for three years, that is, until a year ago. Then in the third form at elementary school things began to change, because it's nasty when people judge you badly before even getting to know you, and that's what I have in common with other Albanese. So according to me one shouldn't judge from first impressions, even if often it is that which counts. You should think more carefully about the first impressions, and not say, for example, she's ugly and so she must be unpleasant.

Even though not easy with young people from her own background in Italy she was very positive about Albania and its customs. Thus, in answer to a question how much she enjoyed going to the community festivals, she commented:

> I went to a wedding once, ours are much more beautiful than your weddings. Without meaning to offend you. It took place at C. It was organised brilliantly There was the reception – beautiful. Afterwards everyone sat down to eat, with music from the 1970's. I was really struck by it all ... there were tables for the Italians and for the Albanians. I asked my dad: 'Dad when is it going to finish?', and he said at eight o'clock and I replied 'But it's only three o'clock! We're going to be here eating from three to eight o'clock?' and he said 'Oh yes!' So then a friend of his said 'If you can't manage to sit all that time still neither can I' and began to sing in Albanese. From that moment until half past nine you should have been there to see it. Everyone got up from the tables – they were playing Albanian songs – so everyone was dancing – it was just amazing. The owner of the restaurant said that it was the most wonderful wedding that he had ever witnessed in his place. Because we get really happy at weddings, it's really beautiful. Truly a sacrament.

Led by this connection to talking about marriage, however, the interviewee then went on to reflect on the role of the woman in the Albanian family. Here her views were less black and white.

> With us divorces are very rare. Firstly because people become really united, even apart from the fact that marriage is a sacrament, and then, because they are very rare also for a negative reason, because, let's say, if my husband treats me badly I can't divorce him because where would I go if I did? If I went back to my parent's home they would think that I was not a worthwhile person because I shouldn't have left my husband. It's said

> that people don't believe what women say about what happened. They don't believe you if you say that your husband beats you up, or that sort of thing. And, anyway, it would be pointless to get divorced because then where would I turn? I'd be forced to stick with it.

In answer to the question how much she agreed with the statement 'It's a women's role to look after the family' she went on to reflect further on the cultural differences.

> … it's not only that. It's because women are still considered to be inferior despite ... even now when women have made big strides, even now sometimes you can start to say something and they say 'Be quiet, you, you're only a woman!' In Italy this doesn't happen but, in Albania, it's a thing … that is to say women are seen as very inferior to men. As for me it is as if I'm torn inside over the practices of my own country. Because I respect my country, if I'm in Albania I might put up with even those things, but here now I'm in Italy and yet my parents would like me to behave as if we still lived in Albania.

For her on the other hand, living in Italy means having to adapt to Italian ways, so as to live in the present not in the past.

> But I can't live in one country with the practices of another country. I'm seeing a psychologist because I've been unwell, that is to say, I fainted and they told me that it's not a physical illness but something psychological. Basically, when I arrived I was ten years old and very confused about whether to keep doing what I had been used to doing in Albania or behave according to Italian ways, I still haven't quite worked it out. In practice I have cancelled a part of my past. In fact since leaving Albania I can't remember anything of what happened before when I was living there.

In answer to the later question what she felt she had in common with Italians she replied:

> What I have in common with the Italians is my cheerful approach, wanting to take everything in a light-hearted way, so as to live life to the full. There are times when I think, when my mother says to me 'you can't do that because you're Albanese, 'I think, oh dear, I should be Albanese really, and I want to kill myself. Sometimes I think, since I'm Albanese I'll put an end to it all so then I won't be Albanese any more. Full stop. But then I realise I wouldn't be Italian either. Sometimes I do want to be more Italian.
>
> And what would you have to do to become more Italian?
>
> Well, what I mean to say is it's not that I want to be an Italian. I don't want to be immodest but actually I like myself as I am, in terms of my character. Because I've taken some things from the Albanians, and others from the Italians. Some positive things from both sides. But what my mother thinks of me is very important to me – my parent's opinion is crucial. But what I think of as the positive characteristics of the Italians they think of as negative ones. Sometimes I try to throw out even these positive Italian ways of being and I try to think like a real Albanian.

Conclusions

This chapter has tried to give some insight to what integration involves subjectively for some young immigrants in Italy. It started from the premise that no amount of 'facts' describing integration can answer the question what form integration *should* take, but that debates over this question are badly in need of more evidence about the different forms it actually does take in given times and places. Only on this basis, it claimed, can we start to understand the correlates of different choices by communities and individuals towards closer or less close integration into the host society, and the way these relate to the actions and reactions of the host society itself. It was suggested that such research is all the more valuable when it helps us get beyond the unsystematic and often crudely instrumental reports of problems with integration that tend to be circulated by the mass media, such as the example with which this chapter began (Maneri 1998).

In terms of the way youngsters reconcile their different identities the findings of this study confirm much that Ostberg was trying to get at with his concept of 'cultural navigation'. The adolescents interviewed were almost all engaged in the exploring and testing of boundaries, especially where this involved rules about mixing with the other sex. Young immigrant women in particular showed interest in seeing how far they could go in using the spaces opened up by the more egalitarian approach to gender issues in Italy. On the other hand, Ostberg's metaphor, though suggestive, perhaps finds less applicability to the groups studied in this research than to the Pakistani youngsters he studied. This may be because the youngsters in Emilia Romagna and the Marche are less part of settled communities (It seems that you have to be well 'settled' in your own culture to be confident enough to navigate round it). The challenges that those in this sample need to navigate have mainly to do with balancing the expectations of their families as against the new opportunities opened up for them as individuals. The Chinese girls, for example, were trying both to satisfy family requirements which presuppose massive investment of time and energy in the family business, whilst also participating as long as possible in the Italian education system. And the cultural navigation by the immigrants interviewed here was not always focused on their own cultures of origin. Many young Gypsies and Albanese went so far as to say they would be willing to marry Italians and become a fuller part of Italian society: the problem for them is whether they would be accepted. It is also likely that Ostberg's research methods, involving a follow-up of his sample after some years, offered him better opportunities to capture changes in attitudes to cultural identity over time than is provided by interviews in which it is left to the subjects themselves to describe how their attitudes or behaviour have developed. Further research is therefore required into the value of his idea for different kinds of immigrant groups, and for the circumstances such as those found in Italy.

On the other hand, as shown by the three lengthy case studies, for some young immigrants, having multiple identities can indeed represent a 'problem' with which they have to struggle. In these, albeit untypical cases, identity seemed to be treated more as an 'all or nothing' choice, rather than as a matter for 'cultural navigation' to be handled according to the situation and context. We do not witness here the skilful cultural navigation Ostberg would lead us to expect. Whereas the first young Moroccan woman seems to have suffered a shipwreck, the other is unwilling even to leave the safety of the port! And the Albanian girl remains becalmed at sea.

The troubles of the Albanian girl seem to stem in large part from her attempting to identify simultaneously both with Italians of her own age and her parents expectations of her as an Albanian. The interviews also illustrated the mixed feelings that young people can have about themselves in relation to their group. One of the Moroccan girls, for example, said she would like to spend more time with idealised Moroccan boys. So would the Albanian girl. But they are unhappy with the examples of young men actually available. Yet they are both upset at the view that Italians take of their group. One of the other two young Moroccan women, on the other hand, has already made her choice in favour of a Moroccan partner, to an extent having convinced herself that the real is the ideal – though she has yet to put this to the test.

These three cases thus show something of the very different ways problems caused by multiple identities can work out in practice. Put together, they show a much more complex picture than that implied by the case of culture-conflict leading to rebellion against parents as described by *the Resto di Carlino* newspaper at the outset of this chapter. Whilst some young people do make a decision to resolve their problems by opting for the master identity provided by membership of the larger society, there is no basis for assuming that this is a common or the most common reaction. The first interviewee in the three case studies does make such a choice. Despite claiming still to be proud of her Moroccan roots, she looked down on Moroccan boys available, and found a new family with her Italian boyfriend and his family. In the third of the case studies, on the other hand, the young woman from Albania feels she is faced with an 'excess' of identity which she cannot easily reduce. She complains 'I can't live in one country with the practices of another country'. But in trying to make her identity more manageable she has still not succeeded in finding 'her-self'.

The second of the cases studies, however, shows us how some young people decide to deepen their engagement with the culture of their parents rather than identify strongly with the new culture of the place where they now live. This young woman, even though she found herself in Italy, takes strength from wearing a foulard like her mother, and seeks to preserve a way of life that is rather different from that lived by her Italian youngsters of her age at school. She identifies more with her religion than her national group; for her, many Moroccans behave just like Italians. Insisting on the need for men and women to occupy sharply contrasting roles, she constructs an image of the Moroccan male as the embodiment of that which she seeks in a husband. Confining herself to the home as much as possible, she is reluctant to 'go out' to meet other people – if this means being open to other ways of being. When she does go out she is ready for glances of disapproval, but is not willing to spend her life compensating, as she sees it, for other's ignorance. Interestingly, though, she does also claim that Italians of her own age became *more* interested in her once she made the choice to dress as a religious Muslim.

Examining the other answers provided to the interview questions allows us to identify some of the correlates of different life choices. The three cases we have described in detail, for example, show great variety in the degree to which the subjects mix with Italians. The first girl, who went on to move in with her Italian boyfriend and his family, previously mixed only with Italians, whereas the second did not mix with Italians at all. In addition, even though we have to be careful not to exaggerate how far an individual herself can be fully aware of all the factors that influence her decisions, it does seem fair to say that these girls played a large part in choosing how to live their lives. After all, in all three cases their siblings can and do make different choices from that of the interviewee herself.

But choices are made within a framework of constraints and are subject to contingencies. The Moroccan girl who falls in love with a lorry driver comes from a family where the father has left home. Interestingly, she attributes the breakdown of her parents' relationship to her father's failure to adjust to the different role women are both allowed and expected to play in Italy. Having abandoned school, and got into some conflict with her mother, it may not be far-fetched to say that she integrates into this new family precisely because hers is less integrated. The second girl, by contrast, comes from a large and extended family. Being part of a different 'world' – at home she speaks Arabic – she finds she has much more in common with her own group than with her Italian schoolmates. As she puts it, 'Language, yes language. And the same country of origin. The same way of thinking'. When asked to explain her choice to deepen her Muslim identity she links this to the conduct of her schoolmates, who, when she first came, made fun of her poor Italian. But she herself is uncertain how much to make of this, saying 'I don't know, I feel as if they are bad types ... both. Bad not in the sense that... I don't know how to explain it.', before going on to explain how they made fun of her. More than once she explains her withdrawal and lack of friends by saying she has what she calls a closed character. In her view, her life choices have at least as much to do with the type of person she is than with the alleged failings of the host society.

Even the most difficult cases of identity conflict discovered in this sample do not resemble the extreme case of family conflict portrayed by *the Resto di Carlino* report. Whereas in that case parents are described as acting against the expressed wishes (and objective rights) of their children, in none of the three cases described here was there any question of parents beating or segregating their children, or in any other way breaking the law. In none of these case studies are parents described as actually forcing their preferences onto their children. And in none of the cases (not even the first) did the young person's choice lead to a breakdown of relationships with her parents. The relationship that the young people had with their parents varies on a continuum from initial conflict, followed by closeness and affection even where a different path has been taken, as in the case of the first Moroccan interviewee, to total identification with her mother, in the second case. The Albanese girl, for her part, wants to be more 'Albanese' to please her parents, but also seeks an excuse not to have to do so.

The research findings reported here, limited as they are, should be enough to demonstrate that any one theoretical 'solution' to the problems of peaceful co-existence between people coming from different cultures is unlikely to be able to accommodate the many possible different group, family and individual circumstances. What one group may appreciate as a solution could for another group be a way of making the problem worse. Philosophical debates about how far a liberal society should go in seeking to protect the rights of individuals who belong to minority groups should perhaps take more account of the fact that such conflict often presents itself not so much as a matter of protecting the individual from the oppression of her community, but as the problem of the individual wanting both to be part of her family but also to have the freedom to make choices that they may not approve. On the other hand, it may be that, as immigrant communities become more settled in Italy, what is currently experienced by those involved as a battle within the family will change shape and meaning so as to be fought out as a question of the legitimate extent of minority rights. And, as we have seen, the mass media is prone to reframing the issue in these terms.

Both the host society and their own group can be tempted to make members of minorities feel that they have to choose for or against them. But both can also do what they can to avoid forcing the individual to face such stark dilemmas, and, if this research is to be believed, in the majority of cases an individual is unlikely to want to make zero-sum choices. It is some achievement even to maintain the type of society in which there is room for individuals to make the difficult responses to the challenge of multiple identities that have been illustrated here in the detailed case studies. But it may be an even greater achievement to build a society where youngsters do not feel they have to make hard choices for or against different identities but are encouraged to show a large amount of interest in and knowledge of the many cultures that surround them.

References

Bauman, Z. (2000), *Liquid Modernity* (Cambridge: Polity Press).

Bauman, Z. (2004), *Wasted Lives* (Cambridge: Polity Press).

Benhabib, S. (2002), *The Claims of Culture* (Princeton: Princeton University Press).

Catanzaro, R. and Nelken, D. (2003), 'Come si costruisce un problema sociale: Il commercio ambulante degli immigrati sulla riviera adriatica', in G. Sciortino and A. Colombo (eds.) *Stranieri in Italia 2* (Bologna: Il Mulino), 25–67.

Ciarloni D. (2000), *Sei modi per dire integrazione:* Tesi di sociologia generale (supervisor D. Nelken) (Macerata: Facoltà di Scienze Politiche).

Cologna, D. and Breveglieri, L. (eds.) (2003) *I figli dell' immigrazione (Comune di Milano)* (Milano: Franco Angeli).

Favell, A. (1998), *Philosophies of Integration* (Basingstoke: Macmillan).

Favell, A. (2002), 'To belong or not to belong: the postnational question', in R. Grillo and J. Pratt (eds.) *The Politics of recognising difference: Multiculturalism Italian Style.* (Aldershot: Ashgate).

IRES (1991), *Uguali e Diversi: Il mondo culturale, le reti di rapporti, I lavori degli immigrati non europei a Torino.* (Torino: Rosenberg and Sellier).

Kymlicka, W. (1995), *Multicultural Citizenship: A liberal theory of minority rights.* (Oxford: Oxford University Press).

Lapassade, G. (1998), 'Un conformismo deviante', in M. Delle Donne (ed.), *Relazioni etniche: Stereotipi e pregiudizi.* (Roma: UP), 77–85.

Maneri, M. (1998), 'Lo straniero consensuale. La devianza degli immigrati come circolarità di pratiche e discorsi', in A. Del Lago (ed.), *Lo Straniero e il Nemico* (Genova-Milano: Costa e Nolan), 236–274.

Nelken. D. (2005), 'Integrazione soggettiva e 'navigazione culturale': un'indagine sui giovani immigrati in Emilia Romagna e nelle Marche', in D. Nelken (ed.),

L'integrazione subita: (im)migrazione, flussi, trasformazioni (Rome: Franco Angeli), 230–268.

Ostberg. S. (2003) 'Norwegian-Pakistani adolescents: Negotiating religion gender, ethnicity and social boundaries', *Youth* 11(2), 161–181.

Papastergiadis, N. (2000), *The Turbulence of Migration* (Cambridge: Polity Press).

Parekh, B. (2000), *Rethinking Multiculturalism* (New York: Palgrave).

Pollini, G. (2000), 'Sistema migratorio come sistema di appartenenza molteplici: gli immigrati marochini, tunisini, ghanesi, slavi, senegalesi, cinesi e filippini', in G .Scidà (ed.) *I Sociologi italiani e le dinamiche dei processi migratori* (Milano: Francesco Angeli).

Recchi, E. and Allam, M. (2002), 'L'assimilazione degli immigrati nella società italiana', in A. Colombo and G. Sciortino (eds.), *Stranieri in italia assimilati ed esclusi* 1 (Bologna: Il Mulino), 119–142.

Sayad, A. (2002), *La doppia assenze* (Milano: Raffaelleo Cortina).

Scourfield, J. and Davies, A. (2002), 'Children's negotiation of national identities', paper presented at the annual conference of the British Sociological Association 'Reshaping the social', March 2002

Scourfield, J. and Davies, A. (2005) 'Children's accounts of Wales as racialized and inclusive', *Ethnicities* 5/1, 83–107

Staring, R., Van der Land, M., Tak, H. and Kalb, D. (1997), 'Localizing cultural identity', *Focal* 30/31, 7–21.

Index of Names

For Product Safety Concerns and Information please contact our EU representative GPSR@taylorandfrancis.com
Taylor & Francis Verlag GmbH, Kaufingerstraße 24, 80331 München, Germany

www.ingramcontent.com/pod-product-compliance
Ingram Content Group UK Ltd.
Pitfield, Milton Keynes, MK11 3LW, UK
UKHW021302190926
475701UK00009B/581

* 9 7 8 0 3 6 7 6 0 3 6 3 2 *